My Conflict with A Soviet Spy
the story of the Ron Evans spy case

Robert Corfe is the author of a number of thought-provoking books in addition to several autobiographical works describing his varied and adventurous life. He is best known for his authoritative 3-volume work, *Social Capitalism in Theory and Practice*, which is not only a critique of an irresponsible and failing economic system, but a detailed study of constructive measures for ensuring a stable, free, and prosperous society. The present book tells the story of a project he embarked upon in Finland leading to a personal conflict with a man who was uncovered as a Soviet spy. The cloak and dagger adventure involved a broad range of startling personalities from differing national backgrounds.

By the same author –

Autobiographical –

Death In Riyadh
dark secrets in hidden Arabia

The Girl From East Berlin
a romantic docu-drama of the East-West divide

This Was My England
the story of a childhood

Sociological –

Land of The Olympians
papers from the enlightened Far North

Deism and Social Ethics
the role of religion in the third millennium

Islam and The New Totalitarianism
fundamentalism's threat to world civilisation

Populism Against Progress
and the collapse of aspirational values

Political –

The Future of Politics
With the demise of the left/right confrontational system

Social Capitalism in Theory and Practice
(3 volumes)

Egalitarianism of The Free Society
and the end of class conflict

The Democratic Imperative
the reality of power relationships in the nation state

The Death of Socialism
The irrelevance of the traditional left and the call for a progressive politics of universal humanity

My Conflict With A Soviet Spy

the story of the Ron Evans spy case

―――――――――――――――――

Robert Corfe

Arena Books

Copyright © Robert Corfe 2017

The right of Robert Corfe to be identified as author of this work
has been asserted in accordance with the Copyright, Designs and
Patents Act 1988.

Second edition 2017*

First edition published in 2001 by Arena Books under the author's pseudonym
of Eddie Miller with names of leading participants in the drama referred
to under aliases to protect their privacy.

Arena Books
6 Southgate Green
Bury St. Edmunds
IP33 2BL.

www.arenabooks.co.uk

All rights reserved. Except for the quotation of short passages for the
purposes of criticism and review, no part of this publication may be
reproduced, stored in a retrieval system, or transmitted, in any form or
by any means, electronic, mechanical, photocopying, recording or
otherwise, without the prior permission of the publisher.

Corfe, Robert- 1935
My Conflict With A Soviet Spy the story of the Ron Evans spy case

British Library cataloguing in Publication Data. A Catalogue record
for this book is available from the British Library.

ISBN 978-1-909421-96-7

BIC categories:- BGA, BGHA, BM, BTH, HBTW, 1DNF.

Printed & bound by Lightning Source UK

Cover design
by Jon Baxter

Typeset in
Times New Roman

To The Memory of my
friend & contemporary

Pentti Kiiskinen

Scholar & Writer

On whose persuasion I embarked on a journalistic career in the land of his forefathers, and whose untimely death occurred on 20th July 1971.

***

Foreword

The fascination of spy stories, irrespective of whether they are fact or fiction, lies not in the technicalities of what is acquired by one group or another, or in the secrets in themselves, but rather in the surrounding circumstances of the drama. Indeed, it is seldom that an author is concerned with, or is sufficiently informed to create a convincing drama based on what is really at the crux of all modern espionage activity, viz., a detailed exposé of the latest secret technological weaponry from one power and offered to another, usually a potential enemy.

The secrets, of course, remain with the spies, for it is knowledge entrusted to them by their employers (or otherwise obtained), the confidentiality of which is held as a stewardship for the community. What is of popular interest are the peripheral circumstances of espionage: most notably the personalities of the accused; their motives; how they operate and pass on their information; how their activities affect their personalities; their relationships with those around them, and how eventually they come to be caught.

The drama of espionage, and its excitement, or prurient interest to the man or woman in the street, stems from the clandestine environment in which it is forced to exist. All is made to seem different from what it really is, for that is how it has to be. Secrecy is its essence. Therefore, seemingly meaningless events take on a strange significance; innocuous incidences unexpectedly arouse offence; tension is created in unusual circumstances, and petty spite springs from motives very different from those suspected. Nothing follows a direct course. All seems incidental, even irrelevant, yet everything contributes to the central drama as it inevitably unfolds.

If that is typical of those events surrounding espionage in general, it is certainly true of the Ron Evans spy story. Evans emerges as a complex personality, certainly as a man of "irreproachable respectability" in the eyes of those with whom he came into contact. If he was disliked (and he was) it was because of his fussy anxiety, and because he was "law abiding" to a fault. You could dislike the man because of his finicky manner and almost morbid obsession with correct procedure - but mistrust him? Never! No one could have taken him for a man who was not ruled by the fear of his conscience - and no one did. Evans was the worthy and reliable functionary on whom anyone could depend - or almost anyone. His character or intentions had a rock-like dependability.

But he was much more than just a mere spy. He was a relentless intriguer, but when he found himself in a confrontational situation, he became implicated in a wider sphere of activities for which he had never bargained. The story then becomes a tale of conspiracy. The *Suojepoliisi* (Secret Police) became convinced they were witnessing a political conspiracy. In a country once placed (perhaps still) in a delicate geo-political situation, in their wisdom, the authorities had always been sensitive to those kind of political plots entailing the besmirching of personal character or the infiltration of voluntary associations. In their eyes, Evans was staging a Communist conspiracy on the classic model. There was plenty of circumstantial evidence to support this - quite apart from the offences for which he was eventually convicted. The KGB had made their presence visibly felt well before the storm was to break. Evans, the conspirator, his methods and motives, are therefore no less interesting than Evans the spy.

A large cast of varied characters, of many nationalities, are drawn into the story, which began in Finland in November 1963 and finally ended with the last act of the drama in February 1965. Apart from foreign nationals resident in the country, diplomats, KGB, MI6 and other agents, and Finns who were drawn into the maelstrom, the story includes clowns and eccentrics (often British) and a depraved Finnish aristocrat who was well known in his time in a certain milieu. Few come off with much credit in the story, and those few are usually the much-suffering Finns who were obliged to endure the intolerable goings-on of a weird foreign community.

The author's part in the story is occasionally little more creditable than several of those other foreign "nuisances," but I cannot accept the more serious insinuations to which some have alluded. If I was accused of becoming a Secret Police agent, it should be remembered that it was I who approached the police in the first instance in the wake of what can

FOREWORD

only be described as a murder attempt. If what followed was eager co-operation, then this was because I was engaged in a defensive battle against a group employing some very dirty methods. I needed the law on my side. If this mutated into a cloak and dagger episode involving the espionage activities of foreign agents (which it did), then my role was a moral one, in helping to clear up a mess for which I was partly responsible. Unwittingly, I had created a scenario where espionage could take root and flourish.

When I wined and dined with the KGB, I was unaware of the fact - i.e. unaware of the fact that I was dining with the KGB. I was merely receiving and returning hospitality, in the normal course of social contact, with a gentleman who is curiously described in the book as being of apparently "stockbroker respectability." If he had had ulterior motives then I had a use for him too, as becomes clear in the account which follows. As for the other KGB agent with whom I had contact, he alternated from being the most jovial party companion to becoming an idealistic purveyor of philosophical musings as to how one should properly conduct one's private life.

At the time, a more serious charge laid against me, was that I was directly and solely responsible for destroying the entire British intelligence network in neutral Scandinavia. This is an accusation, the guilt for which, I must emphatically refute. Not only were all my actions undertaken in good faith, but I went further, in taking apt precautions to prevent a situation where British intelligence might have been compromised. As becomes clear, I covered my back by contacting both American and British intelligence at an early stage in the proceedings. British intelligence were tardy in responding to my approach, and when they did so, it was too late, and in the form of an official buff card, identifying the sender, and not even placed in a plain envelope! Considering that I must have been under some kind of surveillance at the time, and that for my part I had taken the trouble to be discreet by using trusted channels in England, this was an example of clownish stupidity of almost unbelievable incompetence. The comment of the British Consul in Helsinki was that "they must be mad in London!" Since that time we have learnt much about the blundering of the British security services in the 1960s, and the suspicion now exists that the London headquarters may have intentionally undermined their own agents in Scandinavia.

The Finnish authorities alone come off unscathed in the account which follows. I do not think that anyone would question the fact that the Finnish police acted in any way that was other than fair and honourable in the story which follows. They fully respected the obligations of national loyalty in my relationship with them, and from the beginning, they were forthright and specific as to the basis for that co-operation. If in fact events were to take a turn whereby it might be seen that I had compromised myself, then this was neither my fault not that of the police, but purely the result of an objective and logical process which had to take its course.

This book could not have been written unless I had kept a detailed diary at the time, retained numerous documents, and actually wrote an account of the story (approaching twice the length of the present book) shortly after the events occurred. The accuracy of all events, including dialogue and reflection, is therefore verified by recorded fact. All personalities in the case are given their correct names, apart from Finnish police officers who are referred to with aliases. I felt it only right that this gesture of protection should be given.

More than fifty years have passed since the Ron Evans spy case, but some of those in the foreign community in Helsinki, described in this book, are still there, such as Peter Martin, Geoff Gee, the Liverpudlian, and Martin Summerhill and his friend, Rolf Erlewein. Martin, after for so long having been regarded as a stick-in-the-mud bachelor, married in the 1970s and has recently been widowed. Rolf Erlewein, meanwhile, was chosen to be the Duke of Edinburgh's interpreter when he visited Finland in the 70s, for which he was awarded the MBE.

Peter, the ex-public schoolboy and buffoon of the foreign community, after many years of post-marital bachelorhood, and worrying his conscience as to whether he should "finally" settle down entered into his third (consecutive) matrimonial relationship, in what his friends sniggeringly described as a "shoehorn" marriage in his fiftieth year. His spare time preoccupations are now a little less frenetic than those indicated in this book, since he spends his leisure hours walking his beloved dachsunds in the woods in the suburb of Espoo, or watching

FOREWORD

foreign TV news channels that so often upset his sometimes ultra-conservative views. He now seems settled and reasonably happy - as a man should be by the time he has reached his mid-eighties.

Digmar, who plays no small part in the story which follows, only died in 1978 at the age of seventy-nine. There are several other Finnish friends of that time with whom I also come into contact from time to time during infrequent business trips to the country. As for the highfalutin North American, Jim Hammond, with his swank and heroic lies, his generosity, and talk of those "Goddam Russkies" who had "once again bugged his apartment" (which became a joke in the foreign community) I last saw him in London at the start of the 70s. He had been posted to the Canadian Embassy in Trafalgar Square. He has now been dead for just on forty years.

If some of those I knew more than fifty years ago have changed little, Helsinki has changed a lot. Its new metropolitan railway and underground system, and huge suburbs in the outer forested areas, have totally altered the character of the inner City I knew and loved so well. The cafés mentioned in the book are still there, but they are different, and so their clientele has changed, and my friends are no longer to be found in their old haunts. In the light of these facts, the story which follows could therefore almost be seen as of "historical interest." After the final act closed on the Ron Evans drama, I remained four more years in Finland, enjoying a successful career as a freelance journalist.

As for the central character in the drama, Ron Evans himself, on his release from prison and deportation to Britain, he was not grabbed by the "Russians or Chinese" as he vainly anticipated, but ironically by the West Germans (a country which he loathed for ideological reasons), where he was used to pursue his research development work in a supposedly "security risk-free" capacity by a major electronics company until his death in 1981 at the age of sixty-three. Before taking steps to write the first draft of this book in the late 70s, I had to carry out my own confidential research in tracing Evans' whereabouts. I traced his elderly relatives in Sheerness, and at a geriatric home where his mother spent her last years as an invalid, with little (if any) remembrance of the past, I was given an address of a small town in southern Germany. "This is a friend of your son - a visitor - isn't that nice luv," shouted the Sister into the ear of the old woman, who wrapped in a blanket was confined in a chair, together with a dozen or so others. I took a gnarled hand, but there was no response other than the faint and meaningless smile of those in advanced senility. "Her son never visits her," said the Sister, and I sensed that she knew nothing about the drama surrounding Ron Evans life.

At this point I handed over my findings to the *Stern* press agency and they reported back to me on Evans' whereabouts and occupational status. That was in 1980, and since Ron Evans was still alive and employed, it would have been impossible at that time to publish the story because of the damage it could have done to the reputation of a major German company. With Evans' death, that danger passed by, since a deceased employee need seldom embarrass his former bosses.

Espionage is a deadly serious business in the literal sense. Nevertheless, in the following story, as passions and tension rose, it gave rise to many comic incidents, and some absurdly sardonic situations of high drama. As I look back over fifty years, on many of the events that then occurred, I am finally left with a grand impression of comic absurdity at the entire episode. What comes over throughout is the foolishness of human nature, its vanity, hurt pride and petty spite. There was much that we all had to be ashamed of, and it is hoped that after nearly half a century most of us have undergone at least some inward change. In the telling of the story which follows, no attempt has been made to change the perspective of events as they were seen and felt shortly after their occurrence. There has been no whitewash, and if the reader sees through the subjectivity of the narrator, he or she will perceive there is often no clear division between "goodies" and "baddies," and so in that sense, this is a spy story with a difference. What is presented is a slice of life as found in the world around us. In this way a greater authenticity of mood and realism is retained. Any other approach would have meant artifice and the fictionalising, or at least the blurring of the truth, so long after the events.

In this story, as indeed since the post-War period, the Finns have been witnesses to espionage rather than participants in it, and because of this, in their peaceful and lovely land, they have needed to have a high-tolerance level for the warring factions of the world around them, and

FOREWORD

especially for those weird and quarrelsome resident foreigners enjoying the privilege of their hospitality. No attempt has been made to remove those slighting remarks about the country expressed by a number of characters in the book. Whenever foreigners gather together - wherever they may be - they like to grouse about their country of adoption in no uncertain terms. "Abroad" is never quite like home. With regard to Finland, however, it is anyway questionable if those critical remarks were meant with meaningful sincerity. The final test, of course, is to be found in the duration of residence.

The greatest part of Evans' punishment was not his imprisonment but his subsequent deportation. He would have preferred the former to be trebled if the latter could be rescinded. In Peter Martin, in his wilder moments, the country never encountered a critic so withering in satirical outpourings. Yet this character has been resident there for over fifty years, and it is now unlikely he could bear to live anywhere else - if indeed any other country would be prepared to take him.

Finland is a country I shall always love, and its people I shall always hold in the highest regard. Quite apart from their prosperity, the Finns have a model society, and cherish values from which we would have much to learn in improving our own country.

Robert Corfe   2017

Contents

Foreword   -   page vii

1	The Secret City	3
2	Who is Jakowleff ?	9
3	Twelve take a bow	20
4	The reticent little man	32
5	Omen of misfortune	42
6	We are not political	51
7	This is intrigue	66
8	The Big lie	75
9	An open breach	86
10	Braving the opposition	97
11	Enter the diplomats	106
12	To work for peace	120
13	Conspiracy most foul	129
14	Let's be legal	138
15	This is libel	150
16	Scrape with death	160
17	No opposition, please	168
18	Only an April fool	181
19	A man is missing	190
20	Festivity macabre	204
21	It's on the headlines	217
22	What happened at Haiko	225
23	Death takes its toll	234
24	MI6 becomes a cropper	247

*

List of illustrations

Soviet spy, Ron Evans, convicted by the Finns in May 1964, on his arrival at Heathrow on 24th February 1965, after his release from prison and deportation from Finland.

facing page – 32

Vladimir (Waldemar) von Etter, Finnish aristocrat, playboy, and friend of the author, suspected by the Finnish intelligence service of working for the CIA.

facing page – 102

Helsinki Appeals Court (the Marble Palace) formerly the Villa Keirkner, where Ron Evans was tried behind locked doors. It is now Finland's Labour Court.

facing page – 150

Haiko, formerly the palatical country home of Waldemar von Etter, overlooking the Gulf of Finland, where at a weekend party information was passed between Soviet and Western intelligence agents. Today the villa is the luxury Haikon Kartano Hotel.

facing page – 200

Eric Cross, head of MI6 in neutral Scandinavia. On deportation to Britain he asked for police protection before being whisked away into secret hiding.

facing page - 250

CHAPTER 1
The Secret City

"There is no place where espionage is not possible."

Sun Tzu, *The Art of War*, ch. 13.

Towards four o'clock on Saturday the 23rd November 1963, numbers of people began to assemble in the Primula café in Siltarsaarenkatu, which is the main street of Kallio, a suburb of central Heslinki. They came in groups and singly, young and old, students and professional people, and others from many walks of life. They came wrapped in thick winter coats and fur and sheepskin hats pulled well over their ears, in protection against the icy wind which blew from across the frozen wasteland of the distant Siberian tundra.

They came in answer to a letter published the previous day in three of Finland's papers, *Helsingin Sanomat*, the country's largest daily, *Huvudstadsbladet*, the leading paper of the nation's Swedish speaking minority, and *Ylioppilaslehti*, the official organ of the student body.

As they pushed their way into the café, removing their hats and heavy Winter coats, they settled into a section that had been partitioned off and reserved for the meeting which was to follow. As the hour drew near, the café became so crowded that the partition had to be removed, and the meeting was to take up all space that the café offered. There was a great din of voices and moving of furniture, as chairs were lifted from one part of the room to another, and as groups crowded around tables or were pressed against the walls, so occupying every square yard of available space.

They had come in answer to a letter announcing the formation of an international society in Helsinki. There was an atmosphere of anticipation and hopeful curiosity as to what would follow, for most had come singly and were strangers to the rest of the assembly present, and that small group who had called the meeting were perhaps the most surprised by the great throng who had come in response to the letter.

I glanced round the room in trepidation, over-awed by the threatening implication of having to form a club from so large and heterogenous a crowd - for it was I who had first thought of forming the club, and it was on my shoulders that the burden of chairman was to fall. I was obliged to delay the opening time of the meeting, for as the hands ticked passed the hour, still more groups of people pushed their way into the café to attend the meeting. My letter to the press was doing the work of the Sorcerer's apprentice! How could a working committee be duly elected from so large a crowd of total strangers? What procedure could be used to nominate those most suitable to undertake the task of founding an international society?

Those were my thoughts just before the opening of the meeting, but of one thing I was certain: there was no ambiguity over the fact that there existed a widespread popular demand for the founding of an international club. The great crowd assembled bore witness to that! My letter to the press had merely voiced the feelings of great numbers of people resident in Helsinki, and indeed, in other parts of Finland too. Autumn was drawing to a close, icy blasts were beginning to sweep over the land, and the dark gloomy days with only a few hours of light penetrating through an endless expanse of grey cloud lay ahead. November and December, those are the bleakest months of the year in northern Scandinavia, dark depressing months when the sun rarely smiles, and an occasional lonely Finn hugs his bottle of wood-distilled liquor as he totters through the colourless streets of the capital, whilst the potential suicide driven to despair by the "purposelessness" of life may seek to destroy himself.

A glance through the great glass wall of the Primula café from its first floor view on the afternoon of that eventful meeting was a reminder of those days ahead. The café looked onto Hakaniementori, a vast empty square and market place and the junction of some busy main streets, and a gusty wind blew over the bleak square. Through the grey dimness of the parting light could be discerned a number of drunks staggering by the bus station, and a group of swarthy gypsies - *mustalainen* (the black people) as the Finns called them - the men in jackboots and fur caps, the women in leather jackets and colourful ankle length skirts. They would stand on street corners and sell illegally home-brewed alcoholic intoxicants or sometimes enter into other shady transactions with the native Finnish population.

That was Helsinki on a November afternoon, and now a meeting was being held to found an international society - a social club for encouraging friendship between Finns and foreigners - something to drive away the doldrums on many a Winter evening, and bring people together in a spirit of convivial gaiety. Such a club would surely help to solve one of the most widespread social problems in Scandinavia: the depression of loneliness with all its resultant ills. Finns are a retiring people, a nation of rugged individualists, often recluse and modest in their needs in a sparsely populated land; but nonetheless, they are amiable when approached - "scratch a Finn and you find a friend," goes an old saying, and I felt that the club I had in mind would answer a need in the nation's capital. The great throng assembled waiting for the meeting to open - so many faces expressing hopeful anticipation - all this bore witness that the founding of such a club lay close to the hearts of many.

But unknown to the others, somewhere in the throng of strangers, lurked some who had come to the meeting for an ulterior purpose. Dark motives had driven them to the Primula café on that gloomy November afternoon. They sat there, quietly concealed in the crowd - the significance of their identities hidden from those around. They belonged to the life of the Secret City, for in Helsinki was a city within a city, and a life that was rarely revealed to the light of day.

The existence of the secret city is not apparent to the casual visitor, and neither is it apparent even to the average *Helsinkilainen*, for there is nothing to betray the city to a possible cloak and dagger existence as in some capitals of Europe: there are no shady back streets or maze of sewers, or bombed tenement blocks, that might be used as a convenient rendezvous for dark intentions. Helsinki is a clean well-lit place - a city of reinforced steel and concrete buildings, massive and ultra-modern. Ten storied glass-walled office blocks, set up only yesterday, look down onto wide streets or tree-lined avenues. It is a capital which lives up to its country's reputation of having produced a half dozen or so of the world's leading architects of the 20th century, and the white classical early 19th century Lutheran cathedral of Carl Ludvig Engel, dominating the skyline of the city and a beacon to ships far out at sea, together with the buildings along the waterfront of the South harbour, had long ago given Helsinki the name of the White city of the North. If the design and architecture of a city reflects the character of its people, then this was never more true than in the case of Helsinki, for the Finns are an orderly and honest people with a strong appreciation for aesthetic form. Belonging to a small nation, they remain ever aware of their limitations; being sceptical in outlook and practical in application, but their self-effacement dictated by a constant fear of attracting adverse attention hides their stubbornness - their proverbial *Sisu* (or grittiness) in the face of difficulty.

No one would suspect that amongst such a people and in such a city, where the daily routine of life passed uneventfully from day to day and from year to year, there reigned a secret life hidden from the outer world. Helsinki is not a city to arouse the suspicion of strange doings and ulterior motives, for of all capitals of Europe it is perhaps the most uneventful - reflecting, surely, a happier set of circumstances. Its wide streets and plain buildings do not suggest the possibility of such a place harbouring mystery or ambiguity. But then, perhaps, the very factor of these plain functional qualities makes it the perfect city for secret intrigue, where suspicion is rarely drawn from one person to another.

Between the streets of Tehtaankatu and Vuorimiehenkatu, in the suburb of Kaivopuisto, Helsinki's most exclusive residential area, stands a large grey structure, more imposing that any other in the immediate neighbourhood. Together with its grounds, it takes up a space greater than that of the Presidential palace situated by the South harbour, or that of the City's large Town hall in the avenue of Esplanaadikatu, or that of the Great Church overlooking the skyline from the South harbour, or even greater than that of the massive red granite Parliament house dominating the city centre from a mound of high land. This particular building, in the suburb of Kaivopuisto, with its heavy monumental style, reflecting the inevitable solidity of its grey granite, with its Doric columns and classic decoration, stands well back from the roadway suggesting purposeful isolation from other buildings around.

Its windows which look down onto the grounds have an unimpeded view of the adjacent streets, for there are few trees or bushes in the grounds that could help conceal an approaching object. The windows, though, are heavily curtained with white netting and so they are eyes

THE SECRET CITY

which look out without the possibility of being seen into. The railings which surround the grounds are too high for a man to scale, but for the twenty-four hours of the clock there stands a police constable on the pavement without.

The building stands silent and remote, and it is rare to see anyone strolling in the grounds, and only sometimes can one perceive a huddled figure in a black coat and broad-brimmed homburg emerge to the great outside. People walking along the adjacent streets on their daily business, pass by with a feeling of awe and trepidation, and only furtively do they glance up at the massive pile, for they know that what goes on inside belongs to the great unknown. On many a moonlit night it casts its shadow threateningly over the neighbouring streets. On some days of the year a scarlet flag can be seen to flutter from the roof, for this is the embassy of a major power! In this building may be found the origin of the secret city!

Yes, Helsinki is a city of secret intrigue - an unhappy situation made inevitable by the force of political circumstances. As a country defeated *de facto* in war and subjected to a dictated Peace and a Treaty of compulsory "Friendship," she has had to look eastward for her political neutrality, whilst culturally and constitutionally remaining an entirely Western state. The awkward ambiguity of her situation, and her 800 mile frontier with a giant power has instilled her people with a feeling that perhaps the sufferance for their autonomy lies elsewhere than with themselves. Finland is a small country, but her people meet their situation with passive acceptance; and without bitterness or cynicism, they expect no change in the conceivable future; concerning themselves only with their own affairs, they refuse to brood over the implications of their delicate international situation.

But the life of the secret city does not so much concern the Finns themselves as the many foreigners resident or passing through their country. It is, then, as a neutral state, lying close to the frontier of a great power that the secret city has been built-up in an aura of international intrigue and espionage. Thousands of foreigners of many nationalities pass annually through the small capital of half a million souls, and some come on strange or inexplicable missions, and some as political fugitives from justice, and some *en route* to the land of the

"New Civilisation," and self-deceived, their hearts are filled with hopeful anticipation. These are the factors which have made Helsinki what is contended on good authority to be the greatest espionage centre in Europe - if not in the world.

As I raised the hammer to declare the meeting open, I glanced round once more at the crowded assembly in drawing their attention. At that moment I could never have guessed that within the space of a year, one person concealed within that throng would receive a prison sentence for a major political crime, whilst another would suffer a horrible death in unusual circumstances not five miles distant from where we stood.

CHAPTER 2
Who is Jakowleff ?

"Plot me no plots."

Beaumont & Fletcher, *Knight of the Burning Pestle*,
Act II, Sc. 5.

As I brought down the hammer at precisely twenty minutes past four and declared the meeting open, no one in that room, least of all myself, could possibly have anticipated that by so doing, I had set in motion the wheels of a process, which were to shake the diplomatic staffs of a dozen embassies; lead to a criminal prosecution and conviction in the High Court of Finland; and shatter the intelligence network of a Western power.

When order and complete silence prevailed, I proposed that we stand for a two minute silence, in remembrance of a great liberal statesman who had met with a tragic death on the previous day. It was the 23rd of November and the world had awoken to a day of mourning, and on every public building and in front of every apartment house in Helsinki, the Finnish flag flew at half-mast.

As we stood there, men and women of all ages and kinds, in the tense and solemn silence, my thoughts flowed back to the immediately preceding events of that afternoon. I had already received a number of letters that day from correspondents expressing eager interest in the formation of the Society, and that in itself was an omen of future success, and that afternoon, I had arrived early at the Primula café. I had fixed up some cardboard posters and direction signs advertising the meeting. Then at 3.15 pm I ordered lunch which I ate secluded alone, behind the partition, in the silence of the empty room reserved for the meeting.

It was, therefore, with some surprise when at 3.30 my lunch was interrupted by the pulling back of the partition and the entry of two ladies. One was middle aged, a short woman with a clumsy flat-footed gait, whilst the other was a much younger companion with an anaemic complexion. The elder woman, with a broad American drawl boldly announced that they had come to attend the meeting of the International Society. I rose and went over to welcome them, apologising for not having finished my meal.

"Why, are we early,?" exclaimed the elder woman in astonishment, and she grasped my hand in a pincer grip, shaking my arm up and down by the elbow some five or six times, as if greeting a long lost friend at a reunion.

"We're Mormons," she emphatically declared. "This club, it's going to be good, isn't it?"

"I hope so," I replied.

"Friendship, that's what we want, an international friendship club," she said, her large blue eyes gleaming through her spectacles. "I want to work for such a club."

"I'm sure you've come to the right place," I assured.

After continuing lunch in silence for some minutes, she again fixed me with an enthusiastic glance, and then leaning over the table, she asked in a significant undertone: "Say, do you speak Russian?"

"No," I replied.

"I do," she responded with emphatic pride.

These were the first arrivals and I was momentarily apprehensive as to whether my letter might tend to attract the more odd or eccentric kind of person.

The room was filled with people well before 4 o'clock, and I was pleased to see a number of old friends, both Finnish, British and foreign. Peter Martin, who had spent ten years in the RAF before arriving in Finland, an eccentric wit and buffoon, arrived at four, and his immensely tall figure, straight as a ramrod, long face and prominent nose, made him everywhere conspicuous. He bounded into the room with comically affected strides, pushed his way to the centre table, and snatching off his hat which he flourished to attract attention, he cried out to the assembly, "*Mitä kuulu?*" (How are you?)

The company were amused that such an exotic looking foreigner was capable of speaking their language, and they laughed self-consciously.

Peter Martin was not content with this though. He was a great mimic. After removing his coat, he began pulling comically teasing faces at people across the room, and several girls reacted with embarrassed titters and blushes, and at this, he adopted the feminine pose of the shy schoolgirl glancing sideways at an interesting male. This evoked some reluctant laughter from several of the men in the assembly, and to this, Peter indignantly answered by complaining about "all the miserable faces" present, and the gloom of the Finnish temperament.

He opened a brief case and pulling out a portable tape recorder, he began playing back an old Churchill War speech: "We shall fight on the beaches, we shall fight in the streets, we shall never surrender!" This caused immense hilarity, and he lit up a pipe, slapped the behind of a passing waitress, and leaned back in his chair to await the start of the meeting.

At about ten past four, a group of young people, known to me, entered the room whom I had certainly not expected to see. Several of them had even been signatories to my letter to the press, but on urging them to attend the meeting a week previously, they had nonchalantly answered that they had changed their minds and weren't really interested enough in the founding of such a Society, and it was a pleasant surprise, therefore, when I saw them enter *en masse*.

Seppo Lipponen, a Finnish student friend who was helping me with the practical arrangements for the accommodation of the meeting, said there was a journalist outside. I left the noisy assembly and went to the far end of the café where it was quieter and less crowded, and met a lady from *Huvudstandsbladet*. After describing how moved she had been by the pathos of my letter to the press, she asked about my plans for the Society for it was her intention to write a "human interest" story about the loneliness of foreigners in Finland. I had not spoken with her many minutes when I was interrupted by a great din and shouting from the direction of the assembly.

Peter Martin was becoming impatient, and I could hear him shouting, "We want Caesar! We want the meeting to start," and then he set up the refrain of, "Why are we waiting?" I left the journalist, who invited me to her office on Monday morning, and on re-entering the noisy assembly, Peter sprang up from his chair, and making the Roman salute, he cried, "Hail Caesar,!" and amidst laughter and other disturbances, there arose a great clapping and cheering. I smiled, and waving to the happy and exultant throng, I pushed my way through the crowd towards the place at the head of the long table, but before reaching there, I was accosted by Geoff Gee, who was amongst the group who had arrived so unexpectedly at the meeting. He nervously stepped up to me, saying he had something of importance to tell me, and I told him to say it quickly as he could see we were pushed for time.

"We want Jakowleff to speak," he said.

"Who's Jakowleff,?" I asked apprehensively.

"This is Jakowleff," said Geoff Gee, and a tall fair-haired young man, nervously sucking at a pipe, stepped up offering me his hand.

"Let Jakowleff speak,!" chimed in Ray Reed with threatening rudeness.

"Of course - everyone will be allowed to speak," I answered, " - at question time."

"No, let Jakowleff speak first," said Ray knocking the butt of his pipe into my stomach. "He has something important to say."

"We all have something important to say," I answered with a smile, and moved on towards the chair to open the meeting.

At the end of the two minute silence, the assembly relaxed, whilst Peter Martin switched on his tape recorder, pushing the microphone to the head of the long table to record my opening remarks for posterity, and my little speech was punctuated with clapping and cheering and cries of, "Here, here!" I outlined the kind of club I had in mind: there would be regular mid-weekly meetings throughout the year in a hall or other suitable premises in the centre of Helsinki, and at these meetings there would be an organised programme of general cultural interest. As the aim of the Society would be to promote international understanding, these programmes would mainly take the form of talks and film shows devoted to current affairs and other countries, their peoples and problems. The representatives of embassies and consulates would especially be invited to participate in such programmes. On other evenings there would be debates (something I intended to introduce for the first time into Finland), and discussions on general but necessarily non-political topics, the showing of full-length classical films, fancy dress parties, card evenings, etc.

WHO IS JAKOWLEFF?

A question time would follow every lecture or educational film shown to the Society, for I believed that no one should be allowed to present a programme whilst avoiding the opportunity for the expression of divergent opinion, and article 12 of my original draft Constitution laid this down as a condition imposed on visiting speakers. Following question time, or during an interval just prior to it, coffee and cakes would be served, and members could move round and meet one another.

Meanwhile, the Social Hosts would introduce new members to existing members. This, too, would be another purely English custom implanted onto the Finnish way of life, and fortunately, we were in a country sufficiently Anglophile to accept such unusual innovations. Towards the end of the evening, there would always be a time (an hour or more) reserved for dancing, and if a band was unavailable, a gramophone would serve the same purpose - for the word discothèque was not then in existence, or at least, had not penetrated as far north as Finland.

The regular weekly meetings of the Society, however, would only serve as the heart or centre of the club's activities. Numerous other functions to take place outside the premises of the Society would be organised, as outings to night clubs and dance restaurants, guided tours around museums and art galleries, week-ends in skiing chalets and participation in other sporting activities, visits to theatres, the Opera, concerts, etc.

Membership of the Society would be open to all persons over 16 with a manageable command of English, and subject to the discretion of the Committee. The Society would, of course, not be obliged to give reasons for refusing membership to an applicant, and membership would be subject to withdrawal at any time and the Committee would reserve the right to refuse the giving of reasons for such withdrawal of membership. A subscription of 10 marks would be paid annually, and in addition, members would pay a nominal entry fee of 1 mark to enter the Society at its weekly meetings. Each member would be allowed to bring in a guest, but guests would be obliged to pay an entry of 3 marks.

In helping to enhance the name and reputation of the Society, it would be headed by an Honorary President and an Honorary Vice-President, and these would be chosen from respected and distinguished public figures. It was my earnest wish that the famous Finnish novelist, Mika Waltari, best known in the English speaking world for his novel, *Sinuhe* or *The Egyptian*, be elected President, and that a younger man, perhaps the editor of *Ylioppilaslehti*, or the remarkable and controversial intellectual, Jörn Donner, who was friendly with the beautiful Swedish actress, Harriet Andersson, who had starred in some of the greatest films of Ingmar Bergman, be elected Vice-President.

The Society would hold annually a formal dinner at one of the smart Helsinki restaurants, and this would be attended by members in full evening dress. I already entertained grand visions of what such a dinner would be like: magnificent in all the stiff formality of Scandinavian etiquette - bowing, nodding and handshaking - everywhere long tails and starched shirts, and here and there a Star or a row of medals - an august assemblage - hundreds of serious faces awed by the solemnity of the occasion. I flattered myself with the magnificent vision of supporting the President, Mika Waltari, by the arm and formally leading him into a palatial reception hall with crystal chandeliers, and introducing him to members of the Society who would be lined up ceremonially in two ranks facing each other along the length of the room. The blinding light of flash cameras would attend us down the length of the room, and accounts of the dinner would be rushed to the press for the morning papers. This, indeed, would give excellent publicity and prestige value to such a Society!

A working Committee of twelve members would run the affairs of the Society and a sub-committee would be formed to include all other subsidiary officers of the Society, as a commercial artist, Social Hosts, Stewards, and room orderlies to arrange seating and help tidy the hall at the close of meetings.

After this opening address, I announced that we would now get down to the brass tacks of attending to the first practical details in founding such a Society. I would walk out amongst the assembly and ask for volunteers who would be prepared to work on such a Committee as I had outlined, but at this point, I was suddenly interrupted by half a dozen voices from the far end of the room crying, "We want Jakowleff to speak! Let Jakowleff speak!"

"Everyone will have his chance to speak when we come to any

other business," I replied.

"Let Jakowleff speak now," cried Ray Reed threateningly. "He's from HISC,• and he's got something important to say to these people here."

"The procedure for this meeting has been arranged in advance," I replied. "It cannot be changed at this late stage."

"Look here, Bob, this is not a proper way to conduct a meeting," said Mike Spencer, another of the group, dropping any pretence to maintain the formality of the meeting.

"In the circumstances, it's the only way to conduct the meeting if we're going to achieve practical results," I replied.

"Let Jakowleff speak first," cried several voices from the group.

"Jakowleff will have his turn later," I replied. "We haven't got all day to spare, and half an hour's gone already since the start of the meeting."

Loud and angry shouting broke out amongst the small group, and words like "tyranny" and "dictatorship" were thrown out indiscriminately. Ray Reed turned to the rest of the assembly, and flourishing his pipe with angry gestures, he appealed for support that Jakowleff might be allowed to speak. With this act of insubordination against the Chair, I realised there was a risk of pandemonium. Several persons from various parts of the room began shouting, "Well then, let him speak! Give him five minutes," and at this, I surrendered to the request of the group.

Speaking from where he stood at the far end of the room, Jakowleff addressed the assembly in a strained inaudible voice, all the while turning his pipe nervously between his fingers. There was a murmur of voices and whispering throughout the crowd, for the interruptions and irregular behaviour of the group had broken down the orderliness and respectful attention of the rest of the meeting. Unable to catch what he said, I interrupted, inviting him to come up to the Chair and speak from the head of the table. This he did and spoke in a cautious manner, but inaudibly, and his hands which held a slip of paper with scribbled notes, moved convulsively with nervous tension.

• Helsinki International Student Club.

He began by expressing his pleasure on hearing that an international society was to be founded, congratulating me on my initiative, and went on to explain that he was the President of the Helsinki International Students Club which organises social activities and outings for Finnish and foreign students during the Summer months. He said that HISC was affiliated to the National Union of Students of Finland, and outlined the facilities and popular success of the club. He explained that HISC, which up until then had only operated in the summer, now intended to open in the Winter months also.

He put the rhetorical question to the assembly, "But why am I here now,?" and began to express his opinion that any international club in Helsinki would most appropriately be led by a student organisation, as students tended to speak English better than non-students. This statement proved to be tactless for there were angry cries of dissent from the assembly. He concluded by appealing to those present to allow the student body to organise the founding of the projected society, and he assured them that although the student body would run such a society it would be open to non-students as well, and that the name of the club would not contain the word "student." He politely thanked me for taking up ten minutes of the meeting's time, and then returned to his place.

As may be anticipated, I was justifiably angered by the presumption of this individual, who appearing out of the blue, should address the assembly in such a way without having attempted to consult me in advance. He had plainly come for no other purpose than to knock me out of the Chair, in exploiting an exceptional situation for the benefit of the student body, and the fact that he could have done this with a straight face, without a qualm of misgiving, only tended to make his behaviour seem all the more reprehensible.

As soon as he had taken his place again amongst his companions I boldly replied that this meeting had been called for an immediately practical purpose; that he and his friends had come without any practical design or authority from the student body (and this Jakowleff admitted), and that finally, the majority of those in the room were above student age and would not be comfortable in a club controlled by students. This was followed by cries of "Here, here!" from every part of the hall.

The HISC group, however, were not to be appeased. They shouted abuse. Ray cried out, "We have ideas quite different from your ideas," and Barbara, his wife, gave an irrelevant little speech about my knowing "nothing about HISC" and not having attended any of its meetings the previous Summer, and then Mike Spencer insisted in a pedantic manner on drawing the attention to the assembly to the fact that the meeting had not been called and opened in a proper manner. He said there had been no proper nomination of a Chairman and other officers to ensure the correct procedure of the present meeting (which of course was true) and that I was acting arbitrarily.

It was in the middle of this speech, whilst Mike Spencer was drawling in a heavy monotone, that a little bespectacled man with receding grey hair, and an irritable manner, suddenly stood up at the back of the room and interrupted the speaker.

"Mr. Chairman," he began in a petulant tone, "this meeting's gone on for almost an hour, and it's being conducted in a ridiculous fashion. We've been continually subjected to disorderly interruptions from a group that I, and probably many other people here, have never heard of. We haven't got all night to spare - and I'm sure there are many other people here, like myself, who'll have to be leaving shortly - and I would propose, Mr. Chairman, that this group be asked to leave the meeting and form their own club elsewhere."

There were loud cries of "Here, here,!" from all over the room. A gentleman seconded the proposal of the little bespectacled man, and I asked for a raise of hands, and by a unanimous vote, the HISC group were requested to leave.

Piqued by the humiliation of the interruption to his speech, Mike Spencer turned angrily on his heel, and followed by the others, left the room. There were cheers and hooting, and some stamping of feet. As the group left, breathing threats and dire vengeance, little did I realise the enormous resentment I had aroused, and I could never then have imagined the mischief they were subsequently to cause.

But they were gone and the meeting could now continue in an orderly manner. I again said that I would walk out amongst the crowd and ask for volunteers for those prepared to work on the Committee of the Society. This business would bring approximately a fifteen minute break in the meeting, and during this interval, coffee and cakes would be made available to those present, and I signalled to Seppo Lipponen, who was at the back of the hall, to bring in the waitresses to take orders for refreshments.

To ensure that a responsible and competent Committee would be elected, it was my intention to only approach persons of a mature age and distinguished bearing, who at the same time looked compliant, trustworthy, and as if they were assured of a financially secure position in life. The reputation and success of the projected Society would naturally depend on the ability and character of the persons so chosen. Picking a Committee on sight of face is not a good basis for judging the character of those chosen, and I was soon to learn that none of them stood up to the ideal bourgeois stereotype I had formulated in my mind.

As I moved amongst the throng, climbing over the backs of chairs and squeezing between tables, I knew that my task would not be easy. I looked round at the sea of faces, and on being struck by what seemed a fairly stable and ordinary sort of person, I would scrutinise his or her face, asking myself: would this man or woman be suitable to serve on the Committee of the International Society?

Judgement and decision had to be made within seconds. Usually the persons so scrutinised would register no reaction to this cursory examination of their features, but continue sitting with vacant expressions, but sometimes, a face would break into a friendly smile, and then I was obliged to pop the question with a, "Good afternoon Sir (or Madam) would you be prepared to serve on the Committee of the International Society?" He or she might make an embarrassed excuse to avoid selection, or sometimes willingly comply.

Meanwhile, several of the HISC group had surreptitiously rejoined the assembly, taking up their old place again by the glass wall at the back of the room.

Nearer at hand I was interrupted with tips or advice, or even assisted more directly with the business of the moment. The insignificant bespectacled little man, with the receding grey hair and fussy manner, who had interrupted Mike Spencer, came up behind me, suggesting that I don't forget to nominate more women to the Committee. A couple of minutes later, he approached me again saying that the waitresses couldn't get to the front of the room to take orders as it was overcrowded with people and furniture. He suggested that some tables be shifted in a certain direction and that people be requested to move more to the back, and I said that this was a good idea, and he began to attend to the matter himself.

Five minutes later, he again came up behind me, with yet another suggestion: that those sitting at the head of the long table be asked to move, and that it be reserved for Committee members and I agreed, and he busily went off and attended to this. This caused a certain amount of protest - some had been sitting there since well before 4 o'clock - and some refused to budge, but the little grey haired man was nonetheless acting in a very officious manner, as if already an authorised official of the Society, and most were thereby persuaded to move. He was a tentative little man with a constantly worried expression, but there was no doubting he was making himself useful - he had probably saved the meeting, even, from collapsing into anarchy - and I was grateful for his assistance.

CHAPTER 3
Twelve take a bow

"All violent feelings ... produce in us a falseness in all our impressions of external things, which I would generally characterise as the 'Pathetic Fallacy.'"

John Ruskin, *Modern Painters*, Vol. 3, pt. 4, ch. 12.

At last a full Committee had been randomly selected, and it was now time to have it properly nominated and voted into office, and on returning to the head of the table, I was mildly surprised to find the little bespectacled man sitting meekly on my right hand side.

The fact that I had not chosen him for the Committee, had obviously not deterred him from the intention that he was anyway going to sit on such a Committee, but if I had not selected him, it was not through purposeful avoidance, but simply because he was always behind and not in front of me. I had decided to nominate each Committee member to a specific post, so that there could be no confusion from the start as to the exact obligations of each member to the Society. I asked first for a Treasurer.

A distinguished looking man in his sixties, with dark and silvery grey hair, sitting on my immediate left, put up his hand and volunteered for this. He was proposed and seconded, and this formality completed, I intended going on with the next item, when I was unexpectedly interrupted.

The Hon. Treasurer, the first duly elected official of the International Society, rose from his chair and pulling himself to his full height, he began to deliver a bombastic and irrelevant speech.

"Mr. Chairman," he began, bowing to me respectfully, "Ladies and gentlemen," and he bowed towards various directions of the room, "as the first Treasurer of the International Society of Helsinki - a very responsible position - as indeed the Treasurer of any society holds a very responsible position - I feel it incumbent upon me that I should introduce myself to members of this newly founded association." He spoke in a resonant voice amply reflecting his feelings of awe at being suddenly thrust into a position of such importance. "My name is Enblom. I am a

TWELVE TAKE A BOW

resident of many years standing in this country, having lived here since before the last War. By profession I am a teacher of languages - particularly of the Swedish, English and German languages. I am by birth, education and citizenship of Swedish nationality. I was born in Karlskrona, which is situated in that most beautiful province of Southern Sweden, Blekinge. I come from an old military family, at one time distinguished in that province, although I myself rose only to the rank of Sergeant of Cadets."

A number of people began grinning in amusement at this time-wasting speech and I was gradually overcome with a feeling of increasing impatience, but could only look on with an expression of good-humoured tolerance.

"My wife is a Finnish citizen, and in her name, I am fortunate to have become a man of property in this country. On the island of Lille-Pellinge, I possess a villa of considerable proportions, capable of housing some thirty to forty persons. I should like, Mr. Chairman," he said turning towards me, "to put this villa at the disposal of the Society."

I thanked the Treasurer for the generous offer of this useful facility, and thought I had cut him short, but then he continued: "My hobbies are learning languages and reading the poetry of different tongues. I am at present engaged in studying Spanish. I hope the International Society will encourage the reading of poetry, for I should like to found a poetry reading circle of different nationalities."

I assured him that I thought this a wonderful idea and after bowing to the assembly and then to me, he sat down amidst cheers and clapping.

I next asked for a Programme Director, and a tall bespectacled man of about fifty, with an awkward manner and a face which always wore an expression as if startled by surprise, said he would undertake this task and he was duly nominated, but then there were cries from the back of the hall of, "Let's have a look at him! Make him stand up!" These shouts came from the HISC group, who had surreptitiously re-joined the meeting.

In great confusion and embarrassment, and keeping his head bowed, the Programme director rose and made himself visible to the assembly.

"What's his name,?" came a shout from the back of the hall.

The Programme Director leaned towards the head of the table and tried to tell me his name, but he spoke so inaudibly, as if wishing to whisper it into my ear, that I failed to hear him. At last, a third person repeated his name to me, and when I announced to the assembly: "Programme Director, Mr. Aldar Runela," the gentleman concerned seemed so embarrassed at hearing his name pronounced in public, that he went red in the face and quickly sat down again.

Next came the Film Projection and Technical Director, and at this point I had to address the entire assembly, in enquiring if anyone present owned or could operate a film projector. One woman stood up saying she had a magic lantern, and then a tall bespectacled man of about fifty with a lean boyish face, sitting beside Mr. Runela, rather shyly put up his hand. Speaking slowly he explained that he was the film instructor at SOK, Finland's largest co-operative, and that he could let the Society have use of a film projector and also films. Like Mr. Runela he had a timid manner, and in fact both gentlemen looked so similar in appearance, being of the same height and build, and bespectacled with long grey faces, that they might easily have been taken for twins, but as I subsequently learned, they were unrelated but good friends.

This gentleman was duly nominated the Film Projection and Technical Director of the Society, and the formality over, I anticipated encountering the same trouble in getting him to tell me his name and show himself to the company as I had had with Mr. Runela, but in this I was wrong, for he suddenly jumped up and turning to the assembly, he boldly announced of his own accord: "Film Projection and Technical Director, Mr. Heikki Jokimäki," and then he bumped down onto his seat again with lightening speed.

There were loud cheers and clapping at this uncalled-for gesture - some of it mocking applause from the HISC group at the back of the room, and smiling awkwardly at those seated near him, it was clear that the newly elected officer was proud of his initiative and flattered at the thought of having made such an impression on the assembly, as if to say, "Wasn't I a brave fellow!"

Next came the Entertainments Director, and I had already settled in my mind as onto whom this post should fall. A good-looking fair haired man, of average height and slim build, in his late thirties, had been amongst the first arrivals at the meeting that afternoon, and one of the first to take a place at the main long table. He had also been one of those sitting at the table whom the fussy grey haired little man had been unable to shift.

He had followed every minute of the meeting with lively interest and humour, sometimes laughing at the interruptions or my sharp replies, and during the interval, joking and talking loquaciously with those around him. It was obvious he was a "charmer" as far as the women were concerned and I thought this a valuable prerequisite for an Entertainments Director. Before the meeting had begun, he had already struck up an acquaintanceship with Peter Martin, opposite whom he sat, and during the interval, he had chatted-up several women sitting on his right - one of whom (a German girl) he was to subsequently marry on divorcing his current wife.

On his consenting to serve on the Committee, I asked whether he was a Finnish citizen or a foreigner.

"I'm a Swede," he replied.

"Then you're a foreigner," I exclaimed.

"A Swede a foreigner,!" he answered in mock scorn. "A Swede is never a foreigner in Finland. We ruled this country for the first six hundred years of its existence."

This piece of insolence was met by a peel of laughter. He was duly nominated the Entertainments Director and gave his name as Gösta Kelter, and then Peter Martin volunteered for the post of Music Director, to which he was accordingly nominated.

"But what will you do for music,?" I asked him a little too late, for I was doubtful as to whether he could supply appropriate equipment.

"This," he answered pointing to his tape recorder which he carried around in a brief case all day, and used for instruction in phonetics.

There was an outburst of laughter, and this spontaneous show of scepticism annoyed Peter intensely, and he jumped up from the table assuring the assembly that although his machine was small, it was a "good machine" and "a lot louder than it looked." He turned the tape over and began playing back the Churchill War speech, and this brought an uproar of laughter from everywhere in the room. (He obliged his pupils to learn and recite Churchill's speeches in improving their elocution.) But this laughter annoyed him all the more.

"It does play music as well," he assured, and he began searching frantically in his brief case, took out another tape which he placed in the machine, and began playing some music.

"Is this loud enough,?" he cried, turning on the full volume.

The assembly judged his equipment satisfactory, and he assured the meeting that of course there would be much better dance music than that at the meetings of the club. Peter, the scatty buffoon was going to take his task as Music Director of the Society in real earnest!

Then followed the nomination of the Catering Manageress, but there was confusion over this matter. At first, the thickly bespectacled dumpy woman, who had been the first arrival that afternoon, was nominated to this post, but subsequently, she discovered she didn't know what she had been nominated for, and the shock of realising she was the Catering Manageress filled her with agitation. She said she could not take on the responsibility of buying food for the Society, and so her resignation was immediately accepted.

She afterwards became the Assistant Subscription Manageress, but eventually, even this became too much for her. She did not fulfil my stereotype of the ordinarily conventional person, but her enthusiasm and friendly manner induced me to select her for the Committee. Her name was Miss Inge Kainulainen.

A plump woman in her middle forties, with platinum blonde hair, a pink fleshy complexion and a snub nose, altogether conveying a pig-like impression, volunteered for the post of Catering Manageress. She was sitting nearby, but against the wall of the room, and therefore had not actually been pre-selected for serving on the Committee.

Before I duly nominated her to the post, she hesitated in a concerned manner saying, "This club's going to be quite non-political, isn't it?" I assured her that it would be.

"You see, I work at the American embassy and I mustn't get involved in anything political." She gave her name as Miss Elisabeth Vaajajärvi.

The next member to be nominated to the Committee was someone to fulfil the function of Press and Publicity Manager. A tall distinguished looking man in his middle sixties with dark neatly cut hair, said he could undertake this. He had a deeply furrowed fleshy complexion and pouted lips giving his mouth a sensuous appearance, and his fingers and neck were perceptibly stained with nicotine and tobacco smoke.

His brown suit was creased and hard worn, although clearly it had been cut from a cloth of good quality and style - a design sharply contrasting it from the charcoal greys and dark worsteds preferred by most Finnish men. He wore a scruffy tie, and an ill-fitting collar over a striped shirt - but again, his shirt was another distinguishing feature of his dress, contrasting him from the majority of Finns who preferred plain white nylon. Despite any adverse qualities that might be seen in his appearance, his aristocratic manner and slight limp, and a worldly sensuous smile, together with a habit of rolling his tongue in his cheek, intuitively persuaded me that he could be of credit to the Society. He was to play a major part in the drama to follow and a more than passing description of this colourful figure is fully warranted.

He had previously told me he held dual Finnish-American nationality, and whenever asked as to his citizenship, he always gave this ambiguous answer attended by an awkwardly complicated explanation. I later learnt that his correct nationality was Finnish, but he always seemed reluctant to admit this. He was even more ambiguous about his ancestral origins. Sometimes he said he was of Austrian descent, and on other occasions that it was Swiss. Perhaps he was justified in claiming an ancestry from both countries. When I now enquired as to his occupation, he said he was the Scandinavian representative for the *New York Herald Tribune*, and naturally, I accepted this as being an excellent qualification for the Press and Publicity Manager of the International Society. He spoke a perfect Queen's English in a pleasantly reverberating tone of voice. He gave his name as Waldemar von Etter, and as I had half anticipated, I now knew that a Finnish aristocrat from a famous old family was to honour us by accepting nomination onto the Committee of our Society!

This being done, the Subscription Manageress was the next to be nominated. She was a girl in her late twenties, blonde, with a full face, small eyes and an icy manner, imposing rather than attractive. Earlier in the meeting she had frequently nodded to me with encouraging gestures to take a firm stand against the HISC hecklers. Her serious and intelligent countenance had persuaded me that she would prove an efficient personality in working for the Society. She was a Swedish Finn, and her name was Ingrid Andersson.

Next came the question of nominating a Legal Adviser and this proved to be of some difficulty. Peter jumped up and insisted that the Legal Adviser would hold the most responsible post in the Society, as he would be obliged to answer for any kind of wrongdoing committed on the Society's premises, and furthermore, would need to defend members if at any time they fell upon a "legal misfortune" within the premises. He concluded by saying that the Legal Adviser must necessarily know all the ins and outs of the Finnish penal code. This rhetorical speech, together with its irrelevant implications, tended to generate a reluctance on the part of anyone to undertake the post.

None of the persons I had originally chosen for the Committee would volunteer, and when I appealed to the entire assembly, no one would come forward and there arose a murmur of voices as a number tried to persuade friends or acquaintances near them to take up the post of Legal Adviser, by way of pushing it from the conscience of their own shoulders.

At last, Gösta Kelter, the Entertainments Director, signalled to me pointing to a very insignificant looking man sitting against the wall of the room, and cried, "He'll do it!" The man concerned was acutely perplexed at this unexpected gesture of his friend, Gösta Kelter, but seizing an opportunity, I leapt over to the little man exclaiming, "Why, good evening, Sir! You look just the man to take on the post of Legal Adviser. I hope you won't disappoint the Society by refusing at this stage in our proceedings." After some embarrassed indecision and an exchange of words, during which the entire assembly waited in intense expectation, he consented, and there were cheers, and he was duly nominated, and gave his name as Hilding Westerholm.

Next came the nomination of one of the most important posts on the Committee: that of Vice-Chairman. I had exhausted the small group originally selected by me for the Committee (although I believe several had managed to slip away unobserved), and so I appealed to the assembly for nominations for Vice-Chairman. Several pointed to a small respectable looking man in his late fifties, seated at the side of the room.

He reacted with an affectedly embarrassed gesture, waving his hand aside at those signalling to him, but I sensed at once that he might be willing to take on the post, and I went over to him and asked if he would be Vice-Chairman of the Society. "If I can be of any help," he only replied. I exchanged a few words with him: he was a Danish language teacher of English, German and his mother tongue. He taught Danish at the University, and was the senior English master at the Swedish Lyceum, the largest and one of the oldest Swedish boys' schools in Finland. He gave his name as Stig Lambertsen.

"Will you take on the post of Vice-Chairman,?" I repeated to him again. He looked stolid and well situated in life, and he could give the Society a good academic front.

"Well, if I can be of any help," he said again, without seeming to care one way or the other, and I took his manner for exaggerated modesty.

"You can be of use to the Society by accepting nomination to the Vice-Chairmanship," I said.

"I'll be glad if I can be of any help," he only said again.

Little did I know then (an ironical reflection on remembering the first sentiments he expressed with regard to accepting the Chairmanship of the Society) that he was to be the man who finally sealed the destruction of the Society just at the moment when it might have been saved. However, he was duly nominated Vice-Chairman, and then came the matter of nominating the Secretary. Inevitably, there was only one person on whom this post could fall - the fussy little man on my right.

During the nomination of the Committee members, he had been continually fidgeting to offer advice on all sorts of matters: he had chided me for bullying Mr. Westerholm into the post of Legal Adviser, and now he had begun to pass round a sheet of paper for Committee members to write down their names and addresses, and despite his fussy manner, his constantly worried expression and neurotic chain smoking, I judged him a useful sort.

He was accordingly nominated Secretary of the International Society, and with this nomination, the ultimate destiny of the Society was finally to be sealed. On his being nominated, though, he did not rise from the table and take a formal bow as had the others, and neither did he give me his name, and as there was a certain amount of fidgeting and murmur of voices amongst the assembly, and as I wanted to progress the meeting, I did not bother worrying the Secretary into showing himself to the crowd. Lastly, I myself was nominated Chairman of the Society - I nudged the Secretary into proposing me, and one other person in the crowd seconded this.

There followed a discussion on a number of essential points of policy determining the composition and future of the Society. First came the question of the Society's name, and it was suggested that the Society be called the International Society Finland and not the International Society Helsinki, as I had proposed, and the motion was voted and carried, and accordingly, the Society's name was changed. Gösta Kelter proposed that the minimum age of members of the Society be raised from 16 to 18, as it would be embarrassing to the Society if a 16 or 17 year old girl was to be compromised by another member, and the motion was put to the meeting and carried unanimously.

The Secretary proposed that the foreign members of the Society should only be those registered with the police as residents in the country, and with a fussy manner and in his cautious nasal tone of voice, he stressed the importance of seeking to satisfy the authorities from the very start of the Society's existence. The motion was put to the vote and carried.

Next followed a lengthy and argumentative discussion on the actual day for the weekly meetings, and finally, Wednesday was settled upon. Then on my agenda came the question of electing an Honorary President. I had set my heart, as I have said, on Mika Waltari, but after a heated discussion, during which Hilding Westerholm rose and implied that the gentleman suggested was a "drinker" and might therefore cast doubt on the Society's good reputation, a vote was taken and Mr. Waltari unanimously rejected, despite his fame as a writer of international repute. This decision, expressing moral reprobation, annoyed me, coming as it did from a nation not renowned for its abstinence, but the candidature had to be dropped, and Alvar Aalto (the architect) was voted in his place, and Miss Inge Kainulainen agreed to contact him with regard to this.

Next followed a discussion on membership and entry fees and the initial financing of the club, and it was agreed that all present should contribute to a voluntary donation of one mark per person, and several ladies under the authority of our Treasurer, went round the room with sheets of paper collecting names and addresses and one mark donations.

By now the business of the founding meeting was almost over and it was proposed and carried that the first weekly meeting of the Society should beheld on Wednesday 4th of December - only eleven days hence. In the meantime, the Committee would make up a programme, secure premises, and send out a circular to members informing them where and when.

At this point, the Secretary nudged me, asking if he could have a word, and he rose from the table and speaking in a worried tone of voice, he informed those present that this meeting could not really be regarded in the strict sense as a "founding meeting." He granted that the present meeting had succeeded in achieving a great deal of work, but that it had been "unconstitutional." No secretaries had been appointed to take down the minutes, no proper agenda had been read, and the Committee had been chosen and nominated in a very "weird and irregular manner."

His little speech dampened the spirits and expectations of the assembly, and in view of all the strenuous work which had been accomplished that afternoon in the face of considerable difficulty, his discouraging tone and attitude annoyed me intensely - especially in view of the fact that he had been the most irregularly chosen Committee member of all. He proposed that the existing Committee should only be regarded as provisional, and the motion was voted on and passed.

At that moment, a young Canadian, one of the HISC group, demanded an immediate re-election of the Committee - he made the demand purely as a disruptive gesture - and after some shouting on both sides, and a vote of confidence in the present provisional Committee, he was so infuriated at the snub, that he stormed out of the café crying, "Then I wish you all the worst luck in the world!"

The assembly was momentarily stunned by this gesture, gasping in disbelief at the outrageous rudeness, but unfortunately, with those few words, the curse had been laid on the Society, and as events were to prove, no exorcism could remove it.

The lists with the members names and addresses, together with the donations which had been collected, were returned to the Treasurer, and I thanked those present for attending the meeting, and brought it formally to a close.

By now it was 7 o'clock, and I asked the Committee members to stay just a few minutes longer so that a meeting could be arranged for later in the week. As the crowd began to move hurriedly away, Seppo Lipponen pushed to the front of the room, saying that a journalist from *Uusi Suomi* (Finland's third largest daily paper) wanted to speak with me on the phone.

"That's a job for our Press and Publicity Manager," I said nodding towards Waldemar von Etter, and Seppo led the gentleman to the phone.

Sitting down with the rest of the Committee, we checked the finances of the Society - the Treasurer sat behind a great mountain of notes and coins - and discussed and settled several matters of immediate concern. Glancing cursorily at the list of the names and addresses of Committee members, to ensure they were all quite legible, I was surprised on reading the name of the most important functionary of all. He had written his name, address and phone number in legible but very small block letters - a handwriting reflecting the reticence of his character.

"Evans! That's not a very Finnish name, is it,?" I pondered in surprise, for I had thought our Secretary was a Finn, and I had anyway resolved that he should be.

The Secretary moved uneasily on his chair, and then replied, "No, I'm not Finnish," and as if reluctant to admit the fact, he said in an off-hand manner, "I'm British."

Without giving further thought to the incident I moved onto other business, handing out carbon copies of the fifty-four paragraph draft Constitution of the Society, and after some moments perusal, Stig Lambertsen commented, "This reads like the rules for a boys' reform school!"

My inspiration for the Constitution had been Beau Nash rather than "a boys' reform school," entailing an up-dating of the ideas of the great 18th century socialite of Bath to suit the needs of 20th century Helsinki. But I said nothing in answer to the Vice-Chairman's sour comment.

Seppo returned and sat down at the far end of the table, where he followed the meeting with interest, and I called upon the Programme Director for any suggestions he might offer for our first Wednesday. He became confused, looking more startled even than he usually did when he merely sat and did nothing, and he stammered about inviting a man from the Indian Embassy. Then Mr. Jokimäki said he could bring his projector and films along to the first meeting, and so on this occasion, Mr. Runela was saved further embarrassment.

Von Etter returned to the meeting, and Peter outlined his plans for recording music from suitable radio programmes for re-play to the Society, and Evans warned him against the dangers of contravening the music copyright laws.

Then came the most urgent topic, that of securing premises for the meetings of the Society. Waldemar von Etter volunteered to look into this matter, and promised to phone me on Tuesday of next week as to the results of his enquiries. Finally, it was decided that a Committee meeting be held at the Primula café at 8 o'clock on the following Wednesday, and then, exhausted by the strenuous proceedings of the long afternoon, we rose from the table and began to leave.

"I think this club's going to be very successful," remarked Gösta Kelter to several colleagues across the table.

I noticed Evans edge his way up to Enblom and Lambertsen and secretively whisper some confidential words.

Peter strode over to me, and said aside: "I like the people here. I think the Society's going to be a success."

CHAPTER 4
The reticent little man

"We were in some little time fixed in our seats, and sat with that dislike which people not too good-natured usually conceive of each other at first sight."

Sir Richard Steele, *Spectator*, No. 132.

Unknown to myself or to anyone at the time, the first seed had already been sown for putting into operation a conspiracy which was to grow and ultimately take on the form of a political plot. The seed of this conspiracy was to be found in slander and half truths, calculated lying and the credulity of those dull persons only too ready to accept any malice spread about others.

After the meeting, I invited Seppo back to my flat for a glass of wine and a bite to eat. I lived not three minutes from the Primula café, in Pitkänsillanranta, the most beautiful street in Kallio, overlooking a narrow inlet of the sea and the city centre of Helsinki. As we made our way to the street, Seppo urged that we should make our peace with the HISC group, for they had been so distraught by their rough reception that afternoon and by what they regarded as my "tyrannical dictatorship," that they had sworn vengeance at any cost. Seppo had sat with them in the company of the *Huvudstadsbladet* journalist, and he had been very disturbed by what they had said in her presence.

As we came into Pitkänsillanranta, we bumped into a couple of drunks, for on the street corner there was an alcohol shop, and dozens of drunks and alcoholics frequented the street during all hours of the day and night, and when the alcohol shop was closed, then gypsies from the countryside would loiter in the street selling their home brewed intoxicants, and this was the only adverse characteristic of an otherwise pleasant environment.

I lived on the fourth floor of a fine apartment block and my window looked onto a magnificent skyline view of the city, stretching from the Great Church, Stockmann's (the main department store), the famous railway station of Elial Saarinen, the Hotel Torni, the Post Office, the Parliament house and the National museum. The shoreline of

Soviet spy, Ron Evans

convicted by the Finns in May 1964, on his arrival at Heathrow on 24th February 1965, after his release from prison and deportation from Finland.

the sea inlet was lined with many pleasure boats, which had now been brought up onto the bank and turned upside down to rest on trestles for the duration of the Winter months, and across the water lay the Botanical museum and gardens of the city.

"*Kipis*,!" I exclaimed raising a glass after we had comfortably settled ourselves in my flat.

"To the club," replied Seppo.

"They're not a bad crowd, the Committee we've chosen, don't you think?"

"They're all strangers. No one can tell yet," he replied thoughtfully. "Some are a bit weird though. That von Etter - he's a queer fellow."

"I believe he comes from a well connected family," I replied.

"I've heard the name before, but I don't know anything about him," said Seppo.

"He should make a good Press officer," I remarked.

"I don't think he speaks Finnish," said Seppo.

"Doesn't speak Finnish,?" I exclaimed surprised.

"When I took him to the phone to speak to the journalist from *Uusi Suomi*, he only spoke Swedish," replied Seppo. "He didn't seem able to speak any Finnish."

"I expect that's just his form of cultural snobbery. He's one of those too proud to speak Finnish - there are still plenty around of his generation," I said. I sensed instinctively that my friend had taken a dislike to von Etter, and knowing Seppo's Finnish language patriotism, I decided not to discuss the matter further.

"Do you know many of that HISC group well, who attended the meeting this afternoon,?" enquired Seppo curiously after a thoughtful pause.

"Some of them quite well - not that I choose to associate with them," I replied. "And you yourself know that I know that Swedish fellow, Anders Carlén."

"Who was that dark looking chap,?" he asked, " - very small."

"That was Geoff Gee, an Englishman," I answered.

"He's dangerous!"

"How do you mean?"

"He was telling everyone you were expelled from Sweden as being a person unfit to live there."

"Surely not,!" I cried astonished. "Who was he saying that to?"

"To everyone! To everyone who would listen. He told everyone at the back of the room not to vote for you."

"He actually said I was expelled from Sweden as being unfit to live there?"

"In just those words."

"It's defamatory! The accusation doesn't contain an iota of truth," I cried angrily.

"That's why I said the HISC group were dangerous," exclaimed Seppo. "They'll do their worst to wreck the Society and bespatter your name in mud. That's why I said we'd better come to terms and appease them."

"Appease them, my foot, we'll fight them," I cried.

"You can't fight people who tell lies and spread rumour. They'll always remain friendly to your face whilst stabbing you in the back. They're not manoeuvrable to fight with."

"How did other people, not part of the HISC crowd, react to this slander?"

"I don't think they were taken in. The HISC group had already disgraced themselves in the eyes of the majority."

"Then perhaps it's nothing to worry about," I said.

"Still, you should be careful about the future, and try to patch things up with the HISC group," said Seppo.

"I shall do something," I replied.

"You remember how the slander originated," said Seppo after a pause, taking down the rest of his wine. "It was Anders Carlén who started it."

"I remember well," I answered. "You were with me," and my mind flowed back to that evening in the Kolme Kreiviä almost a year ago. The Kolme Kreiviä (The Three Counts) was situated in the heart of Helsinki in the main street, Mannerheimintie, opposite the Swedish Theatre, an ultra-modern comfortably furnished café, and the most frequented haunt of foreigners of all kinds in the city.

One Saturday evening, Seppo and I, amongst a group of friends, were engaged in a lively discussion on Sweden's controversial role with her neighbours during the last War; when a young Swede from a nearby table overhearing our discussion with curiosity and mounting irritation at so much criticism of his country, interrupted our conversation after an apology, and took us to task. None of us, however, were prepared to retract anything we had said, as "history was history and could not be reversed," and the Swede was suffered to listen in silence as we recounted the stories of the Baltic exiles, the Norwegian partisans, the Finnish Lapland refugees, and the Swedish iron ore and railway agreements with the Nazis, and when we had had our say, the poor Swede was left dumbfounded for lack of an argument, but scorching with resentment, he suddenly turned on me (who had said less than the others) with a personal attack, crying, "I don't believe you had to leave Sweden for nothing."

This was a reference to an earlier part of our discussion when I had recounted the annual end of Summer clear-out by the authorities of all foreigners in Sweden carrying student or short term labour permits, and I had been amongst this number in September 1961.

"You must have done something wrong," continued the Swede, whose name was Anders Carlén. "I've never heard of such a thing as these mass expulsions before."

"They're common knowledge," I replied, "and I'd done nothing wrong. It's just a policy of the Swedish authorities in making an annual clearance of their country - nothing out of the ordinary for many countries at that time of the year."

"I'll check on this with the Swedish police," said Carlén whose pride was stung by what he regarded as an affront to his country. "I'm going to Stockholm next week and I'll visit the police."

"Do that," I said.

I saw Anders Carlén on several occasions within the next few months, but he had never bothered to visit the police to satisfy himself as to the truth of my allegations, and he meanwhile allowed the suggestion to circulate amongst the HISC group, of which he was a member, that perhaps I had been deported from his country for a disgraceful action.

"There's certainly a good basis for slander there," commented Seppo.

"I think I'll consult a lawyer on Monday," I said, "to nip this thing in the bud, and clear it up for once and for all."

"I wouldn't do that if I were you," said Seppo. "I should wait and see how things go, and if the HISC group get really nasty, then perhaps see a lawyer."

I decided to follow Seppo's advice and ignore the HISC group. As I was later to learn, it was perhaps a foolish lapse of judgement, but by then it was too late to amend the fault.

Shortly before 7 o'clock on the evening of the following day, whilst busily preparing the agenda for next Wednesday's meeting, my doorbell was rung. I was not expecting visitors and did not much like the idea of being disturbed by callers as I wanted to complete the agenda before going to town to meet friends at the Kolme Kreiviä.

On opening the front door I saw a small thickly set bespectacled man, with short wavy grey hair receding at the forehead, and wearing a heavy although crumpled trench coat. On seeing me, he shifted from one foot to the other, and the folded skin of his worried countenance relaxed into a half smile.

"Good evening, Mr. Evans," I exclaimed brightly. "Welcome! Please come in."

"I only thought I'ld come to see you about one or two matters," he said pushing passed me into the hallway and snatching off his coat.

"By all means," I replied, a little apprehensive at his worried tone.

As I took his coat, he walked straight into the living room without further ado, and on asking him to take a seat, he sat down in my only armchair crossing one leg over the other as if quite at home.

"I'm glad you've come along," I said. "I was needing some help just now."

To put him completely at ease I offered a cigar, which he accepted with a grudging gesture, but on cutting off the end and lighting up, it became an obvious source of pleasure to him, and he soon filled the room with great puffs of cigar smoke. I offered him a glass of wine, and he accepted this too with a reluctant gesture, explaining that he was driving.

"You know, it's a good thing this club has been started," he began in his nasal voice and shifting awkwardly in the chair. "Something like this has been needed for so long in Helsinki. There's no social life at all here in this country."

I agreed with him.

"I've been living here for nine years now, and I've never had the opportunity to mix with student circles," he continued, crossing one leg over the other and taking down his wine. "My life has been very dull here." He was a nice quiet modest little man. "Those damned students, though, they really got my goat yesterday," he said with an unexpected burst of petulance which surprised me. "It was good we took a firm stand against them. What really got me was when they said students speak English better than non-students. Now I've found quite the opposite since I've been here: it's the students who can't speak English, whilst there are many ordinary working people who can."

"The main foreign language here is still German," I explained, "but that's changing with the rising generation."

"I hope I wasn't too rude when I got up yesterday and told them to get out."

"Not at all," I replied.

"You see, I'd been to my firm's annual Xmas party the night before," he explained, "and I had a hell of a hangover. You know what it's like after a hangover - you're tired and fed up, and someone only has to suddenly get your goat when you explode."

"I know," I answered sympathetically.

"Still, we'll have to make it up with the student body," he continued. "They're very powerful. We don't want any quarrel with them. - You got very excited at the meeting yesterday. You'll have to control your nerves," he said suddenly after a pause.

"It was a difficult meeting to handle," I replied.

"I'm glad I've been elected onto the Committee," he said a moment later, and I was at once reminded of the irregular way in which he had secured his own election. "I feel I can do something useful at last - something with purpose. For a number of years I've been a member of an amateur radio club here in Helsinki, and do you know, they're so damned nationalistic, these Finns, they won't give a foreigner a chance to get onto a committee, or play an important part in a club."

It struck me he was a man always trying to compensate for a feeling of deficiency.

"I'ld like to make a suggestion," he began awkwardly. "I thought it would be good if we could have a kind of honorary president who would sit on the Committee occasionally. I was thinking of Prof. Paloheimo - an old friend of the family. He was formerly director of the Mannerheim League - my wife knows him very well - she was his secretary for many years."

I agreed that it sounded a good idea and said he could approach the professor with this object in view. He then began to outline more exactly how Prof. Paloheimo's position in the Society could be fitted in with the Constitution as according to the laws of Finnish association. I was impressed by the care and thoroughness and legality of the Secretary's approach to the affairs of the Society. The potentiality of his usefulness was plain to see!

"Prof. Paloheimo's a psychologist, and if he was to preside at our Committee meetings there'ld be a wonderfully calm and relaxed atmosphere," concluded Mr. Evans, and I took this to be another veiled reference to my failure in properly controlling yesterday's meeting. As we spoke I continued typing out the agenda.

"We must go very carefully to begin with," said Mr. Evans fussily. "The authorities in this country are very particular. They could make things awkward for us if we took a wrong step. We must go very slowly at first, so that we can feel our way."

I agreed in principle with the Secretary, although I did not quite understand what in fact he was driving at.

"This club could turn out to be something much bigger than you think," he continued. "It could be made to serve some very useful purposes."

"Such as what,?" I enquired.

"Well, for example," he said shifting awkwardly in his chair, "I was thinking of a good way the club could make a lot of money from big business. There are many large firms here like Philips and Aga - the firm I'm working for - and I was thinking that perhaps we could open a special subscription to these firms, of say a hundred marks per annum, so that their many agents visiting the country could be brought along to the club."

"That's an excellent idea," I put in enthusiastically.

"Hundreds of technicians and engineers visit this country annually from all parts of the world, and in the evenings they have nowhere to go, and it's hellishly lonely having to sit in hotel rooms every night of the week."

I agreed with the Secretary - he certainly seemed to have struck on a clever idea - and there was a pause of some moments as I typed. Then he said to me, "Have you ever been to the British Embassy club?" I replied that I had attended the opening party of the club but had never applied for membership.

"Well, it's all a damned racket," he burst out irritably, and he pronounced the word "damned" with peculiar emphasis. Then a moment later, he added half aside, "They wouldn't let me join."

He scrutinised me through his spectacles and a cloud of cigar smoke that made his complexion look greyer than it really was. I returned the glance and noted the drooping mouth through which he had puffed the cigar smoke, and the tension of his features which were already showing signs of advanced middle age.

"You have what I'ld call a very cultured voice," he said at last, and I somehow sensed he disapproved of the fact. "You speak with a college accent."

I shrugged my shoulders with embarrassment.

"I've been outside England for so long, that I haven't really got any distinguishing accent," he said. He was correct in that assumption, I thought, but I said nothing.

There was a ring at the door and I went out and answered it to find Mr. Enblom, the Treasurer. I welcomed him into the flat, and after my hanging up his hat and coat, he came into the living room and greeted Mr. Evans.

The latter rose only half out of his chair in greeting the older man, and Mr. Evans gave him a weak handshake and a reluctant smile, before sinking back into the comfort of his chair. I offered Mr. Enblom some wine and he accepted half a glass only saying that alcoholic beverages worried his ulcer. I offered Mr. Evans a second glass, and he reluctantly accepted a "drop" more, reminding me he was driving.

"The police are so damned strict in this country," he said. "If they discover you've had a drop before driving, they arrest you immediately, and you get put away in prison for six weeks, however sober you may have been. It's a damned impertinence!"

"I don't think you need worry about one and a half glasses of Beaujolais putting you away in prison, Mr. Evans," I replied. It seemed as if the irritable little man was haunted by a host of petty terrors.

Mr. Enblom handed me a list of member's names and addresses that he had neatly typed out, saying he had made up a balance sheet of the Society's accounts. In his loud ceremonial voice he then confirmed his promise of the previous day of allowing members of the Society use of his Villa Soltorpet on the island of Lille-Pellinge.

Whilst I completed typing the agenda and letters to be sent out that night, the two gentlemen discussed the future of the Society in hopeful and glowing terms.

"We'll have to go very carefully at first," said Mr. Evans again in his finicky manner. "The first thing we must do is to get the Society registered, and to ensure that, everything we do must satisfy the authorities. We'll have to be very careful of the members we're going to allow into the club. There are lots of undesirable types in Helsinki, who could do harm to the club at its start."

Enblom punctuated the Secretary's remarks with, "yes, yes,!" and "Quite so, quite so!"

At last I had finished typing out the agendas and letters, and they were sealed in addressed envelopes ready for posting, and Mr. Evans kindly said he could run us both up to the city centre in his car. We left the flat and the Secretary's orange and cream coloured East German Wartburg was parked in the street outside.

He drove us to the city centre and dropped Mr. Enblom and I outside the railway station, and as he moved away from the kerb, both of us waved crying, "Till next Wednesday."

Mr. Enblom turned to me, and exclaimed, "A very good man, Evans, a very good man, don't you think?"

"Yes," I replied, "he seems a very good man."

Evans was a "good" man, and he was already out to make an impression on members of the Committee. But good for what,? That was the question; and only later - too late, were we to find the answer.

CHAPTER 5
Omen of misfortune

"The moment one of the people took one of the truths to himself, called it his truth, and tried to live his life by it, he became a grotesque and the truth he embraced was a falsehood."

Sherwood Anderson, *Winesburg, Ohio*, "The Book of the Grotesque."

The international Society was conceived through the accident of a single episode. It resulted from a momentary inspiration. There was no gestation period in my mind between the sudden realisation of a potential need for such a club and the practicality of its existence, and my determination to go ahead and start it. There was less than a fortnight between the first idea and the realisation.

One cold windy November Saturday night I turned up at a dance hall to find that all tickets had been sold out - not an uncommon occurrence - and then I went to a second hall and then to a third, and again I was met by a full house, and by then it was too late to buy tickets for any dance *Lokal*. I was in the doldrums!

What's so good about these dance halls, anyway,? I asked myself, they're jostling, crowded uncomfortable places, where you can't even buy a drink. I went to a café and meditated on this, and on all the other ills of such places, and finally thought myself lucky that I had not been able to buy a ticket. What's needed is a social club with a more cultured environment: where one can sit, talk, drink coffee, listen to lectures, participate in debates, meet charming girls and dance - all under one roof. What we need is an International Society!

The thought had no sooner struck me than I was determined to carry it out. I told my friends. "You're mad,!" they said. "You can't do a thing like that - it wouldn't be done." - "You're a foreigner - leave it to the Finns to do," said another. "They'll never think of it," I said, "so I'll do it myself." - "You must be joking," they answered, and they satisfied themselves that I would forget the "foolish" idea after a good night's sleep, but they were wrong, and I awoke the following day more determined than ever to implement my plans. I sat down at my desk that

Sunday morning and wrote out a fifty-four paragraph Constitution for such a Society, outlining its rules (with the thoroughness of a Beau Nash); its function; the structure for its governance, and the activities it would organise for those who would join.

Then arose the question of how best to launch the club: through a human interest letter to the press, I thought, bearing the signatures of a number of foreigners interested in the project and wishing to increase their circle of Finnish friends. This letter I soon drafted, and along with it I went to the Kolme Kreiviä. At first there was reluctance to sign - such a new and unheard of project - but I soon overcame this with glowing descriptions of the benefits of the club.

My good friends Rolf Erlewein (a Swedish Finn) and Martin Summerhill, both translators working together in their own business, and Phil, an American diplomat, were sceptical though.

"I'm not signing," said Martin, a great bull of a man. "The idea's far too dangerous. It's attracting the attention of the authorities. It's best for us foreigners to keep our heads well down in a country like this."

"How do you mean,?" I asked.

"Suppose it got used as a front organisation,?" said Phil.

"But I'm founding this club single handedly," I replied. "I'll control it myself."

"That's what you might think," said Martin, "but if it got taken over and used, you'd get into real trouble with the police and you'd lose your permits."

"The Communists or a Fascist organisation could infiltrate and take it over without your knowing it - or not until it was too late," said Rolf.

"And there are plenty of Communists in this town," said Martin in a significant undertone pointing his finger threateningly in my face. "And mark my words, some of them are very nasty people it wouldn't be wise to get mixed up with."

"If you were ever to found a club that was to be taken over by the Communists, you'd be marked for life," said Phil. "And it wouldn't matter if it wasn't your fault either - you'd still be a marked man! The United States government has proscribed thousands of organisations all over the world, as Communist or Fascist infiltrated associations - and ninety per cent of them have nothing directly to do with politics."

"And in this country, with Big Brother just looking over the border, it's best to keep well out of the limelight," said Martin significantly. "And remember, the Communists in this country are stronger than anywhere else this side of the Iron Curtain - twenty-five per cent of the vote, remember!"

"If you started a club here in Helsinki, and it got taken over by the Communists, you'ld never be able to get into the States," said Phil. "They'ld mark you down immediately as suspect - and you'ld never get an appeal."

After we had discussed this for an hour, we noticed two young Russians, each with a copy of *Pravda*, seated at the table behind us, quite clearly eavesdropping on our conversation. The Russian boy nearest our table, seated with his back to us had turned round on a number of occasions and looked us full in the face - a most audacious gesture of observation.

The four of us were so absorbed in the lively discussion on my projected club, that at first we took no notice of this intrusion, but it later became disturbing. At last, Martin exclaimed in a confidential whisper, "Those two haven't been reading their papers for the past half hour."

"Let's move out from here," said Rolf leading the way, and we went to another table at the opposite end of the café, and less than five minutes later, we saw the two Russians make a hurried departure down the staircase to the street below.

"Now they're going to report everything we've said to the Big boss," remarked Martin.

Phil continued to expatiate on the dangers of my starting any kind of club in Finland, arguing that I would almost certainly become a cropper, whilst Martin spoke in a paranoid fashion, conjuring up visions of Communist spies and agents who were lurking in every corner of the city, ready to pounce and exploit any new thing which came into existence. In view of this drumming I could only sit back passively, and when at last my friends tried to extract a promise to give up the "foolhardy idea," I appeased them with the answer, "I'll re-consider it," but I had every intention of pursuing my plan.

On reaching home that night, the only effect of the dire warnings of my friends was a decision to write two letters to different authorities, informing them of my intentions and inviting any advice or caution which they might feel was necessary: a letter to the British embassy and a letter to the Lord Mayor of Helsinki.

The next twelve days were spent in the busy task of preparing for the founding meeting: revising the draft Constitution with my friend Seppo Lipponen, and visiting premises in different parts of the city with a view to hiring them for our Wednesday night meetings. Martin Summerhill's feelings were so strongly opposed to my founding the club - "You'll end up by getting us all thrown out of the country," he had cried - that he urged others in the foreign community to boycott my project, even approaching those who had been signatories to my letter.

Several of the signatories, Ray Reed, Geoff Gee, Mike Spencer (of whom more anon) and Geoffrey Diamond, from Tiger Bay, were HISC members, the first three of whom were soon moved over to Martin's way of thinking. Consequently, within a few days their ready sympathy for the need of such a club was turned from doubt, to fear, and finally to total cynicism to the idea of any such society, and they even went so far as to repeat the crazy mouthings of Martin Summerhill.

"I think you should forget it," said one. "It can't possibly work," said another. "It could spell trouble for us all," said a third. Ray Reed even said he wished to scratch his name from the letter, but this I was reluctant to allow.

"When you were in a soberer state of mind, and you considered the matter yourself, you said you wanted the club," I reminded him. "It's too late to withdraw your signature now. The letter is completed and ready for publication."

With Martin I was most annoyed, and openly expressed resentment at his underhand behaviour in discouraging others behind my back from participating in this exciting project. "You'll regret this nonsense, Bob," was all he could answer.

The idea to found the Society, which had originally stemmed from a purely subjective experience, now broadened in aspect to take on the form of an altruistic project, and as the days passed, I struck upon further benefits that the club could offer its members through a diverse programme of activities.

The letter calling the founding meeting bore eight signatures from natives of the following countries: England, Wales, Canada, Switzerland and West Germany; and the three copies of the letter were delivered by hand to the newspapers in which they were to appear on the Thursday before the meeting, and on the following morning, they were in print in each of the aforementioned publications. The original English text of the letter read as follows:-

Sir.
    This letter is written on behalf of the many foreigners resident in Finland, to point out the great need for an International Club and to help promote the founding of such a club in Helsinki.
    Many foreigners working here as teachers, technicians, chemists, engineers and as agents for commercial firms, as well as graduates staying in Finland to gain technical experience in several disciplines, have frequently complained of the difficulty of making suitable contacts with Finnish nationals.
    With the advance of Winter, and the shortening of the day to a few hours of light, and with the thought of Christmas looming in the not too distant future, many foreigners are made to feel particularly lonely at this time. Last Christmas still remains a vivid memory in the minds of many of us then in Helsinki. The streets were dark and deserted, all restaurants and hotels were closed, and we finally congregated to the station, where our spirits were regaled by a beef sandwich and a hot cup of coffee. On that day the station restaurant became the Mecca of many foreigners of all nationalities!
    Some foreigners in Helsinki live and work here purely by choice, others are sent here by large commercial concerns, but almost all are engaged in skilled or semi-skilled work - indeed, in many cases their work permits are only granted by the police on the condition that their services are specifically Necessary to the country. Nearly all are a credit to the country in that they help contribute towards the national weal without holding any special privileges or rights.
    It is to be hoped that the feeling of rootlessness and loneliness of many foreigners in Helsinki springs from the need

OMEN OF MISFORTUNE

of a suitable club or society, rather than from any lack of friendliness or callous reserve on the part of the Finn. Indeed, an International Club could very well serve the interests of the Finn, and such a club could be of great mutual benefit.

It would best take the form of a cultural society, meeting weekly and holding talks and debates, with long coffee intervals at every meeting to allow for introductions and light conversation amongst members. Entry to such a club would be exclusive (although not based on specific educational qualifications other than a manageable command of English) and subject to the discretion of the Committee. The chief purpose of such a club would obviously be to promote sociableness amongst its members, otherwise it would defeat its own use, and although there should be no age limit, the under-30 group should be especially encouraged.

The foreign members could give talks on their countries and subjects allied to them and participate in discussion groups, whilst at the same time entertaining and usefully imparting knowledge to the Finnish nationals present. In return, the Finnish members could invite and entertain their foreign co-members in their homes. Besides the weekly meetings, many other activities could be organised; in Summer: trips to the country; barbecues, and sailing, and in Winter: skiing parties, visits to the Opera, and dances. Well known personalities could be elected to the Presidency and Vice-Presidency of such a club.

To help promote the immediate founding of an International Club in Helsinki the first signatory of this letter cordially invites all those interested to attend a meeting at the Primula café, Siltasaarenkatu, at 4 o'clock this Saturday on 23rd of November, where the management have kindly agreed to lay aside so many tables as are necessary to accommodate all who will attend.

At this meeting will be formed a Committee of founding members, and a Chairman and a smaller committee to run the affairs of the club will be elected. Also, a set of rules will be drawn up to form the Constitution for the management of the club, and an immediate programme and other matters will be discussed. The proceedings of the meeting will be in English.

Any persons interested in the promotion of this club who would be unable to attend the meeting are kindly requested to write to the first signatory of this letter.

Yours, &c.

My elation at seeing the letter printed in all three papers without omissions in any, and the publicity which this would inevitably give to our founding meeting can well be imagined, and late that evening, after the last of my pupils had gone, I rushed to the Kolme Kreiviä to drum up some enthusiasm and promises of active support from friends for the morrow.

"Have you seen the papers? The letters have appeared in all three," I exclaimed to the Welsh signatory of my letter, who was seated nearby, as soon as I reached the top of the staircase.

"Have you heard the news,?" retorted the Afro-Welshman significantly.

"What news?"

"President Kennedy's dead! He's been assassinated."

"I don't believe it," I replied incredulously. "You'll be sure to be at the meeting tomorrow?"

"Who cares a damn about your Society now," cried the Welshman violently with tears in his eyes. "Kennedy's been murdered."

The news was still too shocking to be believed, and for a moment, I thought this was a piece of Welsh leg-pulling in bad taste.

"Don't talk nonsense," I only responded.

"I bet you a thousand pounds he's been murdered," cried the Welshman jumping up from the table and seizing my hand.

"I haven't got a thousand pounds. And anyway, I don't bet," I replied.

"It's true, Bob," said Martin nodding at me from another nearby table. "They say he's been assassinated by a Russian fanatic. Nothing's clear yet. The news only came through on the radio an hour ago."

My incredulity overcome, I sat down with Martin, Rolf and several other companions, and we discussed the terrible outcome that might spring from such an event, and meanwhile, Geoffrey Diamond, the Welshman, went round the café collecting signatures to a paper addressed to the American ambassador, expressing the "deep regret of the foreign community in Helsinki on hearing of the tragic assassination of John F. Kennedy, President of the United States of America."

That night, after the café closed, I walked home with Martin, for we both lived in Kallio, and his talk was full of the imminent dangers of war.

"Do you realise if they drop the bomb on Leningrad, all the windows will be shattered in Helsinki,?" he said as he held his coat collar around his neck against the biting wind.

"If there's war I've no intention of staying in Helsinki," I said.

"If there's war you won't be able to. We'll all be interned in some God-forsaken place in the middle of Finland."

"It's no good losing our heads Martin. If there's war we can pack our bags and take the next boat to Stockholm, and teach English there. Or maybe Iceland's a safer place. I've certainly no intention of returning to Britain to re-enlist." (I had had a recurring nightmare of being drafted into the Army once again on the occasion of the outbreak of nuclear hostilities between the great powers, and the wrench that this would entail in parting from loved ones for the last time in the certainty of final extinction.) "I've done my stint in the Army," I continued, "and I've lived through one World War and the bombing of London, and I've no intention of getting mixed up in another."

"Don't worry, Bob, once they start throwing that stuff around, no one's going to be safe anywhere on the globe," said Martin.

"A plague on both their houses, is what I say," I concluded.

At home I stayed up until the early hours, tuning into different radio stations to glean a few more facts surrounding the assassination report, but these were conflicting. Radio Moscow contended that the President had been murdered by a right wing extremist, whilst an American wavelength reported the opposite.

In any event I took the assassination to be a bad omen occurring, as it did, on the eve of the founding meeting of our Society. Would this discourage attendance, or dampen the prospective enthusiasm of those who would otherwise be keen? Would the American Embassy regard those calling the founding meeting of the Society as acting in bad taste if they failed to postpone it until a later date?

This last possibility was something I could amend in putting our new Society in a better light, and the next day I drew up a letter of condolence to be signed by all those attending the founding meeting of the Society. Unfortunately, in the bustle and storm of that meeting, I forgot about the letter, or at least, did not find an apt opportunity for circulating it, and this was probably to prove unfortunate to the future of our club as will be seen.

CHAPTER 6
We are not political

"A conspiracy is everything that ordinary life is not. It's the inside game, cold, sure, undistracted, forever closed off to us. We are the flawed ones, the innocents, trying to make some rough sense of the daily jostle. Conspirators have a logic and a daring beyond our reach."

Dan De Lillo, *Libra*, pt. 2, "In Dallas."

On the Tuesday following the founding meeting, I was pleased to see a prominently placed article on the new Society together with a photograph of myself in *Huvudstadsbladet*. Much had happened during the course of the previous three days. On Monday morning I had been interviewed by Mrs. Kristina Rotkirch of the above paper, and it was as a consequence of this that the excellent publicity article appeared the following day.

During our discussion she expressed her disapproval of the tactics of the HISC group, telling me that her husband had founded the club three years ago, becoming its first president, but that now he had nothing to do with it. She then tentatively enquired as to who the "short dark Englishman" was amongst their number, and I said I thought that this must be Geoff Gee.

"I didn't like him," said Mrs. Rotkirch, and she offered no more comments on the matter, but I immediately guessed he must have repeated to her what were always later referred to as the "HISC slanders."

Meanwhile, the HISC group had begun to close ranks in pursuing their vendetta against the new born Society in retaliation at the affront to their pride following their expulsion from our meeting. They could not attack us directly, and so they resorted to the most devious methods in a sly attempt at ruining our reputation.

On parting from Evans and Enblom that Sunday night, I went to the Kolme Kreiviä, and met there Geoff Gee himself. I decided to breach the subject of the contemptuous slander being spread about me, but not in such a way as to precipitate an open quarrel between us. I sat down at the table with Geoff Gee, Martin Summerhill and an Irishman who was teaching English at a local school.

"I believe Anders Carlén was telling everyone around him I was expelled from Sweden as being a person unfit to live there, at the meeting yesterday," I said speaking across the table to Geoff Gee.

There was a momentarily uneasy silence, and then Geoff replied that this was so.

"I think it's a filthy thing to do," I said.

"Why shouldn't he do that if he wants to,?" said Thurlow.

"Because it's a lie," I answered.

"It's the talk of Helsinki you were deported from Sweden."

"I was never deported. My application for a work permit was merely turned down."

"I don't see the difference."

"I do."

"What do you intend doing about it?"

"If I catch the bastard - or anyone else for that matter repeating the lie - I'll sue them."

"That'll be difficult."

"And if I can't, I'll smash his face in."

"Then you'd lose your permits here in Finland."

During this strangely evasive verbal engagement with its rising tension, the Irishman sat chuckling, and after some minutes, he exclaimed at last, "Watching you two is the funniest thing I've seen for years. It's like a couple of robots having a go at each other but programmed never to touch."

"Anyway, Anders is going to the Swedish embassy tomorrow to find out about the circumstances of your being thrown out of Sweden," said Geoff finally. "It's important we should try to find out the truth behind this matter."

"He's welcome to visit the Swedish embassy," I answered, "but it would have been better had he tried to find out the truth behind the matter before spreading the slander."

The discussion then switched to the rival club that HISC had said they would found.

"Is this club definitely going to be formed,?" asked Martin.

"Yes, all arrangements have been made - only the premises have to be found," replied Geoff.

The rival club, however, was never to materialise.

Later that night, I met Mike Spencer at the Orso café. He was sitting alone, hunched over a bowl of borsch, looking depressed and grey as he usually did. He soon made it clear he was still burning with resentment after yesterday's affront to his pride.

"I could have socked that weedy constipated looking Finn who interrupted me," he exclaimed, and I could not refrain from a smile at the thought that yet another Englishman should have mistaken Evans for a Finn. "We should never have left the meeting when we did. It was my fault. Had we stayed a bit longer, we could have wrecked the whole affair. I don't think you'll go far. They're all old men on the Committee, and if you try to push them at the rate you move, they'll drop dead before the club's got off the ground."

I was particularly disappointed that Mike Spencer should have taken this exceptionally unfriendly attitude, as only eighteen months earlier we had been quite good friends, lunching together almost daily, and I had briefed him thoroughly on the best way to set up a private teaching practice in Helsinki, and he had been pleased to follow my advice, enjoying remunerative results.

The following day at lunchtime, I met Ray and Shirley Reed and several of their cronies in the Kolme Kreiviä. They demonstratively gave me the cold shoulder, and when I teasingly chided them for their childish behaviour, Ray viciously exclaimed, his pipe still clenched between his teeth, "You're a tyrant!" I was taken aback by this unexpected outburst.

"I can't understand what you've got to be resentful about," I answered to humour him. "It's me who should be resentful, not you. After all, you only came to that meeting to take it over for yourselves, and you failed in the attempt. No one can question the fact you morally deserved to fail."

At this stage something more must be said about the HISC group, and who and what they were, for although they are to play only a minor role in the events which are to follow, their part behind the scenes in setting into motion a number of events (that not even they could have anticipated) is probably of such great significance that otherwise there would have been no such story to be written. Reference to the HISC group in this book, however, should not be taken as a collective term for all members of that body known as the Helsinki International Students Club, but only a very small proportion of these, about fifteen in number, who happened to be influential in governing the club at one particular time. These persons were loosely connected as a group of friends, mostly British, and Swedes and Swedish Finns, and I had known most of them for at least a year at the time that this story opens.

Ray and Barbara Reed were a curiously matched pair of Londoners - she from a more refined background, whilst he had the rough manners of a drill sergeant. She had come to Helsinki to study at the University, whilst he bummed around cleaning cars and painting boats for a year, before being granted a permit to work in the import department of the Academic Bookshop - several employees of whom were to act as a pernicious influence in damaging the International Society, but more of this anon.

Gunther was a Swedish Finn, a law student and alcoholic who had been treated for drug addition. Often he held rowdy parties - I had attended several of them - and when he became morose and wished to bring the evening to a close, he invariably did this by seizing hold of his guests and physically hurling them out of his flat amidst furious abuse. Douglas was a highlander with shoulder length hair, and always dressed in a kilt with socks hanging over his ankles, bad-tempered and filthy in appearance. He worked as a dish washer and was reputedly the first CND activist to land on Finnish soil, surreptitiously littering the streets of Helsinki with thousands of paper symbols and English language leaflets within days of his arrival. He did not remain long in the country.

Geoff Gee was a Yorkshireman, an ambitious and successful commercial artist, and about a year before the opening of this story, he had been commissioned to decorate the Marines mess at the US Embassy, and shortly afterwards, the bar in the American embassy residence. He soon struck up a friendship with the jovial American ambassador, Mr. Cullen, a black journalist and protégé of the late President Kennedy, and boasted that he drank with him regularly.

As a result of this connection, Geoff strengthened his bonding with the marines, and they invited him, and subsequently, those others in his circle of the HISC group to the mess bar on Saturday nights. In return, several of the marines associated closely with the HISC group, and were often seen in the Kolme Kreiviä, and soon the relationship became so close, that the HISC group began to adopt the attitude they might drink in the marines mess as of right.

Ray Reed certainly came to think this, and one night whilst drinking and doubtless passing sour comments on company present, as was his wont, he had a loud exchange of words with the Sergeant of marines, with the result that he was forbidden to enter the mess again.

"I don't care about their stupid ban," he had said in comment. "They're just a lot of boozing drunks making nits of themselves. I don't need their company to live in Helsinki." As to whether these were his real sentiments it cannot be said, but after six months, all was forgotten and forgiven, and Ray Reed was again a regular drinking guest in the mess. By this time it was apparent that the HISC group were the eyes and ears of the American embassy in their relationship with the foreign community of Helsinki.

Apart from myself, Peter Martin was the only other member of the International Society who had a personal relationship with the HISC group, and he might have interceded as a mediator between myself and the group had he not had a violent quarrel with Ray Reed at a party several days after the founding meeting of the club. This was at a gathering held by Victor Danet, a generous well-to-do young French businessman, and late in the evening, after the Whiskey had run dry (although plenty of other drinks remained in the flat), Ray Reed in a bullish manner, reproached his host for not having had the forethought to stock up sufficiently in advance. This piece of rudeness by one barbaric Englishman towards a civilised Frenchman, and the disgraceful light it cast on English manners, so enraged Peter that he execrated his countryman in such strong terms that the other called him outside for a fight. It never came to this, but for a year, the two were not on speaking terms, and with this quarrel died the last hope for any intermediary between myself and the Society in a conflict with the HISC group and their dangerous slanders.

By the Tuesday after the founding meeting I had already received many letters from all parts of Finland, from persons offering all kinds of advice or wanting to join the club, but there was one letter which especially stood out, and that was from a gentleman, who signed himself Rowland G.P. Hill. I immediately recognised this as the namesake of the Englishman who had invented the penny postage stamp and reformed the postal service in Victorian England, but I was struck by the absurdity of his middle initials standing for the great institution associated with his name. The letter bore a coat of arms and an erased London address in Woburn Place, but it was sent from Karis, a small predominantly Swedish speaking town some seventy miles to the West of Helsinki.

Mr. Rowland G.P. Hill (he seemed always to be referred to only by his full name) filled his letter full of advice, especially urging that I should preserve the exclusivity of the club by not allowing "all and sundry" to join as a cheap and easy method of improving their conversational English. He then told me something about himself: he had lived in Finland since 1949; had founded a series of English clubs throughout the countryside, and had become an authority on the Lapp culture, having compiled a book on Lapp problems, and lectured and given radio talks on the Lapps. The letter struck me as being written by a self-important person who customarily looked at people from a higher level - although he kindly invited me to visit his recently acquired villa - and for the moment I was to forget him, although he was to play a major part in the drama to follow.

On the afternoon of that day Seppo (whose mother acted as my telephone secretary) passed on a message that I was to contact Waldemar von Etter, for as yet I had no phone in my flat, and messages could only be relayed on foot. Von Etter said he had found two possible places in which meetings of our new Society might be held and I arranged to meet him in the Primula restaurant in Mannerheimintie.

He was still wearing the same old brown suit when I first met him, and he approached me with a charming smile and slight curiously aristocratic limp. He ordered coffee for himself in his resonant Swedish (I was still lunching) and as we spoke, I noticed his long slim fingers and the many rings he wore carrying precious or semi-precious stones.

There was something distinctively decadent about his appearance - the general disrepair and sensuousness and lack of energy - but it was a decadence in excellent taste, and I liked the manner of the man. He congratulated me on having taken a firm stand against the HISC hecklers, and said he could not possibly have joined a students' club at his age.

He told me something about his travels years ago, and reminisced with pleasure and amusement how he had attended a finishing school in Paris for both boys and girls, but how the sexes were nonetheless strictly segregated. To overcome this barrier, at midnight the boys set ladders up against the windows of the building where the girls lodged, climbed into their dormitories and bedded them every night. They, and the girls too, had had to be so silent and discreet, that sometimes they climbed into the girls' beds before the latter had realised the fact, often unaware in advance of the girls into whose beds they were entering, and in any event, sleeping with many girls before the finishing course had ended.

And the extraordinary fact remained that the prim and disciplinarian authorities of the school never discovered that anything improper had ever occurred, for during the day the boys and girls were as good as gold as if "butter could never have melted in their mouths." We both laughed at the thought of these remarkable escapades of long ago.

After finishing our refreshments, we went first to the Helsingfors Sparbank, to view a hall they gave free of charge to different associations. It was a fine room, although only accommodating 80 to 100 persons, but we could not take it, as it was not the policy of the bank to give it out to an organisation on a regular basis. The room was given for free hire to as many clubs and associations as would use it, for the purpose of giving publicity to the bank. We next went to the Royal Restaurant, behind the Swedish Theatre, but this room was far too small and expensive, and the purchase of expensive refreshments would have been obligatory. We then parted until the Committee meeting of the following day.

On Wednesday, *Uusi Suomi*, Finland's third largest daily, published a short article on the International Society after I had personally approached their editor the day before, and that morning I received a card from a lady who had attended the founding meeting promising she could lend some films to the Society. She asked if she might have an opportunity of addressing the Committee on this offer, and I phoned and spoke with her, and as I was impressed by her personality and the potential value she might be to the Society, I duly co-opted her onto the Committee without further ado - little aware of the repercussions which might follow.

At this time my only concern was with the practical details of making the club a working success for its members, for the cash we had collected as a voluntary donation from so many people was a heavy burden on my conscience, and I was determined that these contributors who had put their trust in us would under no circumstances be disappointed. I was not averse to implementing democratic procedure, but during the founding meeting I had been obliged to lay aside some of this in the cause of preventing disruption, and if the best interests of members were to be maintained, I was fully prepared to continue placing aside useless or time wasting formalities if this was necessary. Therefore, in co-opting Mrs. Kaatia, I did this with a good conscience, not expecting to meet with opposition, and confident that I held the trust of members.

At the Committee meeting that night, however, I was surprised when the Secretary rose from his chair, and with all due respects to the lady present, objected "on principle" to the arbitrary way in which the Chairman had taken it upon himself to co-opt Mrs. Kaatia without reference to other members. People who raise objections on "principle" very often do so as the empty abstraction *per se* is the only objection they can think of, but on this occasion, I bowed my head and said nothing for I was clearly in the wrong in having contravened "correct procedure."

Mrs. Kaatia must have been acutely embarrassed, and she promptly replied by saying that she did not wish to be considered as "a full" member of the Committee.

This, however, was not the only scathing reference I was to receive from the Secretary that night. Having delivered his preliminary remarks, he then went on to read the Minutes of the founding meeting, remarking that this had been made difficult for him due to the "lack of preparation and irregular procedure" of the meeting, no secretaries having been appointed to take down the business, etc. These comments seemed grossly unfair in view of the difficulties I had faced at that meeting, and also inaccurate, as I had been forced to lay aside much of the formal pre-planning of the meeting; and as for lack of preparation, I had been two weeks engaged in this.

There was little I could say in reply to these remarks, and so I merely sat in good humour watching the Secretary, smiling submissively as if accepting this list of faults as well-meant criticism. The Minutes over, the Secretary reminded us that we had to be very careful in not "offending the authorities" and that everything should be done in a "correct" manner, and he then began reading through a partly legible paper he had written out the night before containing clauses and paragraphs from all kinds of law books.

"I'm sorry, I can't read the next sentence," he apologised. "I went to bed very late last night, and my writing's not so clear when I'm tired."

All the while he blew out great clouds of tobacco smoke, stumbled over the pronunciation of Latin words to the embarrassment of us all, and finally gave up after discovering that the last paragraph was entirely illegible.

"I'm sorry, I'll have to write it out again," he said.

I began to doubt in my mind as to whether he was really reading out his own handwriting, or as to whether he was trying to read out the script written down by another hand that at the same time was trying to direct his actions.

Impatient to begin the real business of the meeting, I seized the initiative in calling on the various officers to report what they had done since we last met. First the legal Adviser, Mr. Westerholm: he was absent and his friend Gösta Kelter had been unable to contact him. He never appeared again.

"That's what comes of bullying people," said Evans aside.

Next: the Entertainments Director, Mr. Gösta Kelter.

"I'm sorry but I don't know what to think of," he began. "I was wondering whether any of the Committee had suggestions for entertainment. I do have some imagination but not all that amount."

Anyone would have thought he had been asked to present the

Committee with a novel the way he used the word "imagination." No one else was forthcoming with suggestions.

Next: the Programme Director, Mr. Aldar Runela - and this gentleman almost jumped out of his skin at the pronunciation of his name.

"I was thinking we might get someone from Suoma-Seura," he stammered. "It would be good to get a man from an embassy but I don't think they'ld agree to come along."

By this time Miss Inge Kainulainen had fallen fast asleep, and after two hours at the meeting, she excused herself and went home. Things were not progressing well. I outlined my plans for the printing of application forms and membership cards. Aldar Runela volunteered to take on this responsibility and Gösta Kelter said that we could have use of his spirit duplicator for general circulars and letters. Now things were moving, and at least two people had begun to compensate for their earlier deficiencies.

"Lastly, ladies and gentlemen," I said with distinct emphasis, "before we can go any further, we must secure proper premises for our regular weekly use. If we fail in this, we can call it a day and pack up the whole idea of a club. As I see it, the only way to get premises is for one member to spend the entire day looking for accommodation, having compiled a suitable list of places to visit. What volunteers do I have?"

Mrs. Kaatia volunteered for the task, and then the Committee suddenly broke into action, in suggesting places to be visited and fetching the telephone directories and copying down names and addresses and numbers. When almost twenty places had been listed, Mrs. Kaatia suggested that her task might be made easier if she had someone to drive her around, and Waldemar von Etter volunteered for this.

"We must find premises by tomorrow night," I insisted.

Finally, it was agreed that Mrs. Kaatia would phone the Secretary as soon as the task had been completed, and that he would call on me tomorrow night and that we would both inspect the chosen accommodation.

He arrived late the following evening, and I was expecting his arrival in eager anticipation hoping to be met by a happy face, and I was apprehensive and disappointed at seeing his irritably worried expression.

"Good news, I hope," I said brightly.

"Well, I don't know about that - but it doesn't seem too likely," he replied in an intensely concerned tone of voice, and he held a cigarette in the fingers of one hand, and during the few moments he stood in the hallway, he filled it with tobacco smoke.

"What's happened,?" I asked impatiently.

"The good lady's found some kind of rooms, but they're in the premises of an extremist right wing organisation," replied Evans.

"What are the rooms like?"

"I didn't have a chance to speak with the good lady for long, but she did say the rooms could accommodate up to a hundred and fifty persons, and that there were separate cloakrooms and a kitchen for preparing food," he replied fastidiously.

"Sounds excellent," I said. "Where are the rooms?"

"In Fabianinkatu."

"Couldn't be better! Right in the centre of town."

"Well, I think we should be very careful," said Evans. "I don't think we should settle on the rooms. You see, they're owned by an extremist organisation and people are very sensitive in this country. We might get ourselves boycotted by the Communists - or they could cause trouble for us - and then we'd really be in the soup."

"I honestly don't see why we should be bothered by the Communists or by any other political organisation," I answered. "After all, we're quite non-political, and we have to have premises somewhere."

"But not in the rooms of an extremist group," he said. "Politics is a sensitive issue in this country - it's not like in England where you can do what you like. We must keep on friendly terms with every political association."

"I agree entirely," I said.

There was something disturbing in what the Secretary implied. The Society could certainly not hold its meetings in a building known to belong to a Fascist organisation, if that's what was meant.

"Anyhow, we'll see the rooms," I said, and he agreed to fetch me at noon the following day.

I watched him arrive in the street from my window punctually at twelve o'clock, and as I had forgotten to tell him that the front door of the house was always kept locked when the alcohol shop was open (to prevent drunks and others consuming their intoxicant beverages in the hallway of the building) I went down into the street.

He met me with a cursory gesture and worried expression, saying he had parked his car at the other side of the inlet, and suggesting that we walk to the rooms in Fabianinkatu. He seemed flustered and confused as we walked along the pavement, and then he came out with the reason: "Of all the damned coincidences! Do you know, I've just seen my boss as I came into the street," he exclaimed in a worried tone. "He'll be wondering what the deuce I'm doing in this part of the town during my lunch hour."

"What does it matter what you do during your lunch hour,?" I replied. "It's your free time, not his."

"But I usually lunch in the factory," he answered.

"Why worry about what your boss thinks, anyway,?" I said.

After a pause during which his face wore a contemplative and anxious countenance, he switched the conversation to the premises we were going to visit.

"I'm worried about this place," he exclaimed suddenly. "Only twenty years ago these people shot every fourteenth Finn."

"Twenty years ago,?" I said.

"Well yes, a little more than that," he answered.

"You mean during the Civil War?"

"Yes."

"That was forty-five years ago," I corrected. "It's history!"

"Not when it's your closest relatives, it's not," he insisted. "It's still in a lifetime."

"Everyone knows the Civil War was a very nasty business - as indeed civil wars are always nastier than other wars."

"The Whites carried out a very savage butchery in every part of the country," he said. "They killed men, women *and* children. They wiped out whole communities."

"And so did the Reds," I put in. "And besides, it wasn't only a civil war, it was a war of liberation against occupying Russian troops who had turned Soviet overnight."

"Anyway, I think we should be very careful about hiring the premises of an organisation which shot every fourteenth Finn," he replied by way of extricating himself from further political discussion.

"What organisation is this?"

"The National Coalition party," he answered.

"Is that what you describe as an 'extremist right wing organisation',?" I exclaimed astonished. "That's not my opinion."

"Isn't it,?" he exclaimed irritably. "We'll just have to see what the Committee have to say about it. We can't take these rooms without the authority of the Committee."

"The National Coalition party is a respectable constitutional movement," I said. "It's the third largest parliamentary group. It's no more right wing than the Conservative party in England."

He made no reply to this, but on arriving at the address in Fabianinkatu, and throughout the interview that followed, his behaviour annoyed me intensely. At first we were shown into a waiting room, and he made no attempt to remove his coat and hang it on a stand provided, but instead he lit up a cigarette and began drawing nervously. As he sat back in the armchair, his small figure hunched up in a crumpled trench coat, one leg resting over the other, his face contorted with worry, it occurred to me that he would make a dismal impression on the official coming to meet us.

After ten minutes, we were shown into the room of the general office manager, and introductions were exchanged. I sat down in an armchair and Evans sat stiffly on a wooden chair placed against the wall. As the gentleman concerned could not speak English or German, and as Evans could not speak Swedish, the interview was carried out between the Secretary and the office manager in Finnish. Although my knowledge of Finnish was far from perfect, I understood most of what was said, and all the while, Evans clutched nervously onto his hat that he held between his legs as he leaned forward to speak.

He never smiled, and the serious and fastidious expression of his face was sometimes contorted into an expression of disgust, but most annoying of all was the fact of his reiterating the remark, "We're quite non-political - you must understand we're non-political!" These remarks were quite uncalled-for, since our Society was clearly only a social club, but Evans was intent on driving home the point that our Society could not be expected to share the sympathies of the National Coalition party, as if the latter was somehow to be in the position of compromising the integrity of the Society.

We were then shown the rooms. There was one large hall, complete with comfortable modern chairs and a speaker's lectern, an entrance hall, a large room for cloaks, separate toilet and wash rooms for ladies and gentlemen, and a kitchen complete with all utensils; and upstairs, there was another hall (used during the day by a ballet school) that we could have for dancing. The rooms were modern and newly decorated, and their entrance was in a spacious courtyard, quite separate and distant from the entrance to the central office of the National Coalition party, and so there was no need even for ordinary members of the Society to know that the premises of the club were held in the rooms of this particular movement.

I was keen on securing the rooms immediately, and I continually urged the Secretary to enquire as to their charge of hire, but for some time, he avoided putting this question. Instead, he went on making the same old pointless remark: "You must understand, we're quite non-political." The office manager, naturally enough, passed no comment on this, but it occurred to me that the continual reiteration of this remark would surely at last arouse some suspicion: Was the Society non-political after all? Then it struck me that perhaps Evans was purposely trying to create a negative impression, so that the rooms would be refused us, with the result that his fears of the Communists "boycotting" the Society would no longer be a problem.

On returning to the office manager's room the charge of hire was settled: 75 marks an evening for all rooms together, or 60 marks if the dance hall was to be excluded. We settled for all the rooms and Evans said the arrangements would be confirmed after the Committee meeting of next Sunday. The rooms would be in our possession every Wednesday night of the year, from 7.0 pm until approximately midnight, or later, if we wished. At first the agreement for the hire would be oral, but later it might be put into writing if both parties agreed.

We then left, and on shaking hands with the office manager, Evans again exclaimed to my intense irritation, "You must remember, we're entirely non-political!" Were those apparently fatuous remarks necessary,? I asked myself as we walked down the steps of the building. I could not answer the question then, but I might well have asked myself the same question six months later and have found a very ready answer.

CHAPTER 7
This is intrigue

"Conspiracies no sooner should be form'd
Than executed."

Joseph Addison, *Cato*, Act I, Sc. 2.

On returning from Fabianinkatu towards Kallio with Mr. Evans I made a critical reference to Westerholm's vanishing act. The Secretary gave a little chuckle.

"I expect he decided to get out whilst the going was good," he said. "After the irregular way the business of the Society has been carried on, I expect his friends gave him a tip-off to steer clear of a load of trouble."

"What kind of trouble,?" I asked.

As so often when I put a direct question to which he had no answer, he evaded it by doggedly pursuing his own train of thought.

"If we're going to carry on much longer the way we are now, the police'll track us down and keep a watch on us."

"Nonsense," I replied. "There's freedom in the law of association here, and providing we don't actually overstep the law, there's nothing we should be afraid of."

"We'll find plenty of enemies in other associations before we've gone very far," said Evans, "and they'll see to it they give us trouble."

"What associations?"

"Well, for example, rival associations like the Finnish-British Society."

"How could they get the police onto us?"

"Through the embassy, and they'll get onto some government department to shut us down. You don't know how underhand everything is in this country. The police here have strange ways of operating."

"I think it's absurd to have a phobia about the police. They can't go beyond their limits anymore than you or I. If they want to come to the club to snoop around - just to satisfy themselves that everything's clean - they're welcome anytime."

"We don't want the police nosing their way into our club," cried Evans emotionally. "If they started that, the Society would be finished."

"Rubbish,!" I cried, exasperated by the Secretary's paranoia.

"We'll see what the Committee have to say about it then," he said. "We want to keep clear of the police - they spell trouble."

"I don't expect the police will bother themselves to know of our existence. And as far as Westerholm's concerned," I said changing the subject, "he's been chucked off the Committee."

"You can't do that," said Evans outraged. "It's unconstitutional!"

"Well I've done it," I answered exasperated, "irrespective as to whether it's unconstitutional or not, and if the authorities or the police want to know I've done it, then they're welcome to it."

By this time I had satisfied myself that Evans was a born mischievous intriguer - an irritable Beckmesser - a man who loved empty procedures and principles for their own sake alone - who would go to any length in proving the contravention of a petty rule if he could squeeze political mileage out of it. This was intrigue of contemptible cynicism, typical of the "committee" man of the dullest imagination but out to make a mark for himself. But what did Evans want in our Society?

Here my suspicions were aroused. Certainly he did not react in good faith to the spirit of the Society as a friendship and cultural club; he did not have the sociableness or the friendly optimism of a Gösta Kelter, and neither did he have the yearning for culture of an Anders Enblom. He had shown himself too serious a man to be genuinely involved in a club with purely social aims. I concluded for the time being that he had only joined the Society in seeking some form of status in his dull life that a Secretary's position would give him.

That afternoon I prepared and sent out the agenda for the Committee meeting of the following Sunday, which was to be the last before the first general meeting of the Society - the date of which had already been postponed from the 4th to Wednesday 11th December. The agenda, therefore, was necessarily long in finalising arrangements in preparation for the historic date! There were eighteen items of business to attend to, and members were requested to arrive at the meeting some twenty minutes before the time of its official opening at 3 o'clock, for the purpose of reading through a revised version of the draft proposals for the Constitution which I was busily completing.

Earlier in the week, I had received a friendly letter from a Mrs. Marja-Liisa Toivanen, Secretary of the Finnish Students Christian Movement, showing interest in the Society. She explained that her movement operated a hospitality service for foreigners in Finland, introducing them to friendly Finns, and that for the duration of the Christmas holiday special arrangements were being made for foreigners to stay with Christian families. This opportunity was exceptional, and so I phoned Mrs. Toivanen and asked if she would consent to be co-opted onto the Committee of the Society as the Social Contacts Director.

She gladly accepted this post, and in return, I promised that the Society would help and give publicity to the Student Christian Movement, and subsequently, our club displayed a notice about the SCM on its notice board every Wednesday evening. I realised, of course, that yet another co-option would give Evans a further excuse for accusing me of arbitrary behaviour, but the Society was still in the gestation period, and then the Secretary had himself been insistent that the existing Committee should only be regarded as provisional.

Gösta Kelter and Salme Kaatia promised to be the leading personalities of the club, and I hoped that both would cooperate as a pair in managing the entertainments side of the club's activities. I hoped that Kelter, the charmer, would become MC of the club so that I could take a back seat function in the Society's social activities, and as I had noticed a friendly inclination of each towards the other - she was a divorcée and he in the later stages of completing his divorce - it seemed they would make an excellent pair.

I wanted to meet them both together, firstly for planning their function in the Society, and secondly, for confiding to them my distrust of Evans, as a first move for removing him from the Secretaryship. It was essential that the Secretary be a Finn, and I thought that Evans could be moved sideways to some fine sounding post as a sop to his pride - possibly as Assistant Programme or Entertainments Director - where he would be safely prevented from the possibility of making further mischief.

THIS IS INTRIGUE

After some phoning it was finally arranged that Gösta Kelter and I meet Mrs. Kaatia at her flat in Lauttasaari, an island and suburb of modern apartment blocks approached by a bridge and causeway to the West of Helsinki that Saturday night.

"I must tell you something confidential," said Salme Kaatia after the three of us had been together for about an hour. "I've heard the American embassy are very displeased with us."

"Whatever for,?" I exclaimed.

"They're dissatisfied with someone on the Committee," she replied as we sat round a coffee table with only candlelight in her living room.

"Who,?" I asked.

"We don't know."

"Then we'd better find out," I said.

"Or else forget it as a silly rumour," said Gösta.

"But it's not going to be very nice if the American embassy's going to be displeased with us, " said Salme.

"I agree," I said, "but I think they should have the decency to tell us with whom they're displeased. - Where did you get this information?"

"From a Finnish student called Martti Hirvonen," said Salme. "I can give you his phone number, as he said he'd like to help the club."

"I'd be interested to contact him to get to the root of this," I replied.

"You see, Bob, no one really knows anyone in the Society," said Gösta, "and as Mr. Evans says, we must go carefully at first."

"I quite agree," I answered. "We're all strangers to one another, and the only thing we have to go on is instinct at this stage."

"We've got some pretty strange people on the Committee at the moment," said Gösta, "and later, I think some of them will have to be changed. That Miss Kainulainen - she's weird. She fell asleep on my shoulder during the last meeting."

"I think she likes you, Gösta," I replied laughing.

"When I spoke to her at the founding meeting," continued Gösta, "she kept talking about a 'wonderful festival when all the boys and girls of the world came to Helsinki and danced and sang in the streets.' She was referring to that World Communist Youth Festival of last year - and she said I should have been there to join in their fun."

MY CONFLICT WITH A SOVIET SPY

"Perhaps she's the person the Americans don't like," I suggested.

"I doubt it," said Gösta. "She's too innocent and naive to be dangerous."

Suddenly, Salme seized my hand.

"Please, Bob, don't give me anything more to do with that von Etter," she said.

"Why not,?" I exclaimed in surprise.

"Oh, he's disgusting," replied Salme.

"He does come from a well connected family," I said defensively.

"His behaviour to me the other day was unforgivable," said Salme glancing straight into my face. "Do you know, Bob, the only reason he wanted to be my chauffeur last Thursday was to flirt. He kept trying to kiss me and put his hand on my knee. Oh, it was awful!"

"He's just trying to take advantage of his seigneurial rights," I joked. "After all, he is an aristocrat."

"His behaviour was such that I felt ashamed to be with him," continued Salme. "He's not merely licentious. He's positively lewd!"

"We'll just have to take his good points with his bad," I said.

"And do you know, he only wanted rooms for the Society where there was alcohol?"

"That's not so unusual in this country," I replied.

"And he spoke badly about Gösta and Peter."

"Why ever should he do that?"

"I've heard that von Etter can be very vindictive," said Gösta.

"He said that Gösta and Peter would take all the prettiest girls for themselves," explained Salme.

I laughed at the idea that von Etter could have raised such an absurd objection.

"That's ridiculous,!" I cried. "I hardly think anyone in Helsinki could complain about a dearth of female talent."

"Waldemar von Etter has a large family estate somewhere near Porvoo," began Gösta. "He holds very exclusive parties there - only top people in the country are admitted - and they say he organises the most outrageous orgies. In fact, they've been so bad, that girls have run away from the place in the middle of the night and complained to the police."

"He sounds a very original man," I remarked.

"President Kekkonen's best friend has often attended these parties," continued Gösta, "and they say that even Kekkonen has been himself on at least one occasion. I've tried to go to these parties once or twice myself, but I've never succeeded in getting in."

I laughed at this admittance of unhappy failure, and at that moment we were startled by the doorbell.

"That'll be Mr. Evans," said Salme. "He phoned a couple of hours ago asking if he could come along. He said he had some urgent business to discuss."

I was touched by a twinge of apprehension. Mr. Evans entered hurriedly in a flustered state.

"I can't stay long, I've got some other calls to make," I heard him say to Salme in the hallway, and he seemed worried.

Gösta and I rose to meet him as he came into the living room, and when he saw me, we must have exchanged a glance of mutual distrust. After offering the two guests a weak handshake, he sat down stiffly without removing his trench coat, and there was a momentarily awkward pause as he fumbled with his hat and prepared to speak. Salme put down a cup and saucer in front of him and offered a cake.

"I really won't have anything, thank you - I've just had something to eat," he said, and his mouth indicated distaste as his eye caught the cake. "You know, I'm very worried about the affairs of the Society," he continued in a tone reflecting an intensely irritable mood. "I think we're moving too fast. If we begin to push things too quickly at this stage the authorities are going to get suspicious."

This little speech aroused my shocked astonishment for here was a piece of intrigue intended behind my back.

"I don't exactly understand you," I interrupted. "In what way are we going too fast? Please be more specific."

"We mustn't get into the limelight at this stage," he continued completely ignoring me. "We must stay in the background until we've won the confidence of the authorities, and got ourselves registered."

"Of course we must be careful to begin with," answered Gösta solemnly, nodding in agreement, and it was obvious he had been moved by the Secretary's little speech.

"But what do you disagree with, Mr. Evans,?" I enquired.

MY CONFLICT WITH A SOVIET SPY

"Well, for example, I think the publication of that article in the paper the other day was most unwise at this stage," said Mr. Evans fumbling with his hat. "It's not going to help us with the authorities. We mustn't do anything to displease the Finnish government."

"Personally, I just can't see we've done anything to displease the Finnish government," I answered.

"It is very important we get registered," said Gösta in a quietly serious tone. Then Evans said something that quite astonished me.

"And another thing - what I've really called about - Mr. Martin phoned me earlier this afternoon on a private business matter, and eventually we got round to discussing the Society's problems, and he expressed complete dissatisfaction with the agenda sent out for tomorrow's Committee meeting. And I must say I'm inclined to agree with him. It's far too long, and it's impossible to deal with all that business on a single afternoon."

"Really, Mr. Evans, I think you should have come to me with a complaint of this sort first," I exclaimed indignantly. "After all, I undertook the task of compiling the agenda, and if you were really displeased with it, I think it might have been more proper to have approached me directly on the matter."

"I don't think we can possibly hope to use the agenda," continued Mr. Evans ignoring my remarks.

"We've got to use the agenda, because all the business on it has to be settled before the meeting on the eleventh," I answered, and after an exchange of words which must have been mutually aggravating, he reluctantly nodded, murmuring an affirmation that the agenda would after all be used.

"Of course, the present Committee must be regarded as purely provisional," he continued, addressing the others. "We know very little about each other, and it might be necessary to make a few changes later, before we get registered."

"That's just what I was saying to Bob here, a moment ago," said Gösta.

"I've heard there's been some rumours about several people on the Committee," continued Mr. Evans, and I listened to him in astonished apprehension, "and they might have to be removed before we've progressed much further, if we're going to gain the confidence of the authorities."

"Rumours about what Committee members,?" I asked.

"Well, it's a very delicate matter this," replied Evans half turning towards me, "and I don't think it would do at this time to repeat any rumours about anyone. We must move very carefully at first in feeling our way, and then we can separate the black sheep from the others."

"I agree with you Mr. Evans," exclaimed Salme with enthusiasm, "and do you know, the American embassy are worried about the Society because of someone on the Committee?"

"I expect the Americans are displeased with our Society only because we happened to hold our founding meeting on the day after their president was assassinated," I replied.

"Well, I must hurry along now," said Mr. Evans rising from the sofa. "I've got several other calls to make. Would anyone like a lift into town,?" he added as he reached the door, and the remark was obviously aimed at me.

As soon as we were comfortably seated over cups of coffee and there was a relaxed atmosphere once again, I quietly suggested that it would be a good idea if Salme became Secretary of the Society for the purely practical purpose of helping to compile and translate the Constitution, and negotiating with the registration authorities.

"I don't think that would be at all wise," replied Gösta in a serious tone. "Mr. Evans is a very good Secretary - and he's such a complete contrast to you in his approach. I think you both make a very good pair in complementing each others' qualities."

"I think he's perhaps too much of a contrast," I said. "He seems full of fears and suspicions, but he's always vague and unspecific if you try to pin him down on a point. Haven't you noticed that?"

"He's just cautious. He doesn't want to rush things," replied Gösta.

"But cautious of what? And what is it he doesn't want to rush and why,?" I answered. "He never makes it clear what he exactly means. He hasn't raised a single objection to a specific action we've already undertaken - apart from the press article."

"He's worried, that's all," replied Gösta. "It's in his nature."

"I think he's scheming," I pointedly remarked.

MY CONFLICT WITH A SOVIET SPY

"I don't think he'd do that," replied Gösta. "But even if he did, I think you could rely on the rest of the Committee standing behind you. I don't like the man very much myself, but I think he makes a good Secretary to your Chairmanship."

That night the three of us went to a ski club dance at the Otaniemi Technical School and towards the end of the evening, Salme suddenly seized my wrist in her hand. She was sitting across the table, dressed in a paper hat, and bleary-eyed, she was lolling against the support of Gösta's shoulder.

"Bob, remember, please don't give me any more work to do with von Etter," she exclaimed.

"I'll remember," I returned pressing her hand reassuringly.

"He's the black sheep on our Committee, you know," she said significantly.

"Let's hope so for your sake," I replied with a smile.

CHAPTER 8
The big lie

"The devil can cite Scripture for his purpose,
An evil soul producing holy witness
Is like a villain with a smiling cheek,
A goodly apple rotten at the heart.
O, what a goodly outside falsehood hath!"

Shakespeare, *The Merchant of Venice*, Act I, Sc. 3, 1.130-3.

It was two years since I had first met Peter Martin, and during that time I had come to know him well. He was wildly extroverted and was known by most the foreign community who frequented the cafés in Helsinki, and he was possibly more spoken about than any personality in our midst. He was critical of everyone and everything - like the fool in a medieval court - with little sense of discretion with regard to his own behaviour, and if it was not for the fact that he was a born comedian - a glance at his face was enough to evoke laughter, and in fact did so amongst Finns who often understood not a word of English - his presence would never have been tolerated in any group.

Insults fells as naturally from his lips as compliments do from flatterers, but because of his effusive wit and the constant mirth that surrounded him, it was impossible to take offence at any scorn which fell from his lips. Nonetheless, despite his complaining attitude which amounted to the pathological, I could not for a moment believe that what Evans had said to Salme and Gösta about Peter's phone call was true. I did not believe that Peter could have acted as such a snide, or was capable of such malice.

After returning home from Otaniemi in the early hours of that Sunday morning, I remained long awake brooding over all that Mr. Evans had said to the three of us the previous evening. The Secretary's enigmatic statement that some members of the Committee were under suspicion and might have to be removed at a later date was especially worrying. What did Evans mean by this, and anyway, how much did he know about other persons on the Committee? It then struck me he might have heard the HISC slander at the founding meeting, and the probability of this became more convincing when I recollected that Mr. Evans and his wife had been sitting at that end of the room where the HISC group were gathered. The seriousness and damaging implications of the HISC slander were now fully brought home to me for the first time and I decided that later that week I should contact the British Consul and seek his advice on the matter, but I later dropped the idea, and this lapse possibly proved both disastrous to my interests and those of the Society.

On phoning Peter to tell him about the Secretary's visit to Salme of the previous night he emphatically denied he had ever phoned Mr. Evans on any occasion.

"It was Mr. Evans who phoned me," he said.

"He told us something about you discussing a private business matter, or something," I answered.

"He wants me to do some private work for him - something to do with technical radio equipment," replied Peter. "Mr. Evans is doing a private job for friends, and as he knows I've been ten years in the RAF and know something about radio technology, he wants me to help him work out some data."

"The point is, Mr. Evans said that you expressed complete disapproval of the agenda," I said firmly, "and he's been pushing for it to be scrapped."

"That's totally untrue," replied Peter. "It was Evans who expressed complete disapproval with the agenda, and he said it would be impossible to use it as it was so long. The only critical thing I said was that I thought it unnecessary for the Music and Technical Directors to view the premises in advance to arrange placing equipment. I thought that was a lot of bull."

Peter agreed that Evans was clearly trying to make mischief at my expense, and on telling him about Evans' "suspicions" of various Committee members and that I suspected he had heard the HISC slander, Peter suggested that he might tactfully address the Committee that very afternoon with the aim of stopping the spread of any malicious gossip behind my back, and I gladly agreed to this proposal.

As I replaced the phone, I reflected with concern on the big lie that

THE BIG LIE

the Secretary had invented and from that moment I realised that if the Society was to exist internally as a peaceful association, then Evans would eventually have to be removed from the Committee.

The meeting began punctually at 3 o'clock that afternoon, and after the formal opening, I read the following letter addressed to myself from the Lord Mayor of Helsinki:-

> I am in receipt of your letter concerning the founding of an International Club for foreign residents in Helsinki as well as for others interested in such activities. Later I have seen in the newspapers that the Club has been established.
>
> I take this opportunity to wish you as Chairman and the Club itself success in the work to come. It is good that foreigners living in Helsinki have this opportunity to get in touch both with each other and with Finnish citizens.
>
> Sincerely yours, Lauri Aho.

(The letter was dated 29th "October" 1963 when November was correctly intended.)

After reading this friendly letter, I indicated that Peter should make his short address. Speaking with emphasis, and glancing around the table and fixing each Committee member in turn with his eye, he said: "During the past few days there have been some disparaging rumours spreading around Helsinki about our Chairman. These rumours do not contain a shred of truth, but if they should reach the ear of any Committee member, I hope that he or she will immediately report them to the Chairman. We want no intriguing or backbiting in the Society, and if anyone present has any dissatisfaction whatsoever with the Chairman, would he either speak up now before we begin the business of the meeting, or speak with the Chairman afterwards, or else forever after hold his peace."

After this address, there was an atmosphere of tense silence for some moments as Peter again glanced round at each of the members in turn. No one chose to speak, and so the matter was closed.

The Secretary nudged me asking if he might say a few words as he had to leave the meeting early. He had many pages of scribbled notes, and he began outlining his scheme for large companies subscribing to the Society. His plans were theoretical, without practical proposals to work on, and after a long-winded speech, frequently interrupted by a failure to decipher his own handwriting, the Committee were disappointed by being denied even a motion to vote on.

After this time-wasting episode he then reverted to his old tack that the Society was moving too fast, but again, he remained doggedly non-committal as to "who" or "what" was moving too fast, only hinting that we should be careful as to the kind of people allowed into the club. Mr. Enblom agreed with this, adding that we should be particularly careful as to allowing "Italians, Spaniards and such like onto the premises," as they were too fond of "going after the girls."

The Secretary then cast out some Cassandra-like prophesies in that the Society might encounter many enemies, and that we had been most foolish in inciting a quarrel with the student body, and that Eric Jakowleff and HISC could use their influence in throwing difficulties into our path.

This line of argument shocked me for its hypocrisy in that it was Evans who had finally proposed that the HISC group be expelled from the founding meeting, and as if that was not enough, he then had the effrontery to tell the Committee that he had phoned Mr. Jakowleff the night before, to smooth over the unfortunate relationship and bad feelings generated between HISC and the International Society. Mr. Jakowleff had responded in a friendly manner, suggesting that the two clubs might be able to cooperate sometime in the future.

I read out two letters and a publicity circular for the approval of the Committee, before their duplication and despatch, and after the Secretary suggested several amendments, he said he would like a word before leaving the meeting. He began by reporting on the premises found for the Society - an item down on the agenda for the Chairman to handle.

"The rooms seemed quite sufficient for our purposes," he concluded, his mouth curling into an expression of mild distaste, "but I'm worried about their being situated in the headquarters of a political movement. We must consider this factor very carefully before coming to a decision. If we take the rooms, we may be inviting trouble for ourselves. The Communists in this country, for example, are very sensitive, and they may take an uncanny dislike to us, and brand us as having right wing sympathies."

This was met with sniggers and laughter.

"What does it matter what the Communists think? We've got to have premises somewhere," exclaimed Peter.

"Surely it's better than having rooms in the headquarters of the opposite political movement," said Stig Lambertsen.

"Well, I should like to suggest we send out letters to all the left wing movements, telling them we're entirely non-political, and that their members are always welcome to our club," said Evans fastidiously.

Jeers of derision filled the room and the unwise proposal had to be dropped like a hot brick. Turning to the Secretary to relieve him of his embarrassment, I asked if he had yet approached Prof. Paloheimo with a view to accepting the Honorary presidency.

"He wouldn't do it," replied Evans with an awkward gesture smiling. "He asked about our relationship with the student body though. He had read about the clash with HISC - and of course, if we don't improve matters with the student body pretty soon, no one will accept us."

"I've read nothing in the papers about our quarrel with HISC," I said astonished.

"I expect it was printed in some internal journal of the University," explained Evans.

Several minutes later he left the meeting, and Mrs. Toivanen was introduced to the Committee, but she declined to sit officially on the body, and then final details were drawn up or clarified as to clerical arrangements, publicity, and the organisation of the first meeting on the 11th. Gösta Kelter said that the Society might use the post box of his firm as the postal address of the Society, and this was agreed on by the Committee. I asked for some monetary donations to start the club going - as ready cash was needed for refreshments, postage and smaller miscellaneous items, before any dues could be collected at the door, and after waiting some moments, Mr. Lambertsen and Mr. Enblom loaned 50 marks apiece. As the Catering Manageress regretted she would be unable to attend the first meeting, Mr. Enblom volunteered to organise the catering arrangements for the 11th.

Then came the matter of the Constitution, and Mrs. Toivanen informed the Committee that for registration purposes, this would have to be drawn up according to strict legal form, and Salme and I agreed to visit her office with a view to studying the Constitution of the CSM for comparison purposes and for modelling our own document.

It was also necessary that the founding Committee members produce Church and Judicial Certificates for submitting to the registration authorities together with the finalised draft of the Constitution; and as a preparation for this, I asked the Committee to write down for me their full names and titles, together with addresses, dates of birth and occupations. This was done correctly by all members except for von Etter, who declined to put his date of birth and who ambiguously described his nationality as Finnish-American. I already possessed a Church and Judicial Certificate and the other members promised to secure these documents for themselves within the near future; but on subsequently phoning the Secretary and informing him of the Committee's decision on these matters, he exploded violently with the words, "I'm not going to get any damned Church or Judicial Certificates! I've never heard of such impertinence,!" and he immediately contacted other Committee members urging them not to cooperate with this request.

Towards the end of the meeting, a massive man with a barrel-like figure, wearing a tweed suit that he appeared to have grown out of, pushed open the partition at the far end of the room, and tip-toed quietly towards the table where the meeting was held. He was about forty years of age, with a reddish complexion, and fair hair cut in a schoolboyish fashion that stood slightly on end.

Peter Martin recognised him, and they greeted one another with a wave of the hand, and as I did not know who this intruder was, or what had persuaded him to honour us with his presence, I momentarily stopped the proceedings.

"Mr. Rowland G.P. Hill," he exclaimed ceremoniously, offering a hand.

"The inventor of the penny postage stamp, I presume," I only responded.

"Ah, but that was shortly before my time," he answered

grandiloquently.

I rose half out of my seat and greeted him perfunctorily.

"Are you the gentleman with the Irish wife,?" I enquired, for at the time I only registered the name as being one out of a number of correspondents.

"I haven't had the pleasure of meeting her yet," replied Rowland Hill with a smile, and this brought a round of laughter from the Committee. It could never had been anticipated by anyone in the room that within twelve months he would be married to one of the Committee members sitting round the table that afternoon.

Mr. Rowland Hill recognised Mr. Runela and Mr. Lambertsen as old acquaintances, and before sitting down to hear out the rest of the meeting, he shook hands with them ceremoniously. Afterwards, the gentleman approached me, congratulating me in a patronising fashion for my "forethought" and "initiative" in founding the Society, in much the same way as a Housemaster would congratulate a boy who had just won a cup for the House. By this time I remembered the letter he had sent me and he repeated the advice he had urged then.

As members gathered their cloaks, and Mr. Rowland Hill moved over to join Mr. Lambertsen, I slipped over to Peter and asked him what connection he had with this curiously bombastic character who was to play a prominent role in the following drama.

"I don't know anything about him," replied Peter. "I only met him for the first time in the Kolme Kreiviä, about an hour before the meeting. He invited himself along. I think he's a bit of a stuffed shirt if you want my opinion. I bumped into him buying a coffee in the KK, and when I said 'Sorry,' he looked at me in surprise, and exclaimed in a pompous tone, 'Why, are you British?' 'Yes,' I replied, 'but I always say sorry when I bump into someone, out of politeness.' He asked if he might join me and I said 'Yes,' and then he said to me, 'What do you know about this International Society,?' and I told him, and then he asked if he could come along. I couldn't very well say he couldn't."

"Of course not."

"When we sat having coffee, he asked, 'What do you know about this Robert Corfe,?' and he kept addressing me as 'Mr. Martin.' I said to him, 'Can't we drop the formality? The name's Peter.'"

"Sounds a pompous ass to me," I exclaimed.

"And by the way, Bob, who's that man in the brown suit who always sits beside me at the end of the table?"

"That's von Etter - our aristocratic member," I joked. "Why?"

"He's always talking about sex," responded Peter in the tone of a prudish middle aged spinster, and he pronounced the word "sex" in an undertone as if it was the most shocking noun in the dictionary.

"He sounds like you," I laughed in the realisation that Peter had widely advertised the fact of having bedded thirty-five women in his first three months in the country.

"He's not normal," continued Peter ignoring my remark as he wore an expression of moral reprehension.

"What's normal, anyway,?" I said dismissively. "None of us is normal."

"I tell you he needs watching. All through the Committee meeting he kept nudging me and making smutty remarks about women," confided Peter, and he was clearly shocked. "Honestly, Bob, I was so embarrassed, and there was a woman - that Mrs. Kaatia - sitting on the other side of me. I didn't know what to say to the fellow."

"I think you'll only have to allow him his little bit of eccentricity," I only responded. "Consider his age. He must be in his sixties or seventies."

"That's just it. He hasn't grown up. He talks about sex like a ten-year old schoolboy. He's fixated on sex. To be quite honest, Bob, I don't think he's a good man to have on the Committee. He can't give the club a good reputation," insisted Peter.

"Perhaps he's the man the American embassy have got their eyes on," I suggested.

"Well, you know what prudes those bloody Yanks are, so I wouldn't be surprised," said Peter. "With a nation that hides its piano legs behind soft coverings, anything's possible!"

The following days were occupied in the hectic activity of preparing for the first general meeting of the Society. As soon as Salme and I had had a long working session with Mrs. Toivanen on the Society's Constitution, I returned home with this, typed it out, and then personally delivered it to Salme for her to translate. Again she reminded me of the American embassy's displeasure with the Society, and because of her nagging insistence on this matter, I too began to share her anxiety.

But what could the Americans really know about our Society? If they read the press they only had the names of two top officials, the Secretary and myself, but as Evans conveyed an impression of almost contemptible insignificance and as he had not yet shown any kind of ability apart from intrigue, I could never have guessed that the Americans would have identified him as a marked man. Was it Evans or myself then,? - and then I recollected that our Committee member, Miss Elisabeth Vaajajärvi, was an employee of the embassy, and she might well have passed on information, and this broadened the suspects to include us all.

Then I remembered the HISC group, and Geoff Gee's slander and close friendship with the American ambassador, and it was then that I first suspected that the HISC group were planting a conspiracy against myself and the International Society from within the walls of the American embassy. This was the greatest fear I had to contend with - Evans could be handled in my own good time - and I phoned the American embassy later that day and many times afterwards within the next few weeks, asking for Mr. Ingram, the chargé d'affaires, but he was never available and so I could never reach the root of the problem in destroying this alleged conspiracy.

It was an acutely uncomfortable experience to suspect that the Americans might possibly be circulating malicious lies invented by the HISC group in an attempt to destroy our club, and that Evans was very possibly taking advantage of this situation, and in view of the incredulity of the American mind, I almost believed that this must be so.

The following day I arranged for a telephone to be installed in my flat, for I now realised that as Chairman of the Society, I could not manage without one. I went to Gösta's office, fetched some special paper and carbons to prepare the circulars for his spirit duplicator, and two days later, I bought boards, paint and brushes for preparing two colourful placards to be placed outside the premises of the Society. The placards were to be painted in yellow and red letters on a pale blue background, and for some days, the strong smell of fresh paint, together with much of the floor being covered with newspaper and painting materials, was an inconvenience to myself and those few pupils who still attended lessons during the Christmas weeks.

When the circulars had been duplicated Elisabeth Vaajajärvi kindly volunteered to come round and address envelopes and fold enclosures, and Mr. Enblom called with the Society's cash box, festively decorated with Christmas wrappings, and paid out money to cover the cost of postage. That night I sent off approximately 150 circulars, together with some ten personal letters to persons offering help to the Society, or to act as hosts to foreigners in Finland. Two circular letters were sent out: one addressed to correspondents interested in the Society, and the other addressed to founding members. A publicity circular, designed primarily to be fixed to notice boards, was also sent out with letters.

Apart from essential information as to the name and address of the Society, and the names of its four leading officers, the following notices were included on the publicity circular: "The aims of the ISF are to encourage friendship between Finns and foreigners and to promote international understanding." (This notice was subsequently to become a cause of trouble in arousing suspicion within certain embassies as to the desirability and motives of the Society.) "Organised Programmes every Wednesday - Talks - Film Shows - Debates - Parties, followed by refreshments and dancing and a time for conversation." (Then followed a notice about "Soltorpet.") "A special service to introduce foreigners to Finnish families, to enable strangers in Finland to stay with and get to know Friendly Finns, is operated by the Society. ... Many other social activities as theatre and opera outings, sporting events, hiking, cross-country skiing, barbecues, sailing, amateur dramatics, dinner and dancing parties organised to take place. ALL WELCOME!"

During this week whilst working every night until the early hours of the morning, in typing and duplicating circulars, painting boards, and phoning instructions or begging requests from other Committee members, Mr. Evans was conspicuous by his absence, but I had not forgotten him, and intended to take him to task over his deceit at the first opportunity.

On Saturday morning my phone was installed, and on Sunday, I was holding a party for the Committee, so that members could strike up a closer acquaintanceship. All members had been asked to this party, except for Mr. Evans, who was left out in the cold for obvious reasons. On inviting Peter to the party he was quick to tell me that Evans had phoned him late in the evening on the day of the previous Committee meeting.

"He was very worried and upset," said Peter, "and asked if I thought he had made a fool of himself before the Committee, in suggesting that the Society send letters to left wing movements."

"I hope you told him he did make a fool of himself," I answered.

"I think Evans is just an old woman," said Peter. "He's a compulsive worrier."

CHAPTER 9
An open breach

"All seems infected to th' infected spy,
As all looks yellow to the jaundiced eye."

Alexander Pope, *An Essay On Criticism*, 1.558-9.

I took up the phone and dialled a number. It was Sunday morning, and for the first time in a week, I was free to catch up on those things I had had to put off. On Saturday I had pinned up more than 100 circulars publicising the Society on notice boards in the University, and throughout student clubs and student lodgings, and libraries and institutes. I had also been busy in shopping for food, drink, and decorations for the party of the following day.

A woman answered the phone, and I asked for the person I wanted. I was surprised to hear her call for him in Finnish, and there were children's voices in the background, also speaking Finnish. I was momentarily apprehensive as to the nicety of what I was compelled to say.

"Evans speaking," came a voice.

"It's Corfe here," I replied. "Look, I'm phoning you about your contacting other members behind my back and complaining about last Sunday's agenda. Now I view this with serious concern. And especially in view of the fact that Mr. Martin emphatically denies having phoned you on any occasion."

"Oh yes he did," returned Evans, his hackles rising.

"He denies it, and moreover, he contends he never asked for the agenda to be scrapped."

"Look here, Sir, don't you start telling lies behind my back, or I'll give you real trouble," returned Evans threateningly.

"Well, that's up to me to judge who's lying and who's telling the truth," I answered, "but your contacting Mrs. Kaatia behind my back was unquestionably mischievous."

"Look here, Sir, I'll give you real trouble if you throw me off the Committee - I promise you that," returned Evans.

"No one's threatening to throw anyone off the Committee," I said.

At that moment the doorbell was rung, and I answered it to let in Martti Hirvonen, whom I was expecting. He had volunteered to help the club on the entertainments side, but I was chiefly interested in eliciting from him the truth behind the rumours about the concern of the American embassy over our Society.

"You'll soon run into trouble, Sir, if you try to run the whole show yourself," said Evans when I got back to the phone. I tried to appease his anger and then he back-peddled saying, "Anyway, Mr. Martin said the agenda sounded like a lot of bull - or words to that effect."

"That's different from the impression you gave other members as to what he said," I answered. "If you have any disagreement with Society matters in future, you just contact me first. You're supposed to be the Chairman's Secretary - and by the way, you've been very conspicuous by your absence this week. I could have done with some more help in getting out our publicity material."

"I've been ill all week. My kidneys have been playing up. The doctors don't know what it is themselves yet," he said self-pitifully.

I expressed my condolences and then he claimed there were rumours spreading about several of our Committee members.

"What members,?" I asked.

"Well, for example, this von Etter," replied Evans hesitantly. "They say he runs a brothel."

"It's just tittle-tattle," I answered. "If you've got real evidence for such rumours the Committee will hear them, otherwise just keep them to yourself."

"It's not going to help the reputation of the club if we have such a man on the Committee. There must be some truth in the rumour."

"If he is, he's no common or garden pimp. I know for a fact he happens to be a pillar of society in this country," I replied. "And what other members are there rumours about?"

"Let's forget rumours, shall we,?" said Evans evidently wanting to shake off the topic.

"We want a nice friendly Society without backbiting or malice," I said, "and if you're not prepared to behave in a friendly and peaceful manner you can resign."

"I'll work for any organisation that really wants peace and friendship," said Evans.

"That was the Society's Secretary, Mr. Evans - he's been a hell of a nuisance," I said to Martti Hirvonen on replacing the receiver.

Martti Hirvonen, who was Secretary of the Orthodox youth club, said he would be pleased to help the new Society, especially with regard to lending dance records and musical equipment. I welcomed the offer and after he had told me about a student exchange visit he had made to the States, I broached the subject of the embassy rumour. He could throw little light on the matter, merely saying that a friend had told him about the embassy's displeasure with someone on the Committee but he did not know with whom.

Later that morning I phoned Eric Jakowleff, President of HISC, and arranged to lunch with him the following day at the station restaurant. I wanted to patch up the quarrel between the two clubs. I received a phone call from Salme excusing herself from the party that night on the grounds that her father had been seized with a stroke and that she had to leave for her native city of Joensuu. I asked how she was progressing with the Constitution which she admitted was giving her great difficulty.

"Perhaps Mr. Runela or Mr. Jokimäki could be persuaded to work on the translation," I ventured.

"Why don't you give it to Mr. Evans,?" suggested Salme.

"His Finnish isn't good enough for that task," I replied. "And I don't think his English is too hot either for amending or adding necessary clauses to documents."

"Mr. Evans would be so happy if you could give him the Constitution to work on," pleaded Salme.

"I don't think there's anything that could make Mr. Evans happy," I replied. "He's not that kind of man. Why do you suggest him, anyway?"

"He phoned me earlier today about the Constitution, and asked how much I had translated," said Salme.

"I'm surprised he should have had the audacity to phone you about anything after assisting your removal from the Committee," I answered.

"Oh, he only wanted to help me," said Salme. "Look, Bob, why don't you give it to him? He'ld be so pleased."

"I'm afraid I'm not so pleased with him, though," I answered. "I crossed swords with him this morning."

"He told me about it," said Salme.

"Did he,?" I said.

"You know, Bob, you've really hurt Mr. Evans. He said you'd both quarrelled very badly over the phone, and he seemed so upset about it. Why can't you two make it up? He's such a nice little man really - he can't help being irritable sometimes."

"To tell you the truth, Salme, I've never known him when he's not irritable."

"But he was so hurt and offended when he phoned me," insisted Salme. "Bob, please give Mr. Evans the Constitution. He feels you're ignoring him, and leaving him out in the cold. He wants to feel more purposeful, and do something useful for the Society. He's so keen, and then the Constitution is the Secretary's job. Look, Gösta is driving me to the station this evening, and I'll give him all the papers of the Society to pass onto you, and you can post them to Mr.Evans."

"I'll reconsider the matter," I replied reluctantly.

It was clear that Mr. Evans was putting on an act of offended pride in the guise of self-pity directed in the right quarter. The weak little man was exploiting the mothering instinct of a woman physically larger and a decade younger than himself. Mr. Evans was out to intrigue and play politics, and his latest act was merely an example of his ruthlessness and another aspect of his deceit.

The party that night proved a great success. Gösta was the first arrival bringing along a set of wine glasses to augment my own small collection. Aldar Runela together with his inseparable friend, Heikki Jokimäki were the next arrivals, and they sat close together for the duration of the party like a couple of owls, and then came Waldemar von Etter, Ingrid Andersson, Stig Lambertsen, the schoolmaster, Anders Enblom, and lastly, Peter Martin.

"This party's been arranged so we can all get to know each other by our first names," said Gösta in his pleasantly lilting Swedish accent after we were settled with drinks. The atmosphere began to relax, and everyone shook hands with everyone else as he revealed his Christian name for the first time.

Von Etter became known as "Digmar," and Anders Enblom, who was bolder than the others, began to spontaneously recite some poetry in his ceremonial tone of voice, before again expressing his ideal that the Society should found a poetry reading circle.

On Ingrid Andersson's arrival there was quite a stir in welcoming her as the only lady guest. In re-arranging the furniture, I had placed a couch in the middle of the room, at the end of which stood a long table from where refreshments were served.

After Ingrid had been introduced, von Etter (or Digmar as he now was) began persuading her with limited success to recline on the couch in the same manner as "Elizabeth Taylor had done in the film *Cleopatra*." Ingrid resisted with embarrassment, but von Etter who was not a man to take no for an answer, took hold of her shoulders and tried to press her down onto the couch. The rest of us could only laugh at this scene of feigned seduction.

"You wouldn't be wanting to take advantage of the dear lady before our very eyes,?" remarked Anders Enblom laughing.

"Who wouldn't,?" responded Digmar with jocularity. "What a delicious creature we have with us this evening! What a pity she won't lie on the couch, so we can stand round and contemplate her more delectable parts!"

There was some awkward laughter before the conversation turned to other things touching the future of the Society. Eventually, I lit up candles turning out the lights, and the atmosphere became pleasantly intimate.

Towards the end of the evening Peter offered a mild rebuke to our aristocratic member that momentarily upset the convivial atmosphere by a tense silence. Digmar had made some witty reference to Omo washing powder and "homosexuality" in the midst of an otherwise clean conversation, and being unable to repress a sensuous chuckle over his little joke, Peter suddenly cut him short with a sharp, "No thank you very much!"

Peter was the first to leave the party - his wife was expecting shortly - and as I saw him out, he turned to me and said, "That man in the brown suit is dangerous. He needs watching!"

AN OPEN BREACH

The meeting with Jakowleff the following day at the station restaurant was little more than an exchange of civilities and an oral agreement that our two clubs should cooperate. He even refused to lunch, instead only accepting a pot of coffee, and he smoked his pipe nervously and spoke little. On expressing my sorrow over the quarrel at the founding meeting I explained it away on the grounds that we had been arguing at cross purposes.

As proof of the friendly intentions of the International Society, I said we would willingly display HISC publicity material on our board. Jakowleff asked if he might give me some of their information literature to hand out to our members, and I gladly agreed to this. I told him about the slander of Geoff Gee, but he appeared quite unconcerned, only dismissing it with his opinion that it was not a disgraceful thing to be expelled from Sweden anyway.

"That's not the point," I said taken aback by what must have been intended as a humorously contemptuous dig at Sweden's expense. "The rumour is untrue and I want the slander suppressed."

Jakowleff merely nodded in assent, and it was obvious he was not going to admit that a member of his club had committed such a grave misdemeanour as to spread a slander.

Then dropping the matter of the slander as something best forgotten, I suggested we could both participate in a programme of the International Society as an open gesture that we had really buried the hatchet. Jakowleff agreed to this, and I proposed that the programme could best take the form of a debate between us. I had listed a number of themes for a debate that could be taken either seriously or treated in a humorous vein, and we chose to debate on the motion that "Mankind Is Becoming Dehumanised." I asked Jakowleff to take his choice as to which side of the argument he would support, and he promised to let me know within a fortnight as to his decision and as to whether he would participate in such a programme or not.

That night Mr. Evans phoned. He was in a quiet frame of mind, and asked if he might only speak with me for a few moments on the Constitution. His attitude was yielding - almost subservient. Might he contact a lawyer with regard to arranging the sections of the Constitution? Most certainly! Would I object if his wife undertook the translation of the Constitution, as she had volunteered to do so? No! He asked if it would be possible for me to send him the Constitution and other registration papers by post. I said that the Constitution was all his, that I was pleased to have it off my hands, and I promised to post it to him tomorrow.

This I accordingly did, and it was an action I was consequently to regret more than any other I had taken in the Society.

On the evening of the 11th, Gösta called at 7.30 and we loaded the club notice boards onto the roof of his car before driving to the Society's premises. Five Committee members and Salme had arrived before us, and there was an atmosphere of hopeful anticipation. Anders Enblom, assisted by Miss Inge Kainulainen busily attended to the catering, the former having brought along a wide variety of cakes and biscuits; and several crates of mineral drinks had been delivered that morning.

Eighty-six persons were present at the meeting that evening, and I opened the proceedings with a speech of welcome at 8.30, wishing those present many hours of "pleasure and happiness" as members of the Society, reminding them that it was their club and the Committee members would welcome suggestions at all times. I introduced each of the Committee members in turn, adding that it was only through "their heroic and unceasing efforts" that this meeting had been made possible, and that we had been determined against all odds to get the Society going before Xmas.

Glancing around the room, and noticing that girls out-numbered boys by about three to one, something not unanticipated in this small city of 50,000 more girls than boys, I continued, "I see there are more girls than boys this evening, but this is something we promise to amend by the next meeting. It is the aim of our Society to equalise the sexes in so far as this can be achieved." This was met with laughter. "In fact a special plan for achieving this, as well as for equalising the number of Finns and foreigners is going to be put into operation later this week."

I appealed for more active members, pointed out our club notice board; made an announcement about the Society's hospitality service; related the story of the HISC quarrel and as to how it had been peacefully concluded, and finally, I read the Lord Mayor's letter, before

AN OPEN BREACH

handing over to Mr. Evans who had told me before the meeting that he would like to say a word.

He shifted from one foot to the other, as he stood before the crowded assembly, and he looked more worried and fussy than ever. He began by saying that I had already said what he had wanted to say, and he reiterated that this was a members' club. In his fastidious tone of voice, he continued, "As this is above all a social and friendship club, I should like to suggest that everyone in the room shakes hands with at least four other persons during the evening. If you do this, you will have made this a true friendship Society." I winced in acute embarrassment at listening to this silly suggestion, and at the front of the hall were seated four Swedish girls, one of whom loudly exclaimed in the hearing of all, "How ridiculous!"

After Mr. Evans had finished, I called upon Gösta Kelter to give out some announcements about the entertainments side of the Society, and I was disappointed to see how self-conscious he was in addressing a crowd. He blushed and made self-deprecating remarks to ingratiate himself for his modesty but little else, and although it was clear to most that he was a charmer on the personal level, I soon saw that he lacked that decisiveness so necessary in holding public attention, and in view of this it became clear that I should have to take on the additional burden of being MC.

Nevertheless, the evening was successful, with an entertaining film, and dancing afterwards in the hall upstairs.

The following days were busily spent in planning the next meeting, painting a larger notice board for the Society, and duplicating and sending out 76 letters to consulates and embassies in Helsinki.

By this time Christmas festivities were in full swing. On the 14th of December a number of us from the club were honoured guests of the St. Lucia party of the International Friendship League. This was an association originally founded by Stig Lambertsen in Denmark, and now he was its Honorary President in Helsinki. It was one of those typically formal Scandinavian functions, rows of people sitting in candlelight at long tables before plates of Christmas biscuits and coffee, no one daring to talk to his neighbour until presiding officers had done with their speeches and dispensed with final formalities.

As the Chairman of the International Society, I was led to a place near the head of the table beside my opposite number of the Friendship League, and then Lambertsen delivered an impressive and highly flattering speech in Swedish praising all the work I had done. I returned the speech, as necessary on such occasions, and after several announcements, the assembly were allowed to eat their biscuits before which they had already been sitting for three quarters of an hour.

Peter and Digmar were in particularly good form, and later in the evening Father Christmas came into the hall presenting all guests with a small gift. Peter received a cheese grater, and not knowing what to do with such a culinary object, he first pretended shaving with it, and not finding that satisfactory, scratching his back, and finally, adopting the shy gesture of a young lady, coyly shaving under his armpits, to hoots of laughter from the crowd.

The climax of the party came when a group of musicians entered in national costume playing St. Lucia, and a door was opened at the opposite end of the room, and St. Lucia herself, a beautiful blonde maiden in a white nightdress wearing a crown topped by candles, and followed by six similarly dressed attendants, entered in all their glory, solemnly paraded round the room and then departed.

Two days later, and quite by accident, I learnt from Anders Enblom that Evans was calling a sub-committee meeting of four persons to be held in his flat in Tapiola. The Constitution was to be discussed and Stig Lambertsen, Digmar and Gösta Kelter had been invited. Anders was surprised I had not been informed about this. "Evans is such a stickler for correctness, I can't understand why he didn't consult you first," he said. I expressed my suspicions with regard to intrigue.

"Oh, I'm sure Evans wouldn't do a thing like that," said Anders quite shocked. "Evans is so careful - he wouldn't do anything that wasn't absolutely correct."

To play safe, I phoned Lambertsen to whom I also repeated my anxiety. There were several more days of busy work for the Society before the Christmas recess, and on the 23rd December - when our club was exactly a month old - I went to Ander's flat where we dined before addressing, folding and sealing envelopes for yet another batch of circulars.

AN OPEN BREACH

On arriving there, however, I was taken aback by something that seemed out of character in view of the circumstances surrounding his life as I had imagined it. He had publicly proclaimed himself to the Society as a "man of property" and with his constant references to his "military" background, and the pomposity of his manner, I had been led falsely to believe (due to my own naivety and inexperience at the time) that he was a domineering personality in his private life. His wife let me into the flat, and I was surprised to see him standing on the kitchen table by the window wearing an apron and rolled up shirtsleeves, nervously messing around with a sponge.

"The corners, you fool, the corners," nagged his wife in Swedish from the safety of the kitchen floor. She was elegantly dressed and had clearly been a woman of beauty in her time.

It seemed as if the poor man would have to overcome a terror of falling off the table before he could comply with his wife's exacting instructions. He must have registered my shocked expression, for he gave me a significant smile. And indeed, I had never before seen a woman in real life treat a man in so humiliating a fashion. I now realised that the man of property was in reality a poor henpecked husband - like a character out of a Strindberg play - and before we began our work, she left the flat.

On the 31st of December the International Friendship League - Finnish section, held a party in public rooms in Fredrikinkatu, and a number of us from our Society attended the function. There was a poor turn out, and only half the laid table places were taken, and several murmured, "Wasn't this just typical? Those Finns are just not interested in social events!" Gösta remarked, "I hope more come to our launching party tomorrow night." However, punch wine was served - the Swedish party had been dry - and Digmar arrived with a bevy of admiring and lively fans in the forty and fifty age group, and soon there was an informality and freedom that had been lacking at the earlier function. I met Sonja, the Swedish ambassador's personal Secretary for the first time, interesting her in our own Society, and I sat with Mrs. Kristina Rotkirch, the journalist from *Huvudstadsbladet*, who was following with interest the progress of our unique club. At midnight - as everywhere in Finland - we each melted lead in huge ladles which was then poured into buckets of water, and from the resulting shapes our destiny was foretold for the coming year.

Digmar soon fell so much into the swing of the party that he lost all sense of propriety, and in the course of dancing he kissed and fondled his different women friends with a youthful passion, exploring their bodies with his bejewelled fingers.

"Do you see that man over there,?" confided Mrs. Rotkirch. "That's Vladimir von Etter - but he calls himself Waldemar."

"We call him 'Digmar'," I added.

"He's all degenerated. He was very rich once, but he's spent it all on drink and women. He's got a big estate not far from Helsinki, and there are terrible stories about the goings-on there. They play polo with women riding on men's backs, and in the summer they run naked through the forest."

"I know him well. He's our press and publicity manager," I said. "He's Finland's advertisement manager for the *New York Herald Tribune*."

"He used to be. Do you see that limp? No one knows where he got it from," said the journalist sadly.

"Perhaps he got it in the War?"

"He was too old for the War."

"Then perhaps the first World War."

"He was too young for that," remarked Mrs. Rotkirch. "During the last century his ancestors were amongst the largest landowners in Russia. They were fabulously rich. You want to watch him though. He could make a bad reputation for the International Society."

The true story behind Waldemar von Etter will be elucidated later in this book.

CHAPTER 10
Braving the opposition

"Though those that are betrayed
Do feel the treason sharply, yet the traitor
Stands in worse case of woe."

Shakespeare, *Cymbeline*, Act III, Sc. 4, 1.180-1.

Paper decorations and fir twigs brightened the hall and over 120 people helped enliven our New Year's day festivities.
"There's hardly room for more," said Anders standing over Ingrid Andersson as she filled our cash box from the queue of guests pushing their way into the entrance. "Soon, we'll have to start turning people away."

The programme for the party was so well managed that it would have been difficult for anyone to escape participating in the many different events. I felt this to be the best way of guaranteeing the success of a party where most were not only strangers to one another but also because of the natural reticence of the Finnish character. Merriment could not have sprung spontaneously from such a heterogeneous crowd - irrespective of nationality - and all had to be inveigled into situations where extroversion might be allowed to get the better of their reserve.

There were games of intelligence, competing teams, and impersonations of objects, actions and people. Refreshments were free, and although we were forbidden by law to serve alcoholic beverages, hot grog (a non-alcoholic wine) was served with raisins and nuts. Peter was in fine fettle, and his ten years experience as an instructor in the RAF Regiment had given him a nice ability to handle people in such a way that he attracted volunteers without requesting them.

"Where's our Ronald tonight,?" he asked referring to Mr. Evans.

"He made such a twit of himself last time, I expect he's ashamed to show his face again," I answered.

Digmar was accompanied by a friend from the Canadian embassy, and both spent much time loitering by the toilets.

"Come in here, Bob, I've got something to show you," he said beckoning me into the gents. "This is a proper drink," he continued taking a hip flask from his pocket and thrusting it into my hand. I took a swig to discover it was *koskenkorva* - Finland's hardest and foulest spirit.

About an hour later, Peter took me aside, a shocked expression covering his face.

"Do you know what that man in the brown suit's been up to,?" he exclaimed.

"No," I lied.

"He's been drinking alcohol in the toilets with an American buddy."

"I think his friend's Canadian," I corrected.

"It's disgusting the way he carries on," exclaimed Peter in the tone of a school ma'm. "We'll have to get rid of him somehow."

Later in the evening the Canadian collapsed in the gents in a dead stupor, and had to be rescued by his friend. I never saw the diplomat again, but some weeks later I learnt he had been reprimanded by his ambassador for attending our Society and was forbidden to go near us in the future.

After a Charlie Chaplin and Laurel and Hardy film show, there was a beauty contest for the election of Miss International Society 1964. There was a panel of six judges including Peter and Digmar, and the talent on display would have been worthy of any beauty contest held in a large British city. Some of the competitors were reluctant participants, but one blonde in a slinky satin dress volunteered an exceptionally sexy pose.

"Gor, just look at that. It nearly caught fire,!" exclaimed Peter.

The prize, a set of Christmas candles with a stand, was awarded to a modest dark haired girl, and then the party moved upstairs to the darkly lit dance hall. Here Peter was really in his element as he took up the role of the dancing master teaching the twist that was only then being introduced into Finland.

"No one can pick that up," remarked one girl. "It looks ridiculous!"

It was time to consult our Treasurer on the financial success of the evening, and he proudly announced to a group of Committee members that we had taken in over 300 marks, whilst our total outlay, including rent and refreshments was less than a third of that.

Before the evening drew to its close at one in the morning, Peter again approached me in confidence, his face expressing moral indignation.

"Bob, things are going from bad to worse," he insisted. "That man in the brown suit's been taking girls into the gents cloakroom and giving them alcohol. Where's it all going to end?"

No steps had yet been taken for drawing up a full programme for the season. I contacted Aldar Runela, the Programme Director, but he merely hummed and ha-ed, muttered something about someone who might give a talk on the building of Sisu bus bodies, and then expatiated on the difficulties of his office. I realised he was useless for the task to which he had been elected, and immediately took charge of the duties he should have attended to.

Within the next few days I phoned many of the embassies and foreign associations in Helsinki, asking for speakers and guests who would address our meetings, and soon I had arranged weekly programmes for every Wednesday up until the end of May. The arranging of this calendar of events required considerable thought and diplomacy if no offence was to be given to the authorities; our members; or the embassies, touching accusations of favouritism for nationalities or areas; and I believe the resulting programme could not have been better balanced, or give rise to suggestions of bias or unfairness from any quarter.

Speakers were to attend from countries representing the four corners of the globe, and those lands in conflict with others were always represented by their opposites within a week or two of their rivals. Thus there was both an East and a West German evening; a talk on Israel followed by a film show on life in the Arab Republic; a colour slide show on the United States followed by a lecture on production in the Soviet Union. There were to be talks on Turkey, Brazil, France and India, and lectures on the Lapps and the problems of Scandinavian immigrants in Canada. Those countries usually left out in the cold were also to be brought into the warmth of our Society, with films from South Africa (to represent a state with a rightist ideology), and a film evening presented by the embassy of the People's Republic of China - Finland at that time being one of the only Western countries with such an embassy. In addition to this, two evenings were to be given over to debates, and one to a Grand Party to celebrate the joys of spring.

It was then necessary to draw up an Entertainments Programme for weekend and non-Wednesday outings, and this was the task of Gösta and Salme. I emphasised that a calendar of varying events from January until June would have to be drawn up within a few days, so we could duplicate and despatch our circulars, but they too proved dilatory and confused in performing these duties.

"I haven't got such a great imagination, "pleaded Gösta at a Committee meeting, glancing around at his colleagues, "so before I plan anything definite, I'ld appreciate suggestions from other members."

No other members were forthcoming on anything definite but merely mooted counsels of advice on what might be done. Gösta remained in a quandary and several times complained of the predicament to which I subjected him.

"You're a marvellous slave driver. I've never known anyone with such a talent for making people work," he laughed one Sunday in his office as a team of us were busily engaged in duplicating and addressing envelopes.

He was director of an importing household goods firm based in Katajanokka, close by the Uspensky Orthodox Cathedral. At that time he was marketing a range of frying pans promoted by TV's very first celebrity cook, Philip Harben, whom he had met several months previously. I told him that Philip Harben had been an old school friend of my father at Highgate, and I hoped that this little piece of information would somehow draw us closer together. But as circumstances transpired, it was not to be.

Inevitably I was obliged to assist Gösta by entirely taking over the task of planning an Entertainments Programme. This programme was to consist of several skiing expeditions and a winter barbecue, visits to the Opera, nightclub and concert evenings, and visits to museums followed by mystery outings. All age groups were to be catered for.

On 8th of January fifty members attended a comedy film show at the Society, the turn out being small as it was a week before the opening of the published programme of the season's events. I was happy, however, to entertain our first honoured guests from the foreign community, Herr Bauer and two colleagues with their wives from the German Democratic Republic's *Kulturzentrum*. They were quiet spoken non-English speaking respectable bourgeois looking Germans, neatly dressed and keeping themselves very much apart from the rest of the company.

Herr Bauer was to give a film show followed by a question time at the end of the month, and he wanted to come along and get the flavour of our club. He had some trepidation because of the language problem, but I assured him I would act as interpreter on that particular night, but I felt he should have had more circumspection about the nature of the programme he insisted on showing for this was to lead to a briefly embarrassing incident.

Several days previously I had visited Herr Bauer at his Cultural Centre, told him something about our club, and invited him to present a programme. I had wanted him to present a quality East German feature film (for which the country was renowned) as they had these at the centre for free loan, but he stubbornly persisted in his idea of showing documentaries illustrating the way of life in the DDR - and as if to ensure that I was to know in advance exactly what he intended to do - I was obliged to sit through some four or five insipid propaganda films on factory production, living standards and collective farms - films which I felt would be received with derision by club members.

If he wants to make a fool of himself (which he eventually did to his acute pain and embarrassment) that's up to him, I thought, but I finally persuaded him to show a film about Brandenburg's beautiful countryside, but when the fateful day arrived he had forgotten to bring it. His insistence on showing propaganda films was particularly ironic and incorrigible on his part in view of the fact that he would only agree to present a programme to the club on the understanding that the Society was entirely non-political and that there would be no questions of a political nature afterwards.

"What a nice man that Mr. Bauer is," said a dotty middle aged Englishwoman who attended the club. "Aren't they so quiet and modest these East German diplomats."

A Committee meeting was held on the following Saturday at Anders flat in Kapteeninkatu in Eira, and it soon became clear that Evans had been carefully briefing the opposition as to who should have the greater say in controlling the affairs of the Society. The Secretary held up several letters and circulars that had been sent out to members and others interested in the club.

"I've been going through these letters, and it's been quite out of order that they should have been sent out at all," mumbled Evans with a distasteful expression through a cloud of cigarette smoke. "The Committee should have been consulted first."

"The Committee was consulted, Mr. Evans," I replied. "No circular has *ever* been sent out by this Society until it was read out in full and voted on by the Committee. It just happens that you were absent at the last meeting."

"They should never have gone out," continued Evans unperturbed. "It's customary in Finland that letters sent out by associations should bear two signatures."

"That point has never been raised before," I replied.

"I don't think it's the Chairman's function to put his signature to letters," continued Evans ignoring my remarks.

"You've never been around to put your signature," I insisted.

"If you must know," said Evans spitefully and turning towards me for the first time, "I've been very ill during the past fortnight, and the doctor has advised rest and complete freedom from stress. And if you must know, I've been working very hard on the Constitution, and it's done nothing to improve my health."

There were murmurs of sympathy in the room to which I felt obliged to add, "We're all very grateful to you Mr. Evans."

"Here, here,!" assented several voices.

"And this here is going much too far," said Evans waving the Winter/Spring Programme which had been duplicated and despatched the previous day. "We're getting too much attention for ourselves. We must go carefully. We're a new Society and the authorities are very particular in this country."

"And so are we! But please specify, Mr. Evans - show us where we've lacked caution."

Vladimir (Waldemar) von Etter

Finnish aristocrat, playboy, and friend of the author, suspected by the Finnish intelligence service of working for the CIA.

As usual he ignored what I said, and addressing the rest of the assembly, he continued emphatically, "I think we're going too fast."

"Yes, we must learn to walk before we can run," said Stig Lambertsen the schoolmaster.

There were murmurs of agreement from several quarters.

"I think the Society is becoming too much of a one-man band," continued Evans.

"But not out of choice, I can assure you," I put in, and my blood boiled at the injustice of the accusation in view of the fact that to get the Society onto its feet, I had been obliged to take on all the donkey work of drawing up a programme and of acting as a master of ceremonies. I had not yet myself had an opportunity of relaxing or socialising in the club's premises.

Nonetheless, Evans had stirred up support and Anders, Stig and Gösta (all of whom had attended Evans' own irregularly called sub-committee meeting) added their support. The Finnish members, including Digmar, remained non-committal on the matter, but even Peter commented: "You know, Bob, you've got too headstrong a personality."

Then followed the back-peddling compliments: "Of course, we're all grateful to you, Bob" - this came from Gösta, and then Anders said, "If it wasn't for you, none of us would be in this room this afternoon."

Evans added that he was taking on a very grave responsibility in acting as Secretary of the International Society Finland, and that no events must be allowed to occur whereby the loss of his reputation would be risked, and he said that if the affairs of the Society were to continue to be conducted as they were now, he would have no choice but to resign.

There were exclamations of "No," and finally it was agreed that no correspondence would be sent out in future until the Secretary had first approved of it and I stood by this agreement until the final storm occurred. The meeting ended in an atmosphere of tension, but then an informal party followed, and we were served coffee, smörrebröd, and beer and mineral drinks. The topics raised by the Committee meeting, however, could not so easily be forgotten.

"We've got to be very particular about the type of people we allow into the Society," said Anders. "There were several dark-looking people at the last meeting that I didn't like the look of at all - the kind who chase after women in the wrong way."

"Let's not start showing racial prejudice - there's no need for it in this country," I put in.

"Some of the girls look very young," said Gösta.

"We've got a moral responsibility to ensure that none of the younger girls get into trouble," said Peter taking up the topic, and he seemed quite sincere, and this despite the fact of his outrageous promiscuity which was the talk of the town - and his recent marriage (his second) was no bar to these proclivities.

"Some of them have to be protected against themselves," said Gösta.

"It would create an awful scandal for the International Society if one of our members was to put a bun in the oven, as the saying goes," said Anders in a pompous tone. "If that got out, I don't know how we'd live it down."

"Especially as we haven't a Legal Adviser," added Peter.

"I think we're all agreed the Society's got to be kept respectable," said Anders.

"After all is said and done, the main thing is we don't allow anyone onto the Committe who's going to 'walk off with the silver' as they say," said Peter after a thoughtful pause.

"Exactly," I assented.

"There are a lot of very strange people who've got to be kept out of the club," said Evans.

"What kind of people,?" I queried.

"During the past year a lot of German Nazis have been infiltrating the country," he explained hesitantly. "They've already exploded two bombs in Helsinki."

This was met by guffaws of derision, and Evans dropped the subject and took up his favourite topic of keeping on the right side of the authorities.

"If the police got suspicious of any member and started coming to the club, it would be the end of the Society," he concluded.

"I don't accept that at all," I retorted sharply. "I've told you before, the police are welcome to the Society any time."

"You don't understand," said Evans smiling condescendingly. "This isn't Britain. There you can get away with anything. But in Finland the police'll arrest you on any pretext. It's a Fascist-dominated police state. It's not a free country like Britain."

"As we're non-political I don't see where the question arises," I said.

"If the police move into the Society, I resign as Secretary and from the Committee," said Evans emotionally.

Anders told the party of how he had been an object of suspicion with the police in Finland during the Winter War and the War of 1941-44.

"Coming from a neutral country they observed me very closely," he said.

As the atmosphere relaxed, and we discussed social conditions in different countries, I decided to try a tack in arguing a line of thought with which I hoped Evans would be entirely in sympathy. He had offered an opening by describing his home in the beautiful ultra-modern suburb of Tapiola - magnificent apartment blocks generously spaced in a forest of greenery near to the sea and several lakes.

I praised the fortune of the Finn to be born in a country that enjoyed such vast spaces and such a high standard of living in town and country alike. Finland was a country without slums, without unheated buildings, without unemployment, without poverty. I made a comparison with the appallingly demoralising conditions, whether they be slums or soul-destroying middle class urban areas in Britain, where the majority of people had the misfortune to live out the greater part of their lives.

I looked at Evans expecting his ready ascent - surely he would agree - but he merely looked at me with a non-committal smile. I felt, then, that the conflict between us was only just beginning.

CHAPTER 11
Enter the diplomats

"Everything is done by intrigue, not by loyalty."

Victor Hugo, *Ruy Blas*, Act III, Sc. 2.

There had been a problem in deciding what event should take place on the opening night of our published programme on the 15th January. As films of a purely entertaining nature had been shown on two occasions and a grand party had been held a fortnight previously, I felt that an ordinary social evening would be an anti-climax in launching our Winter/Spring programme.

It had to be something special - to arouse interest and mild controversy throughout the town in serving as a publicity function - and I felt that this would best take the form of a talk by a Committee member in some way attempting to project an image for the Society.

Although I realised it was not strictly the purpose of a chairman to do this, I concluded that no other member could be entrusted with this task, and reluctantly I decided to give a lecture entitled, *Internationalism and Europe*, which I hoped would express opinions coinciding with those of our members, their guests, and the diplomatic staffs of the many embassies in Helsinki. Being free of partisan feelings to the left or right, but nonetheless holding deep and radical convictions, I felt suitably fit to perform this difficult exercise in objective idealism.

Naturally the lecture would have to be prefaced by reminders on the non-political nature of the Society, and for the rest, I trusted in my own good judgement and intentions, that no offence or objection made in good faith could be raised from any quarter. As some interesting repercussions in my relationship with the authorities were to stem from this speech, its outline must be recorded here, so that readers may judge for themselves as to the type of political animal I was, taking into account the different conclusions that could be read between the lines.

Secretly, known only to myself, I entertained certain notions that exceeded the published aims of the Society. These notions did not amount to ulterior scheming, and neither did they reflect a wish for self-

ENTER THE DIPLOMATS

aggrandisement, but I hoped that with the passing of time - after a year or two - that the Society would mutate into a role for which it could be ideally suited. Finland's place in the world as a neutral power was unique; it was not the neutrality of cold isolation like that of Sweden or Switzerland, but a neutrality of obligatory participation with both great power blocs, and this presented a unique example of coexistence, raising the question of a new function that Finland might play as a moral influence in world affairs. It was my idea to welcome diplomats from all countries to the club, but especially from those major powers of Russia, America and China, and with adroitness, I wished to disseminate certain constructive ideas that might diminish grounds for differences between the various powers.

This would be achieved by lectures (similar to the kind I was to give on the 15th), and by taking chosen diplomats aside and speaking with them from an unbiassed viewpoint, I hoped that by the subtlety of the Socratic method to implant certain desirable political concepts. Ultimately, when the club had expanded and we had premises of our own with a licensed bar, I even hoped for the possibility of enjoying the privilege of hosting high ranking diplomats from conflicting powers for the purpose of encouraging open discussion in an environment which was less restrictive than that of an embassy or palace of state. Naturally, the realisation of such a possibility would necessitate an approach of the utmost discretion, but if such arrangements could be entrusted to a single individual of integrity, I saw no reason as to why they should not be viable in the right circumstances.

On the 15th I was overjoyed at seeing an announcement of my lecture to the Society in the cultural column of *Huvudstadsbladet*, and this paper was to freely publish details of our Wednesday activities throughout the duration of the season.

That evening the hall was filled to capacity, and as I stood in the foyer, welcoming members and guests, a small stocky man conservatively dressed in an immaculate suit, his hair newly cut and sprayed, approached me brightly, accompanied by a large awkwardly wary looking man with ill-fitting clothes.

"May I introduce myself, Mr. Corfe," said the first man. "It's a wonderful idea your club. We've needed something like this so long in Helsinki."

"Everyone's welcome tonight," I assured him, shaking hands with several persons passing into the hall.

"My name's A.P. Akulov," he continued, "Second Secretary of the Soviet embassy."

I grabbed his hand warmly for I had not suspected that diplomats from this power would have honoured us with their presence so soon, and especially in view of their reputation for wariness and hiding themselves from the outside world.

"I'ld like to become a member," he said.

"Certainly! I hope you'll always feel at home here," I answered.

"This is my friend, Mr. Ivgorin. He doesn't speak English - only Russian, but he's interested to learn. He won't join the club - he's just come as a guest. He feels lonely here."

The friend wore a deadpan expression and clearly apprehended nothing of what had been said. He wore a wide-brimmed hat that shrouded the upper part of his face, and his huge arms conveyed the impression that he could have crushed two men to death with each of them at the same time.

"I hope we can find a companion for your friend then," I replied, trying to repress any feelings of prejudice, and realising that even a Russian with the appearance of a thug - who in reality was very probably not a thug - was as capable of feeling loneliness as any other person.

"I'll be taking care of him," added Mr. Akulov, and in my mind's eye I formed a vision of a little Russian leading a large bear by a chain.

"Do enjoy yourselves," I exclaimed after them as they entered the hall.

Later several Mexican and Arab diplomats arrived, including the press attaché of the United Arab Republic, Mr. Esan El'din, escorted by his charming and beautiful wife, and it transpired that they knew the Russians, and they joined company with Mr. Akulov who was to play such an interesting role in the drama to follow.

At last the great moment arrived and after I mounted the lectern complete silence fell over the room. I opened the meeting with a few humorous remarks as to how the assembly should be addressed; gave out

ENTER THE DIPLOMATS

some announcements; apologised for introducing myself and also for the presumption of the Chairman delivering a lecture to his own Society. I continued by explaining that I had had several prospective speakers and friends but at too short a notice, and that finally it was suggested by the Committee that I should myself address the meeting. I continued:-

"I felt reluctant to participate in any programme of the Society, but it was insisted that my speaking to the Society would be useful on several counts. Firstly, it was suggested that I give some kind of introduction to the series of talks to follow during the next few months - a general talk on internationalism, or something of that sort. Secondly, it was thought that my addressing the Society would give members an opportunity to get to know what kind of man their Chairman was.

"And so finally, I was persuaded to address the meeting tonight, and I chose for the title of my talk, *Internationalism and Europe*. I must confess, that on picking this subject-title, I hadn't the foggiest notion as to what line of argument to take, or even, as to what I was going to talk about in the broadest terms. For some time I was faced by a quandary, and my feeling of trepidation increased with the passing of each day. However, like the great French philosopher, Descartes, who suddenly struck upon his great guiding thought for his *Discourse of Method*, 'cogito Ergo sum - I think, therefore I am!' whilst sitting in a steam bath; I, in the same way, suddenly struck upon the line of argument for my talk tonight whilst sitting one afternoon in a Finnish sauna.

"Now, I don't want anyone to regard anything I say in the following talk as necessarily reflecting my own opinions, or for that matter, as anyone else's opinions. I want you, if you can, only to imagine that what I say to you here tonight is something that has somehow floated down from outer space, and that I am merely a chosen medium for certain random impersonal thoughts. After all, this is a non-political club, and I am a relatively non-political person. My only purpose in speaking to you tonight is to entertain - not to put ideas into your heads - which anyway would be presumptuous.

"Why is this a subject of great interest to everyone sitting in this hall tonight? It is because the promotion of international understanding is one of the aims of our Society. The creation of a Federal Europe would be an example to the world that international understanding can indeed be made a practical reality. If Europe could be united after so many centuries of strife that are behind us, it would stand as an example to the world that unification of neighbouring yet widely diverse countries in any part of the world should be conceivable. The creation of a Federal Europe would be a beacon to peace loving nations everywhere, and would be a step beyond the political reality of coexistence. What are the problems facing the unification of Europe? They are problems of different kinds, yet each as important as the other. They may be conveniently summed up under four separate headings.

"The chief political problem is that of European neutrality. Unless Europe can attain complete neutrality, so being independent of outside forces, it is unlikely she will ever be strong enough to form her own unified policy in pursuing her own specific interests. Secondly, that of Internal Division: that is, the political and cultural problem of overcoming the centuries of mistrust, prejudice and strife that has kept Europe divided.

"Thirdly, the Technical problem: that is, as to what form of federation a United Europe would entail. A United Europe could not succeed unless on the one hand, there was a strong central government, and on the other hand, unless there were safeguards guaranteeing the cultural autonomy of each European state. And fourthly, the economic aspects. The smaller countries must not be overrun by the larger, and neither must cheap labour from those poorer countries be allowed to flood countries with a higher standard of living.

"Then there would have to be a common foreign policy, especially as regards trade relations with dependent and commonwealth states. Europe occupies a unique politico-economic position in the world and this is perhaps one of the chief factors necessitating her unification.

"I've called this talk Internationalism and Europe, because I believe a Europe unified under a strong federal government would nonetheless present a body of culturally autonomous Nations, and that therefore, such a Europe would still present a study for international understanding. There will never be a European nation. Language is usually the furthest frontier of a nation. It was the great Finnish philosopher and statesman, J.V. Snellman, who said that wherever there existed a people speaking a common language, so there were to be found the basic foundations for nationality. What there can be, however, is a European state, and I want this word to be understood in the strictly Hegelian definition. I now want to consider the above four points a little more closely.

"Neutrality is necessarily the first step towards a unified Europe. Unless Europe can work out a policy of complete neutrality, her unification will never become a practical reality. This follows from several factors, and especially from her necessity for independence. The unification of Europe is basically an internal matter, the details of which can only be worked out by the European powers alone - without prompting from outside influences. The European powers must find a common policy beneficial to all, and like any national state, Europe would have to work out and follow a policy pursuing her own unique interests. Internal strength, self-confidence, and a feeling of independence and a common aim, is vital to the basis of such unification. These things are not possible without a neutrality which would give Europe the freedom and the self-confidence to go it alone.

"What would such a European neutrality entail? Clearly, it would create a third world bloc. A tripartite alliance guaranteeing the maintenance of peace would be a necessity. The developmental trends of military strategy during the past years would seem to argue that such an alliance could be made fully practical. A neutral Europe would lessen tension in that part of the world where for many years the danger of war has been greatest. She would also find herself as an arbiter between East and West - perhaps with the greatest peace mission the world has known in recent times.

"How could such a neutrality be achieve? Every European country would have something of unique value to contribute to a European state. Switzerland and the Scandinavian countries - particularly Sweden and Finland, would be most valuable in leading Europe towards the path of neutrality. Sweden could set the example as to what neutrality means: an attitude of cool objectivity to the affairs of the outside world; a reluctance to pass moral judgements on matters of distant importance; and a policy of self-interest, pursued quietly and with discretion. A United Europe, on the other hand, would not of course share the political isolationism of modern Sweden. Finland, because of the unique position in which she is usefully placed, might even be the country giving Europe the moral lead towards the first practical steps of neutrality.

"The president of that country in which we are now privileged to reside has perhaps closer contacts with the East than any other Western statesman. As a man trusted by both East and West, perhaps he would make an ideal leader for neutrality. Finland's status of alliance with the East, as a power within a European federation, need not in the slightest be altered. A neutral Europe could form an alliance with the East, in many respects similar with that alliance of Finland.

"In considering a neutral Europe, the question of cultural exchange, of course, cannot be ignored. This is something of very special importance. Such a neutrality is not possible unless Europe could retain the confidence of both East West powers. This could be achieved through an extensive cultural exchange programme, whereby Europe would be obliged to equalise as far as is possible its cultural imports from East and West. This would naturally present considerable practical difficulties, but would nonetheless, be vital to attaining a genuine neutrality. It would tend to revolutionise the cultural pattern of Europe. It would not mean that for every Western film there would be an Eastern import, or that as many books would necessarily have to be imported from the East as from the West, but it would mean, for example, that if few higher quality films came from the East they might be given a longer run, to compensate for the greater number of lower grade films from the West, or that if a million books were to be imported from the East and a million books imported from the West, in the first batch, there might be a smaller number of titles than to be found in the second. The final rights and choice of such cultural importation would of course have to be controlled solely by a Federal European state.

"Next, the internal divisions dividing Europe. When glancing at these, the problems confronting the unification of Europe might seem almost insuperable. Europe is still divided by age-old mistrusts, prejudices and hatreds. How can these divisions be broken down, and the way prepared for internal unification? Firstly, we can glance purely at the geographical situation. A number of countries placed in such close proximity clearly have certain potential interests common to them all, as regards defence, communications and trade. Today, some of these interests, especially as regards defence, may seem to make the European countries inevitably interdependent. A divided Europe could soon open herself to disaster. I think history has shown that there are times when countries of widely differing cultural backgrounds can come together if they find a number of purely material interests common and profitable to them all.

"The second factor in overcoming the division of Europe is to find those things which are common to her cultural background. The heritage of Europe could be held up as a common ideal to the European peoples. After all, at some time in the very distant past, perhaps most of us in this hall tonight, originated from a common stock somewhere north of the Caspian and Black Seas, irrespective of whether we be Scotsmen or Russians; Spaniards or Norwegians; Frenchmen or Greeks. Then Europe has a common Greco-Roman-Christian cultural tradition. The common bonds of this in the history of our civilisation are so obvious that they need not be elaborated upon here. The European countries should therefore all belong to one big happy family!

"The internal divisions dividing Europe could be overcome on the one hand by guaranteeing cultural autonomy within the European nations, so that no European country would risk dominating another, and on the other hand, by upholding a common European ideal and encouraging as much international friendship and cultural exchange as possible. A Federal European government would therefore be obliged to standardise certain aspects of education in schools and universities as regards the teaching of history and the social sciences, etc.

"Next, the technical problem as to the unification of Europe. How would it be achieved, and what form would such a federation take? The first step would of course entail the formation of a political movement to sell the idea to the masses, work out a policy of neutrality and the constitution and machinery of government that such a federation would take. When such a government finally took power, it would then participate in a tripartite alliance with the other two great powers and facilitate the removal of the occupation forces in Europe. A question of prime importance, is what form and appearance would such a federal European movement have?

It would necessarily have to be above the suspicion of having any leanings towards existing European left or right political factions. It must be remembered that a federal movement would have to be of mutual satisfaction to such varied governments as those of Spain; Norway; Great Britain; Switzerland; Greece or Sweden. Its political idealism, as far as the economic structures of the community were concerned, would need to be neutral. If such a movement came under the suspicion of being Socialist, Conservative - or anything else in the common political jargon of today - division would creep in. Such a movement would need to remain as indefinable as it could be as to its leanings towards the left or right. Such a movement would only seek to advocate the ideal of European unity, and the consequent aim of prosperity for all. It would be obliged to change its announced policy or the details of its programme as often as it found it convenient to do so.

"What powers would such a federal government have? It could control the armed forces, the police, the extent of free trade, and the movement of labour between the countries concerned. It could exert control over foreign policy whilst guaranteeing individual nations their territorial rights overseas. Domestic policy could still be carried on by the individual nations, although of course, national governments would remain subordinated to federal authority. There might be a system of double passports: national passports for travel within Europe, and European passports for travel outside Europe, including travel to dependencies and commonwealth countries.

"Lastly, the economic problems. Economically, a federal Europe would be mutually advantageous, but each country would need to be guaranteed certain rights safeguarding its economic and cultural integrity. These rights would be of different kinds. There would be the right under certain circumstances to restrict nationals from one country buying up land and property in another country. For example, a growing concern has recently been felt in Switzerland and Denmark because of extensive buying of land by foreign nationals.

"Further, touching the economic aspects of promoting international understanding, I think that yachts and other small pleasure craft should be obliged to fly the flags of those countries in whose waters they're sailing in addition to their own national flags. There are canals and lakes in Holland where can be seen more flags of a certain foreign nationality

ENTER THE DIPLOMATS

than Dutch flags, and I believe this does not help international understanding and friendship.

"The movement of labour would also have to be controlled. Clearly it would be intolerable if on the creation of a Federal Europe, if half a million Sicilians, for example, were to move up to Sweden to look for work. Sweden, quite rightly, would never allow such a situation. Her living standards would then be threatened. Far better it would be for Swedish, German and British commercial firms, etc., to build assembly plants in the southern countries.

"To sum up, what general comments can be made on the creation of such a Federal Europe? It would be a neutral Europe living in peace and prosperity - not harassed by the threat of war, and at the same time, free to pursue her interests, unhindered by occupying powers to observe, criticise and censor her every move. She would, too, not be harassed by the threat of internal political strife. She would be free from those political idealisms of the past, threatening her equilibrium. This is part of the inevitable and historical evolution of Europe. The destructive factions and idealisms of the different economic classes of Europe, is a thing of the past. We live in an age of complacent self-interest, where internal political issues tend to interest us less and less, because they are less acute, and because, we, the ordinary people, have less power to alter the course of events. As the powers of government increase, so our interest in it tends, through an ironic combination of factors, to correspondingly diminish. Whether the results of this be for good or ill, it is only to be hoped that Europeans may retain their dynamic individuality and will to power, which is anyway the source of the only true freedom."

(Those were my views at the time - a long lost age ago - and soon, fifty years will have passed since I made that speech. Its content can only be properly understood in view of the world situation at the start of the 1960s, and particularly in view of the crushing blow to British and French interests, and the consequent humiliation, inflicted by Eisenhower's Republican government following the Suez crisis in 1956.

Those views have long since been changed due both to the progress of history and the results of a much deeper study of politics and the social sciences.)

As I spoke, I noted the attention of the audience and the fact that Mr. Akulov, who was sitting in the middle of the hall, was fixing me with an enigmatic smile. Ron Evans had no time for my lecture, but for the first time he was making himself useful in assisting the Catering Manageress, and several times he busily came into the back of the hall with a tray of cups and saucers which he laid out on some trestle tables before quickly returning to the kitchen. At the conclusion of the lecture it was received with tumultuous applause, and I then took questions for some twenty minutes before the purely social evening began.

"Very interesting," remarked Akulov afterwards. "I agreed with nearly everything you said except for certain terminology."

As the speech went unreported in the papers the following day, I decided to lengthen and adapt it for publication, and this I did, under the title, *Towards A Federal Europe*.[1]

Miss Ingrid Andersson gave an interesting talk illustrated with colour slides on a journey through Turkey, on the following Wednesday, but it was so interminable - she had a thousand slides - that after several promptings which were ignored, Anders Enblom was at last obliged to step in and bring the lecture to an abrupt close.

It was during that evening that I met the imposing Rowland G.P. Hill on the second occasion - he was to give a lecture on the Lapps a month hence - and through a personal relationship which was to germinate from that day, events were to occur bearing considerable influence on the future of the Society.

Rowland Hill strode about the hall during the coffee interval with his patronisingly pompous manner, ceremoniously greeting his acquaintances with a long drawn out "Mister" or "Mrs," and dropping advice whenever he could. He was a particular favourite with our middle aged women members, but he congratulated Ingrid on her "most informative talk" and spoke to her at some considerable length. Maintaining what is reputedly the British countenance, he wore a coldly impassive expression on all occasions, even when it would have made him less ridiculous to appear otherwise.

---

[1] This version of the speech was published many years later in my book, *Land of The Olympians*.

ENTER THE DIPLOMATS

Peter loathed him, calling him the "walking statue;" I called him "Roly-poly," and Elisabeth Vaajajärvi, our Catering Manageress and American embassy employee, positively hated him, from her remembrance a decade earlier when she had been involved in one of his English club ventures. He must have had a personality very similar to his famous ancestor, for he seemed to arouse the same kind of dislike as he had in the novelist Anthony Trollope (as related in his autobiography) who as an employee of the Post Office was directly answerable to the first Rowland Hill.

During the interval Anders approached me with concern, saying, "Mr. Evans is very worried about all these diplomats being around. He doesn't like it at all. I was speaking with him several minutes ago, and he was even threatening to resign."

"Let him," I said.

"He says the police are here."

"How does he know,?" I retorted. "They must be in plain clothes."

"He just says he can recognise the police anywhere."

"What nonsense! He's paranoid," I exclaimed. "Why does he keep worrying about the police anyway? If they are here, the last thing they'll do is disturb other members. After all, everyone's anonymous to everyone else."

"But the police could give the Society a bad reputation," said Anders who was obviously falling under Evans' spell.

"If we're honest in our intentions, the Society should welcome the police," I answered. "They're contributing to the clubs funds, aren't they,?" and with that I walked away.

The first purely social evening I attended was an Opera outing on Saturday 25th of January. Gösta was the chief Social Host and played his part to a tee, and this was by no means easy in view of the fact that girls outnumbered boys five to one. We saw the Viennese operatta, *Victoria's Hussar*, which was enjoyed by all, and afterwards we made our way to Helsinki's most prestigious nightspot, the M club, situated in the basement of the recently built Marsky Hotel.

At the time the club had a restricted membership of 600, Gösta being numbered amongst this elite, and it was the ambition of many women to enjoy the privilege to be taken there once, for a visit was a source of pride. Subsequently, the club was opened to universal membership, and later still, it became a public (even if still an exclusive) dance restaurant, by which time it had lost the magic of its exclusivity. At four in the morning our little party broke up and we made for home.

Herr Bauer was made to feel the folly of his stubbornness on the evening of the 29th. There was a crowded assembly, including three Soviet diplomats, and I introduced the programme by briefly describing the three films to be shown. Except for a film featuring the Dresden Painting Gallery, the others reflected the grey ideology of Communism. There was feeble clapping at their conclusion, followed by a break for refreshments, and then came question time at which I was to act as interpreter.

"You do of course agree there'll be no questions of a political nature,?" said Herr Bauer appealing for reassurance.

"Of course - we're quite non-political," I answered, realising that I could not possibly be held responsible for the tone of the subsequent questions.

Timidly, at first, hands were raised and quite innocuous questions put to the chair. Herr Bauer remained confidently in control of the meeting. All answers were at the tip of his tongue. At last a silver haired Swedish gentleman stood and half concealing a smile, he said: "Mr. Chairman, could the speaker explain why there's a Wall in Berlin?"

There was a murmur of voices in the hall as I translated the question, and then the speaker broke out into flustered anger.

"That question is out of order," he cried. "I thought this was a non-political Society. I didn't come here to answer such questions - if I'd known, I'ld have stayed away."

I apologised profusely and then explained to the Swedish gentleman that the question could not be answered and would have to be ruled as out of order. No other awkward questions were asked and no reference was made to the embarrassing interlude, but at the end of the evening, I overheard Ron Evans mutter irritably to himself as he jangled a collection of cups about on a tray: "What a ridiculous question to ask - 'Why is there a Wall?'"

"Why,?" I enquired.

"Because it was downright bad manners, and you did the proper thing to over-rule him. Honestly," he continued, "I don't know what kind of reputation this Society will get if its members treat guests like that."

CHAPTER 12
To Work for peace

"Smooth runs the water where the brook is deep,
And in his simple show he harbours treason."

Shakespeare, *Henry VI,* Part II, Act III, Sc. 1.

Anders Enblom was due to give a talk on the human problems of Scandinavian Immigrants In Canada (he had himself been such an immigrant for several years) on the following Wednesday, but he fell ill three days before. He was the oldest member on the Committee, over sixty, and his ulcer was playing up and he had spat blood, but I attributed this particular chronic attack of illness to other reasons than age.

Ron Evans had been goading the gullible old man with startling statements - "This place is full of spies," he had contended with a cynical smile. "There's some man from the Canadian embassy keeps asking, 'Who is this Enblom?' They're getting us all taped. The embassy want to look up your file through the immigration department."

This had thrown Anders into a fluster, and he had come to me before going down with illness some days later.

"Evans is quite right," he said phoning me from his sick bed. "We're moving too fast and we could be heading for a load of trouble. I don't like these spies and informers around at all."

"I think Evans is talking a load of codswallop," I said. "I've never seen any evidence of spies around. Why would they want to come to our place anyway - there's nothing to spy on at the International Society? We're just a crowd of nice people enjoying ourselves in a cultural environment."

Not only did I have to make alternative arrangements for a Canadian evening at very short notice, but Anders also requested that I temporarily relieve him of the office of Treasurer for a period of two months. As with earlier casualties that had struck the Committee in one way or another, I was obliged to take over the post of Treasurer, and thanks to the readiness in an emergency of our Technical Director, Heikki Jokimäki, and to the kindness of the Canadian embassy, we were able to present a highly successful film evening vividly describing the Canadian scene. As was later made evident, it was fortunate that I took over the duties of Treasurer for I subsequently used this as a bargaining instrument when the chips were down.

During the Canadian evening an event took place of no small significance. Ron Evans had now tenaciously retained the Constitution for over two months, during which time he had held several sub-committee meetings (at which I had not been present); during which his wife had translated the same into Finnish; and during which he had constantly complained of the difficulties of the task he had persuaded me to surrender into his hands. On numerous occasions I had phoned him in hurrying for its completion - "The authorities are very particular. If there are any mistakes they'll crack down and close the Society," he had contended.

At last the work was completed and I requested copies in both languages. These were not forthcoming: it had not yet been typed - it had been typed but there were only three copies - I was promised a copy as soon as another member had returned his - but I need not worry my head over the matter as the four Committee members and Salme and his wife who had sat on the Constitution for over two months offering their careful consideration, were hardly likely to have made any blunders to which I would object.

It was finally arranged that the Secretary would read the completed draft Constitution in English (and his wife in Finnish) to members of the Society on the 5th of February, to allow an opportunity for amendments and secure a vote of approval. On the night of the 5th I had still not seen this completed draft, and when Evans arrived at the club he casually apologised with the excuse that he had only one copy and was still making corrections. However, he was in the rare frame of mind of being in an amiable disposition, and so I never pressed the point, and before the evening began, he introduced me on several occasions to friends who were visiting the club for the first time.

The first was a colleague, a short middle-aged Finn, the lapels of his jacket be-medalled with red badges of workers' associations. The second was a young Finnish boy - "I do want you to meet Mr. Corfe, I think you'ld both get on very well together," said Evans exuding what charm he could. These two I never met again, but the third was a young dark-haired Pole whose manner was a strange mixture of effusive but false amiability, wariness and gestures of respectful humility. He always approached me bowing and rubbing his hands, often dropping hints as to his wish in serving on the Committee.

He reminded me of Uriah Heep and I disliked him as he remained an enigma and failed to blend with the rest of the company. His name was Andrej Wischzinsky, and he described himself as a student. He soon joined our Soviet diplomatic friends and it was through the kindness of their democratic assistance that he was eventually to achieve his ambition within our Society.

It was also at the start of that evening that Mr. Akulov introduced me to another of his "friends." This was Mr. B.N. Sokolov, a tall good-natured looking gentleman with a round complexion and a fixed smile. He was to become an even keener member than Akulov - rarely missing a meeting - although he rarely spoke to anyone or participated in social activities, merely sitting in the middle of the hall with his faint smile listening to our lectures or watching our film shows with apparent interest.

Despite his remoteness he always seemed contented and he clearly derived something from our meetings. Aren't these Russians self-effacing, modest, and respectable!, I thought to myself as I eyed him sitting alone and in isolation in the middle of the room. So proper and correct! Surrounded by so many temptations and yet he rises to none. Butter would hardly have melted in his mouth! And yet, surely, if he was human he must be bored out of his mind, I corrected myself.

However, unbeknown at the time, deeper and more hidden forces were at work. Mr. Sokolov was to play a key role in our story that ultimately was to have disastrous repercussions for the intelligence service of at least one Western power.

After the interval and the films had been shown, Ron Evans mounted the lectern and apologised for his having to make an appearance and disrupt the social activities of the evening. He explained that a very important piece of business had to be completed that night, and speaking through a cloud of cigarette smoke in his usual fussy manner, he began reading the Constitution to the crowded assembly;

frequently stumbling over words he had difficulty in pronouncing, and several times he stopped and apologised when he was unable to read his corrections over the typescript, and the impression he gave was one of shoddiness and ineptitude.

I sat nearby facing the assembly, and on more than one occasion, when stumbling over a passage, I could not fail to notice the contemptuous expression cast at him by his wife. Few amendments or questions came from the floor - this was merely a formality to be dispensed with as quickly as possible - but coming to the final clause, he read: "In the event of the Society being dissolved the money and property will be distributed to an organisation or organisations which have the purpose of promoting peace and friendship."

This phrase with its ideological cliché hit me like a bolt from the blue. I stood up, exclaiming: "This is impossible! We're a non-political Society and we cannot support such a politically motivated clause."

Mrs. Evans glanced daggers at me.

"What's political about 'Peace and Friendship,'?" cried Evans angrily. "Don't you believe in peace and friendship?"

"It's not a question of that," I answered.

"All of us ought to work for peace in some way," he said emotionally.

Mr. Rowland Hill who was sitting near the back of the hall got up and explained that although there was nothing in itself reprehensible about "peace and friendship," there was nevertheless a connotation in the phrase carrying a politically partisan emotional overtone. A vote was taken on the issue, and the offending phrase was deleted by a unanimous decision.

The Soviet diplomats showed some confusion at this hand raising and glanced around furtively to take their cue from the majority. Akulov had to prompt his duller colleagues, whilst Sokolov almost fell into the fatal trap of voting for "Peace and Friendship" - and would have done so had not his friend held down in his hand in time.

It soon became clear that Ron Evans and his wife were not going to forgive me for the embarrassing interruption I had afforded them, and during the next few days events began to move with greater momentum. On the Sunday following, on taking a friend, Mrs. Anja Hytönen, who was to prove most helpful to my cause in the weeks ahead, to a service at the Russian Orthodox Uspensky Cathedral, I yet again encountered evidence of Evans' cunning mischief.

The Cathedral was filled to capacity, and as I and several hundred others had arrived too late, we were locked out in the snow on the Katajanokka hill where the church was situated. As we stood outside stamping our feet in the cold, awaiting the choral procession of deacons and priests in all their regalia, we met several American girls from the International Society.

"Mr. Corfe, we're so sorry to hear you're resigning - you've done so much for the club," said one.

"I've no intention of resigning," I said. "Who told you that?"

"Really,?" answered the girl surprised. "A little grey haired man with glasses told us at the meeting last Wednesday. The one who read out all that official stuff."

By now there was little to surprise me that came from the direction of Evans. On the 12th of February we enjoyed the best presented programme to date: Mr. Rowland G.P. Hill's illustrated talk on the ancient culture of the Lapps and the difficulties of their adaptation to modern living.

As I sat in the front, watching the speaker, it struck me how similar he was to his famous early Victorian ancestor, as represented by the statue in the City of London standing in front of the main Post Office near St. Pauls. There was the same pose, the same paunch and the same impassive expression. I could hardly refrain noticing his ill-fitting suit, and particularly, how when he took a breath his trouser ends were raised some three inches above the ankles - but the poor fellow could hardly have realised this.

He had studied the Lapps for many years, living with them in Summer and Winter, and it was obvious he must have enjoyed amongst them a feeling of patronising superiority as he carried the White man's burden to the Arctic regions. I subsequently learnt, however, that this particular White man's burden had for many years been a bugbear to the plans of the Finnish authorities in their northernmost territory.

Rowland Hill had not only set himself up as an authority on the Lapps, but as their knight in shining armour in the cause of maintaining their traditional way of life. He had consulted lawyers, barged into the offices of government departments, armed with petitions and legal documents, and generally impeded the building of power stations, paper mills and other industrial projects in the far north.

Doubtless his aims were entirely worthy and in every way desirable from an environmental viewpoint, and they were typical of the man, but his interfering nature and his self-obsession and pomposity blinded him to intrigue, which eventually led him to misapprehend the nature of those with whom he came into contact. Consequently, through the ingenuity and guile of others, this was to lead him along a path which was to destroy our Society. All the same, his talk was excellent, and it reflected the mind of a man who was cultured and widely read; and on that evening, he was of credit to our club.

During the social period that followed, Ron Evans approached several Committee members with a worried expression, exclaiming, "There's not a dog's chance in hell of getting registered if we leave it much longer."

"First you complain we're going too fast, and now you say we're going too slow," I exclaimed. "Can't we ever get it right? What's the delay then?"

"There are all kinds of problems," he answered woefully.

"Such as what?"

"There's supposed to be an English society against us. They've put a spoke in our wheel by complaining to the Ministry."

If there was any truth in this, I could only suspect that such a rumour must have originated in a complaint from the British Council. The director of this institution had in fact written to me requesting that the International Society hold its meetings on an alternative day to Wednesday, as English was the language of both societies, and he feared that the Finnish-British Society might lose members to the competition on its Wednesday night meetings. I had written to him and then made a personal visit, arguing that, firstly, I thought that prospective members would only go out once a week to a cultural club; secondly, that Helsinki was a large enough city to accommodate both our clubs without fear of adverse rivalry to either; and thirdly, I had asked, What was wrong with a bit of competition?

"I see your point, but I don't agree with you," he said, and when I left the Council, I felt its director remained unhappy about the issue. Despite this, however, I refused to believe that the British Council would have gone so far, or would have been so petty to scheme against us.

The attending membership of the Finnish-British Society had been falling for some years. In 1961 (the year of my arrival in Finland) they had hired extensive premises in the Satakunta Student House - enjoying attendances of well over a hundred - and now they held their meetings in the library of the British Council, and were lucky if three dozen attended their Wednesday nights. As it happened attendances were to decline even further - and the International Society claimed its fair rake-off - but I believe the decline of the rival association was to be attributed more to its unimaginative programmes and poor management than to our competition.

"You can only be referring to the British Council," I said to Evans. "They're behind the British-Finnish Society, and there's no other English association in Helsinki that I know of apart from the Embassy Club, and that's merely a drinking joint."

"It's no trouble to them stopping our registration," said Evans. "All they do is go to the ambassador, and the ambassador goes to the Ministry of the Interior, and then you're clobbered."

"There's plenty of corruption around," agreed Stig Lambertsen, who had just sidled up to listen into our conversation - and this incidentally, was the first and almost the last meeting he ever attended at the Society, for tutoring was the excuse which had kept him away.

"These diplomats and Finnish ministry officials are all thick together," continued Evans. "It's the old boy set-up all over again. They just drink together and work out a solution that suits themselves - and damn everyone else."

How wrong he was in drawing this conclusion he was soon to learn. Ron Evans was most busy that evening, rushing around with copies of the Constitution and other documents, soliciting signatures and confidentially taking members aside and obviously urging on them some course of action. My suspicions were well aroused that some evil was afoot but there was little I could do to counteract it. I had committed the supreme foolishness of handing him the Constitution two months previously instead of attending to the matter myself with the help of a few friends, when the task would have been completed in a fraction of the time.

The following day I completed my sixty page pamphlet, *Towards A Federal Europe*, which I had typed in five copies, and I lent them to various friends for their opinions, including a Finnish diplomat and former pupil at the Berlitz Kieliopisto, Heikki Talvitie, who had just returned from a six months term as Consul in Marseilles, but before the morning was out, I was surprised to receive a phone call from Ron Evans.

He sounded as nice as pie, and was so ingratiating in his manner, that I could only conclude he was scheming the very worst. He had something of great importance to discuss with me - a delicate matter best talked over in the comfort of his office. Could I come tomorrow morning? I agreed. Yes, thing's looked a bit brighter on the "Constitution front" and with regard to registration and our relationship with the authorities, but it might be necessary that I resign the Chairmanship. This last bit was said most casually, suggesting that I would not have the slightest qualm over the idea.

My valuable services would of course still be required as master of ceremonies. A sub-committee meeting would be held that night to settle matters pertaining to this. No, it wasn't decided yet where the Committee meeting was being held. I betrayed not the slightest twinge of resentment or suspicion, but adopted a yielding and friendly manner to match that of his own, but inside, my blood boiled. Let him take me for a fool at the moment, I thought. From now on, it's War!

Using a ruse in attempting to find out where the Committee meeting was to be held that night, I phoned Gösta Kelter asking for an additional batch of programmes to send out to enquirers. He was almost rude in his abruptness and I knew he was embarrassed. I put the fateful question. He stammered, saying he wasn't quite sure if there was a Committee meeting that night. Clearly he was in on the conspiracy. I phoned the other weak sheep, Stig Lambertsen, and spoke with his English wife. She was coldly condescending and promised to get her husband to phone me when he came in. I never received his call. I phoned Peter and he expressed astonishment, saying he knew nothing about a Committee meeting but would try to find out.

Hitherto, my tactics in the struggle had been purely of a defensive nature. They had proven both ineffective in themselves or in projecting my image in a better light. Evans was clearly an unprincipled schemer - his single aim since the formation of the Society had been my removal from the Chairmanship - and now was the time for attack! His deviousness; his cowardice in the face of truth; his twisted hypocrisy; his adamant attitude in resisting gestures of good faith, his amiability which only showed through if an ulterior motive was at stake, not only indicated a personality which contradicted the aims of the Society, but pointed to a man who (in my eyes) was of the most depraved and wicked sort.

I cherished the Society, and wished to uphold and enhance the good reputation it had already won during its early days. It gave unalloyed pleasure and cultural sustenance to many, and I dreaded the day - if it should come - when Evans would exert a determining influence on the running of its affairs.

I picked up the phone and made the first contact in a chain of events that were eventually to lead Evans into the walls of a prison cell.

CHAPTER 13
Conspiracy most foul

"For thou art so possessed with murd'rous hate
That 'gainst thyself thou stick'st not to conspire."

Shakespeare, *Sonnets*, Sonnet 10.

At ten the following morning I arrived at the great Aga electrical factory in the industrial suburb of Vallila. Mr. Evans occupied his own office at the end of a corridor, and when he met me, he was dressed in a white coat and all smiles and friendliness.

"I'm afraid you're just too late for coffee," he apologised offering a chair nearby his desk, "but just make yourself at home. Before we begin, Bob, I must tell you that my wife has been most ill during the week. You see, it was her that wrote in that bit about 'peace and friendship' into the Constitution, and she feels you've branded her as a Marxist which of course she's not. Finns take slights to heart that would just run off the back of an Englishman."

"I'm sorry to hear that," I said. "I hope she's feeling better now."

"I should have amended the clause beforehand - it was my fault entirely," he said. "However, let's leave that subject and get onto something more constructive."

He began by reviewing the progress of the club to date, saying that at last there appeared a light at the end of a long tunnel, and that our major difficulties should be resolved in a day or two.

"But if we don't follow the instructions of the authorities now, they'll refuse us registration, and we'll have to call the whole thing a day," said Evans in a reasoning tone.

"What's exactly our situation with the authorities,?" I asked.

"My wife and I were at the Registration Office last week, and they clearly explained to us, that the Chairman of the Society would have to be what's known as a Long-Term Foreign Resident in the country," he continued. "That means, he would have to have lived here for at least five years. Now you've only been three years in the country."

"What do you suggest we do about it?"

"It means that if you don't agree to offer your resignation there's going to be no Society. It's quite difficult enough registering any society in this country, and if it's anything to do with foreigners, they're against you at once. I've been trying to get onto the committee of an amateur radio society for years, and these Finns have used every trick in the book to keep me off.

"They mistrust foreigners - it's the Finnish temperament - I don't have to tell you what they're like. And as for our Society, half its members are going to be foreigners - although we're only allowed a third on the Committee. And if that isn't enough, the authorities are most displeased with us as a lot of other English clubs have been worrying them for registration, and they've got into such a mess, they don't know where they are."

"My only regard is for the future of the Society. But if I resign, who do you suggest should take my place?"

"Well, actually," he began with trepidation, "Mr. Rowland Hill has been suggested. Gösta Kelter proposed him," he added hurriedly.

"Who was at the Committee meeting last night,?" I asked entirely maintaining my cool.

"That was only an informal coffee party at my flat last night - only Miss Andersson and Mr. Rowland Hill were there," he said.

"What was Rowland Hill's reaction to the idea of taking over the Chairmanship?"

"He agreed to it if it was a matter of saving the Society. I think he'll make a good Chairman. He's been twenty years in the country, he's well known, he's got useful connections, and he's had previous experience in starting clubs. - But what do you think about the idea,?" he said after eyeing me thoughtfully for a few moments through a cloud of tobacco smoke.

"I'll reserve judgement on any conclusions until the next Committee meeting," I remarked.

"I'm glad you're reasonable about it," he concluded. "But what I really wanted to talk to you about this morning, Bob, was your future role in the Society. That's what you're most interested in."

He outlined the idea that I should take on the post of Club Leader (an officially defined post in Finnish law), and that I should continue as master of ceremonies - a function I performed quite well - and I sat smiling patiently as he spoke, overwhelmed by the magnitude of his audacity. Finally it was agreed that a Committee meeting would be held on Sunday week at which Evans would present his ideas.

"I'm so pleased everything has been settled amicably," he concluded at the end of our discussion (although I had agreed to none of his proposals), "and now perhaps I can show you something of our factory. You'd be surprised what goes on here - it's not just radios and TV sets - we're doing top research on an international scale for all kinds of projects."

He conducted me around the factory, and in one noisy gallery where stood a mass of switching and generating equipment, he touched the various parts, inviting me to do the same, as he explained their use. I was walking in front of him and I noticed the switches were off until we reached the far end of the gallery.

"You were lucky not to touch that - there are ten thousand volts of live power there," he chuckled.

"Thanks for warning me too late,!" I retorted, but I had already sensed the danger, and if perchance murder had been secretly in his heart, he had underestimated my foresight.

Before leaving I secured a copy of the Constitution, and then hurriedly returned to the city centre to visit my friend, Mrs. Anja Hytönen, as previously arranged, for she was to assist in destroying my rival. She was director of a government health agency, and when I told her of the morning's events showing her the papers which Evans had given me, she insisted that we leave immediately for the Registration Office. Time was all-important! It was vital to ascertain the truth or otherwise of Evans' allegation that I was ineligible for election to the Chairmanship of the Society.

After a wait of some time we were conducted to various officials, and finally found our way to the head of the department, Mr. Kymantaka. He stated that I was as fully entitled to put up for election as a registered resident in the country as anyone else, and that there was no bar touching period of residence. Furthermore, he said there was no such thing in Finnish law, or in any regulations pertaining to it, referring to long or short term foreign residents, and he laughed at the idea. All foreigners enjoyed equal rights irrespective of whether they had been living one week or thirty years in the country - providing that their permits were in order.

"Whose been putting these strange ideas into your head,?" he asked.

We told him.

"Evans," he repeated thoughtfully. "I think we'd better study this matter more carefully. If you have any other questions, come back to us."

That evening I glanced over the Constitution and was horrified by the shoddy English that could only have come from the pen of a semi-literate man. In the last resort this document will be used as my ultimate clobbering weapon, I decided. The following morning I drew up and typed out in twelve copies a Private and Confidential document for the Committee of the International Society Finland. This paper listed the following uncorrected errors: 28 spelling mistakes; 8 serious grammatical errors; one serious punctuation error; one non-existent word, and one incongruity of spelling - and all included on only three foolscap pages.

In addition to quoting examples of his appalling grammar, the paper contained the following remarks: "Mr. Evans Rules for the Society is the culmination of more than two months work on the Society's Constitution. As the document to which this paper refers contains 23 corrected typing and spelling errors, it may be safely assumed that the Secretary carefully re-read the document before passing it onto other members. ... The use of prepositions is necessary in the English (although not in the Finnish) language!! ... Throughout the entire text, there is not a single use of colons or semi-colons although there is a crying need for these. ... If the Secretary of the Society is to be an Englishman, it is vitally necessary that he is able to write a tolerably good English - and more than this - that he is able to SPELL!

"The Secretary is ultimately responsible for sending out all literature to members. The Society would appear ridiculous in the eyes of the educated Finnish public if it were to send out circulars filled with spelling and grammatical errors. Incompetence of this kind, on the part of the Secretary, would be intolerable! The document to which this paper refers is a disgrace to the Society, and if it has by chance reached the eyes of the Finnish legal or registration authorities, then I, as Chairman, feel ashamed and humiliated that such a monstrous thing could have occurred."

The issue of this "confidential" circular may be seen in retrospect as an over-reaction to the animosity I experienced at the hands of Ron Evans, but it was written at a moment when I had decided finally to go on the offensive in no uncertain terms. I felt no compunction at the time as to the loss of face or humiliation to which he would consequently be exposed. The tactic, however, may have been unwise and must have undermined the promotion of my cause.

Peter took me to task, exclaiming, "Why should you expect him to be literate? He's a 'figures' man not a 'letters' man. After all, he's only a bloody engineer, for Christ's sake - you can't expect culture from a type like that."

"As a matter of fact, I do," I replied in response to Peter's snobbish comments.

The following Wednesday could well be the night of the long knives, and to form my own party within the Society, I purchased board and cellophane for the use of publicising with newspaper cuttings and announcements, the good services I had rendered the club, and if necessary, for pointing out where the opposition lay and as to its intentions which were deleterious to members' interests.

With the invaluable assistance of my friend, Mrs. Hytönen, we amended both language versions of the Constitution, and then drew up a paper for circulation to the Committee, outlining the true measures as laid down by the authorities, step by step, that would need to be taken in ensuring the smooth registration of the Society. Committee members had clearly already been led astray by confusion and lies with regard to this.

The formalities of registration were far simpler than Evans had led us to believe, but he had cleverly concealed the real facts from members, possibly because he may have felt some trepidation over complying with certain regulations, and possibly also, because he may have wished to use delaying tactics to ensure my removal from the Chairmanship, so giving him the green light for acting entirely at his own discretion with regard to re-designing the Constitution and generally managing the affairs of the Society. I had long known that I was the only Committee member with the perspicacity to realise his dishonesty, and the only member able to make a gesture in stopping his intrigue.

The first step in registering the Society was to obtain a Concession, and amongst the documents necessary for ensuring this were residence permits and Judicial Character Certificates, and after the approved Constitution of the Society had passed through the Control of the Registration Office, all documents pertaining to the club would have to be laid before the Council of State. After this body had considered the application, they would then pass it to the Ministry of the Interior, who might ask for a report on the aims and activities of the Society from the Ministry of Justice.

If all factors were clear a Concession would be granted, and then direct measures could be taken in applying for Registration. This would entail drawing up the following documents: An Announcement, made out on the appropriate formula; a Declaration of Foundation (bearing at least three signatures), and with regard to foreign members, police certificates of good character issued through their respective embassies; and these documents, complete with the other papers of the Society, were to be submitted to the Registration Department of the Ministry of Justice. Furthermore, any number or all members of the Committee might be foreigners if this was the decision of the association, so putting a lie to Evans' contention that there could only be a maximum of one third foreign nationals.

On Sunday I phoned Rowland Hill to sound him out on his feelings and as to the latest moves that had been taken. He was non-committal, saying, "But what about your place in the Society?" I felt that the time had come for direct confrontation with the Evans clique. I wanted the enemy identified so that an end would be put to rumour, backstabbing and the necessity for secret sub-committee meetings, so I led Mr. Rowland Hill by the nose.

"If Evans' contentions are really true in that in Finnish law I'ld be ineligible for election, then I'm quite prepared to resign, and I'll give you my backing as Chairman," I said, "but mind you, only if what Evans says is true."

CONSPIRACY MOST FOUL

The fat fish took the bait and agreed to accept nomination for Chairmanship.

As I was preparing my debate, the following Wednesday, for the motion that *Mankind Is Becoming Dehumanised* (I was to confront Eric Jakowleff that very night) the phone bell rang. It was Peter.

"Where's this Committee meeting being held tonight,?" he cried.

"I know nothing of any Committee meeting," I said.

Apparently his wife had taken a hurried call earlier that afternoon to inform him that an extraordinary Committee of great importance was to be held at seven in the evening.

"I suspected you might not know," said Peter. "That's why I wanted to tell you."

A moment later Digmar phoned and put the same question. It was clear that whoever was calling the meeting was in such an absent-minded panic as to be so inept in forgetting to tell members the location.

I dialled for Evans. He spoke in a guiltily confused manner lying that he knew nothing at all about a Committee meeting. Next I contacted Lambertsen who spoke nonchalantly pleading ignorance, but after some probing to convey that I knew more than he thought, he said he believed it was a "private" meeting.

"I doubt that in view of what I've heard from Peter," I said.

"Then we'll just have to see what'll happen there," he concluded.

That night none of the conspirators showed up, but a crowd of HISC members arrived to support their friend Jakowleff - and even Ray Reed was there (chewing his pipe as ever) although only a month earlier he had exclaimed, "I'll never come to your bloody club - I wouldn't even be seen dead there," but then he often changed his actions to suit the need of the moment, even when it went against his "firmly held" principles. On meeting him a week later he said, "I didn't think much of your bloody club - it's full of doddering old fools. Half of them will be dead in ten years." Little did he realise that one of his group would be dead within *one* year.

Before embarking on the programme of the evening I delivered a short address hinting that there was an opposing faction within the Society, suggesting that the Secretary was betraying his trust, and I asked for support in the future in the event of an open split within the club. The address made little impression, being met by a mixture of embarrassment and incomprehension, and Peter who was to act as Chairman of the debate to follow, urged me to move over to other things. The debate was successful, enlivened with many questions and much discussion, although by a vote from the floor, the motion was won by Jakowleff, i.e., that mankind was *not* becoming dehumanised.

Towards the end of this function, Mrs. Evans came into the back of the hall and busily conferred with several of her supporters and others, and was apparently collecting names and addresses and circulating some piece of news. I was interested to note her friendliness with several of the HISC group, including a White Russian girl with Communist sympathies who worked in the Academic Bookshop.

No other events occurred that night - nothing was lost nor gained in the widening breach - but it presaged the calm before the storm. On the following morning I could bear the suspense no longer, so I phoned round members for information. Ingrid Andersson merely said that there had been a coffee party last night to celebrate Anders Enblom's return to health, and on phoning Enblom, who was in a state of confused excitement, he said he wanted to resign as Treasurer and that he was fed up with all the backbiting and intrigue.

"Two months ago you expressed the opinion that Evans was not intriguing," I reminded him, "and now you're in the thick of it yourself."

"I'm fed up with everything - it's making me ill - I don't know what to do," he exclaimed exasperated, and put down the phone.

On contacting Aldar Runela and Heikki Jokimäki, whom I took to be my allies, I was told that Evans had been phoning around informing members that he had been subjected to a dastardly attack at the Society last night in his absence. This could only have reached him via an informer who had approached his wife, and I began to suspect that his wife was the driving force behind much of his malice, and this was soon to be made evident. She was the domineering woman behind the irascible little man who only had just capacity enough to carry out her dictates.

That afternoon Martti Hirvonen of the Finnish Orthodox Church phoned for information on the latest political situation of the Society. By this time I was convinced he was working for American intelligence as he showed little interest in involving himself in the running of the club. I gave him what information I had. Others outside the Society were evidently watching for the course we would take.

At the forthcoming Committee meeting I decided on a bold stroke in charging Evans, Enblom, Lambertsen and Andersson with holding an irregularly called meeting, conspiring against the Chairman, and spreading malicious gossip. This would be an attempt to throw them out of the Society. These accusations would be in addition to the fresh information I would bring from the Registration Office, and then Mrs. Hytönen had agreed to sit in on the meeting as a key witness.

Before the end of the week I secured promises of support from Runela, Jokimäki, von Etter, Miss Vaajajärvi, and of course from Peter, and if I could maintain these five supporters - and possibly gain Gösta Kelter - then the Evans clique could be subjugated, and as for Miss Kainulainen, she could vote either way as her unbelievable obtuseness was a credit to neither side. Sunday would be crucial and could well hold (and did) the balance as to the future existence of the Society.

CHAPTER 14
Let's be legal

"O the curst fate of all conspiracies!
They move on many springs; if one but fail
The restive machine stops."

John Dryden, *Don Sebastian*, Act IV, Sc. 1.

It was with a feeling of optimism that I arrived at the Primula café that Sunday afternoon, together with Mrs. Hytönen, and all the evidence and papers which were to destroy any case of the Evans' faction.

The two of us carefully reviewed the documents before the arrival of the other Committee members, and the first to meet us were Lambertsen and Mr. and Mrs. Evans, dressed in their best clothes and all smiles and sociableness. There was handshaking and no sign to betray that an open conflict was about to break out, although there was a certain tension and feeling of apprehension.

All knew that this was to be a very special and historic meeting and at the foot of the agenda I had circulated was the following note: "The entire proceedings of the meeting will be strictly private and confidential. No persons other than the above named Committee members will be allowed entry to the meeting, whether to give factual evidence or to attend as passive listeners, apart from the following: Mrs Evans and the Chairman's Witness." I particularly wanted to exclude the possibility of Rowland Hill blustering into our midst, and as for my witness and her evidence, this was to remain a mystery until the afternoon of the meeting.

As the room filled Mrs. Hytönen went over some points touching the registration of the Society with Mrs. Evans. At five I called the meeting to order and opened the proceedings, although at this point Peter had still not arrived. Standing on my right, the Secretary began to report on his findings as to the registration of the Society, repeating all the lies and misleading information he had reported to me at the Aga factory, and as he spoke, I felt confident he was falling into a trap that would serve my cause. After some twenty minutes Peter bounded merrily into

LET'S BE LEGAL

the room, apologised to the Chair for his lateness and greeted several friends, before opening his briefcase to take out a tape recorder that he plugged into a socket.

"We don't want any of that here - this is a private meeting," said Evans severely.

"I thought you'ld want your voice recorded for posterity," retorted Peter with sarcasm. "This is supposed to be a historic meeting."

"It's out of order," continued Evans. "This is a private and confidential meeting. You've read the agenda."

"I'm resigning anyway," said Peter peeked, and he disconnected his equipment.

He then took out a flash camera and proceeded to take a picture of me, a gesture that must have irked Evans in his pride at that moment as he was still the star of the meeting in presenting his report.

The second item on the agenda was Mrs. Evans report on her findings at the Ministry of the Interior regarding the registration and Chairmanship of the Society, and she reiterated the nonsense about long term residence permits and my consequent ineligibility for election to the Chairmanship. I made no interruptions for my part was to be enacted later in the meeting, and then Mrs. Evans began to hurriedly read through her completed Finnish version of the Constitution, and at such a rate that only the Finnish members could have followed its content, and as it was they who were taking a passive or even neutral role in the struggle, the reading of this document became a meaningless formality. Even if they had spotted a questionable clause they were allowed no time to raise objections.

During the course of this boring process, I noticed Peter become increasingly nervous and impatient. He seemed to sense a gathering tension at the meeting, a coldness towards himself, and he expressed a countenance which indicated mounting disgust. At last, he rose from the table, strapping up his briefcase, exclaiming, "I'm resigning! I'll leave the quarrelling to the rest of you." He then stormed out of the room, and with that I lost another positive supporter.

The following three items to be dealt with on the agenda, including a motion which was to be of considerable significance in this story, urging that the Committee be extended to its maximum of twenty persons, were to be proposed by the Secretary, and afterwards I was then to reply to all that the Secretary and his wife had said at the meeting; but on the conclusion of the Finnish reading of the Constitution, Lambertsen stood up and read out a short statement announcing that I had been removed from the Chairmanship of the Society.

It was stated that the Society had become too much of a "one man band" and that I was not to be allowed to attend any further Committee meetings. This interruption was quite out of order, and in view of its nature and audacity, I realised that now was the time to seize hold of the meeting. Till that moment the meeting had been run without interruptions and in an orderly fashion, and this disorderly break in the proceedings and coming from the Vice-Chairman, threw me into a fit of rage.

"Give me that paper," I demanded.

"No - it's signed by eight members and you're no longer Chairman," said Lambertsen holding the paper away from me.

"I want to see the signatures."

"It doesn't matter who's signed it," he said.

Standing up I denounced the unconstitutional act of my removal from the Chairmanship, and then began to answer the inaccuracies and falsehoods that had been presented by Mr. and Mrs. Evans. My blood boiled, and as I spoke for some twenty-five minutes, banging my fist onto the table, Lambertsen, the Danish schoolmaster, who was sitting on my left, winced with terror, constantly jerking away from me in his chair, as if expecting to be thrashed physically any moment. The speech, although rational and factually supported, was ineffective. The Finns were simply confused, waiting for the cue to be given by the next speaker, whilst Aldar Runela and his friend, Heikki Jokimäki, were so petrified with fear that they dared not open their mouths.

However, this was to be a meeting of carefully prepared statements, for on the other side of me, Evans stood up and read out an announcement stating that Mr. Rowland G.P. Hill intended standing for the Chairmanship, and that temporarily the Chair was to be held by Stig Lambertsen.

"That's quite unconstitutional - not even the Committee have approved it," cried Mrs. Hytönen.

"It's all been discussed and decided before," said Evans savagely, "so you keep your nose out of this - you're not even a member of the Society."

"My witness has as much right to speak at this meeting as your wife who's also not a member," I retorted.

Evans had no answer to that.

"The removal of the Chairman in these circumstances is totally illegal," argued Mrs. Hytönen.

"Nothing's illegal until the Society's been properly set-up and registered with the authorities," replied Evans. "The entire management of this association's been irregular from the day of its inception. It's been a disgrace to democratic procedure, and it's surprising the authorities have allowed it to go so far."

"Then how do you intend to put things right,?" asked Mrs. Hytönen of the rebel clique.

"We're holding a legal founding meeting on the 25th of March," said Evans.

At that moment Lambertsen stood up and announced the meeting closed, urging members to move out of the room as quickly as possible. There was a further exchange of words between Mrs. Hytönen and Evans as the meeting broke up in confusion, and then I returned to my flat with my friend to discuss further moves. It was then I realised that rational argument, even when allied to indisputable facts in the face of falsehood, was of no avail in a struggle against weak-minded men who either had no opinions or refused to hold opinions, or whose actions were motivated by malice.

"You must fight on on principle," urged Mrs. Hytönen. "I've never known anything so corrupt and dirty. I thought that Mrs. Evans was a really nasty bitch. She was rude and snobbish, and most off-hand when I took her to task on the registration question."

"For the moment I'll accept my expulsion from the Committee as a *fait accompli* - I can't do otherwise," I said, "but I'll fight on to get back on, and to win back the Chairmanship, and I'll give them a tough time. There's one thing they've forgotten in all their hurry."

"What's that?"

"I'm still Treasurer and I've got all their cash," I said pointing to the box on the floor.

"Don't hand over a penny," urged Mrs. Hytönen.

"Don't worry, I won't. I'll use it as a negotiating weapon in driving a hard bargain before offering my temporary resignation from the Chairmanship."

"It was quite wrong they wouldn't let you see that paper with the eight signatures on."

"They daren't have done it," I said. "Half of them probably only gave their signatures on the condition it was kept secret."

I was never to see that document again despite several requests for a copy afterwards, and this was subsequently to prove not only a disappointment to myself but also to the police when I came to assist them in their search for evidence against the Evans cabal.

On meeting Peter the following day, he excused his behaviour by saying, "I knew what they were up to and I knew what the outcome would be. You could see it a mile off! And I couldn't see those dozy Finns being very effective in your defence. I'm sorry, Bob, but I just couldn't sit there any more, feeling the tension rising by the minute, just waiting for the bomb to go off."

"Your help could have been useful," I said.

"I can't stand all this in-fighting. My phone never stops ringing. It's been you and Evans all day long for weeks now. After all, it is supposed to be a 'friendship' society, and I've seen nothing but enmity and backbiting. I'm fed up with it all," he added, but then assured me he would continue his function as Music Director, although not serving on the Committee. "I thought it was disgusting the way you were treated. You were the only force on the Committee with any initiative or imagination," he continued. "Most of them are just have-beens - only sitting there for a bit of reflected glory."

Despite his promise to continue as Music Director, Peter never attended the Society again.

That afternoon the Committee began to realise they had committed a tactical blunder in expelling me from their midst whilst I still held the purse strings of the Society. I had worked out conditions for offering my resignation - although I had every intention of putting up for election again on the 25th of March - and when Gösta phoned me about a little matter of the cash box having been left behind, he spoke with a mixture of good humour and diffidence.

I outlined my four conditions:- "1. That I be paid 100 marks incurred in the name of the Society; 2. That I be paid 300 marks to cover the cost of the hired telephone; 3. That my name as Founder of the Society appear where appropriate on all public notices and printed and duplicated literature of the Society; and, 4. That I be created an Honorary Life Member of the Society, and be allowed free entry to the club at all times, and that as the Founder of the Society, that I be put at a place of honour at dinners and social occasions of the Society nearby the Society's highest representative, whether it be a President, Honorary President or a Chairman." I told the Entertainments Director to pass on these conditions to the Committee, and he said that there would be a meeting that night at Anders Enblom's.

The telephone rang four times that evening within a two hour period during the said Committee meeting, and it was clear that the members were in a tizzy at their inability to resolve the question of my holding onto the cash box. There were problems over the conditions I had drawn up, but I was not prepared to budge. First Lambertsen: "We'll contact you again later in the evening," he concluded when his negotiating position had broken down. Then Anders Enblom phoned, and as he conferred with the others whilst not placing his hand properly over the speaker, I recognised the voices of the various members including that of Rowland Hill.

"You're making it difficult for us," sighed Enblom. "Mr. Rowland Hill refuses to accept the Chairmanship unless you surrender the cash box."

"That's your funeral then," I replied.

Mr. Rowland Hill never deigned to speak with me himself, although I heard him constantly prompt the others as to their manner of approach in the negotiations. He knew the limits of his responsibility, and he was not prepared to place himself in a position where he might be accused of thuggery. He had accepted on principle the post of Chairman, but would not take up the offer de facto unless others were prepared to complete the bloodletting on his behalf.

Later Ron Evans phoned and obviously the meeting had reached a state of desperation in its proceedings. He was highly irritable and going to stand for no nonsense.

"Look here, Mr. Corfe, you just can't do this," he began. "Don't you realise it amounts to theft? You could find yourself on a very serious charge. Theft is very punishable in this country, and if you got involved in anything like that, you'd lose your permits."

As with the others, he failed also. Finally, conditions 2, 3 and 4 were accepted by the Committee but number 1 still remained a stumbling block. I remained adamant. The last call was from Gösta Kelter.

"Look here, Bob," he began threateningly, "if you don't hand over the Society's cash box, we'll go to a lawyer tomorrow and open up a civil action against you."

"I'ld feel very privileged to defend such an action," I replied knowing full well that such a case might not come before the courts for two years and after an expenditure of thousands of Finnmarks.

Gösta broke into a temper like an irritable old woman.

"You're being very stubborn, Bob, and very unreasonable. You'll suffer for this - you'll see. You can't pit your strength against the whole Committee. Just you wait until you get a letter from our lawyer."

In the background I heard signs of exasperation, and Enblom exclaimed, "Oh, this is awful! I don't know what we can do," in such a woeful tone as if the end of the world was upon him.

The Committee meeting broke down in confusion and utter failure to achieve the business it had been called upon to resolve. The tide had now turned! The short-lived Evans cabal - a faction that had taken two months hard intrigue to create - had reached the summit of its power on the evening of the previous day. In the name of truth, justice, legality and the best interests of the Society, I was to strike back mercilessly at the enemy until the day when they were to be covered with public shame and embarrassment at the course of action they had been so foolishly persuaded to take.

The following morning Anders Enblom phoned to say that the first of my conditions had now been accepted by the Committee - the matter had been slept on - and that now everything could be amicably settled at tomorrow night's Wednesday meeting; but only an hour later he phoned again to say that Mr. Rowland Hill insisted that the matter could only be settled at his lawyer's office.

"It's so much more respectable to do things in a lawyer's office," concluded Enblom. "There'ld be so much more trust all round."

"I'm agreeable but you'll have to get Rowland to phone me with more specific instructions," I said.

That afternoon Rowland Hill actually phoned me himself confirming that he would only accept the Chairmanship if all points of dispute were settled in writing and signed at his solicitor's, Castrén and Snellman, and he requested that I draw up an Agreement for approval by the Committee tomorrow before implementing its legality at his lawyer's the following day. This I did.

The Wednesday nightclub meeting on the 26th of February was eventful. I arrived with the cash box and draft Agreement for a Committee meeting called for half an hour before our cultural evening was due to begin. Mr. Rowland Hill dictated the wording for my resignation, and meanwhile, I hung tightly onto the cash box for I was not going to surrender it until the Agreement was accepted. This was soon done, and in an atmosphere which must have been embarrassing to both sides, there was some friendly handshaking, and arrangements were made for several Committee members and Rowland Hill and myself, to meet at Castrén and Snellman's the following morning to complete formalities.

"Thank God we have peace at last in our Society," said Anders Enblom, quite unaware of the fact that he was speaking far too soon.

"It's much better when things are settled in a friendly way," said Lambertsen smiling amiably at me.

"Mr. Corfe's done a lot for our Society, and he'll do a lot more in his new function as Club Leader," said Evans approvingly. "And of course, if you still want to put up for the Chairmanship, you'ld still be free to do so."

I smiled, pondering at the relief I had afforded so many consciences. Rowland G.P. Hill was the only non-smiling face as he maintained his dignified nonchalance. Exactly a week previously I had soiled my copy book by openly attacking Evans and making vague references to an opposing faction that at that time was not evident to those in the hall. This week I felt confident that my image would be restored and that the onus of guilt for any intrigue in the Society would be cast entirely on the shoulders of the Evans cabal.

Shortly after 8 o'clock Lambertsen opened the meeting by stating I had resigned, and that the Chairmanship would be temporarily held by Mr. Rowland G.P. Hill until the 25th of March when the official founding meeting would be held. Gasps of surprise and some murmuring filled the hall, and I could see that Rowland Hill was embarrassed as he took a step back and adopted a pose that was as self-effacing as it was possible for him to adopt.

Evans came forward to deliver a few incoherent words on his usual topic, the Constitution, but his elocution was so appalling, that Rowland Hill had to prompt him, correcting his pronunciation on several occasions - almost with annoyance.

The Technical Director, Heikki Jokimäki and his friend Aldar Runela, had not shown up that evening - possibly as a gesture of sympathy at my irregular expulsion - and indeed, they began to fade themselves out from the activities of the Society. As it was the South African film evening, and a projectionist was required, Gösta Kelter volunteered his assistance in this direction at a late hour, and then promptly found himself entangled in yards of film.

"I'm afraid I've never done this before," he apologised to the embarrassed assembly as he tried to disentangle himself and discover the workings of the machine. "Perhaps our guest could talk to us for a few minutes," he added calling over to the Committee members at the end of the hall.

There was an awkward stir for some moments amongst the Committee members as Lambertsen glanced round him, for no one had exactly undertaken to be a master of ceremonies. Mr. Oila of the South African Consulate, who was presenting the films, had only agreed to present his programme on the condition that he would not be called upon to speak or to answer questions - this because of the controversial nature of the country - and he politely excused himself, saying he thought the film would be ready in a moment. At last the projector was ready, and the films that illustrated the national parks of South Africa, were enjoyed by all and warmly applauded.

During the interval, as I had anticipated, a number of members approached me asking in concern as to why I had resigned. I told them frankly that I had been irregularly expelled by a rebel clique but that I would put up again for the Chairmanship on the 25th of March, and that I counted on their votes.

"But you *are* the Society," said one of a group of four American girls. "It just wouldn't be the same club without you."

"It's dreadful what they've done," said another.

"I hope I can depend on your votes on the 25th," I said.

"You bet you can," said one raising her thumb.

"We think you're great, Mr. Corfe," said one of the four diffidently standing behind her friends.

"There's a rat somewhere," said a distinguished looking Finnish gentleman. "I don't like it at all. It doesn't smell good."

"We'll be sorry to see you leave, if that's what it means," said another. "It's taken years for someone to come along with the guts to start a club like this in Helsinki. There's plenty of places for students to go, but not for older people like us - and there's been nothing like it in the opportunity to practice English. It'll be a pity if this is the beginning of the end."

"Whatever have they done to you,?" exclaimed an elderly lady. "I don't know how they'll find anyone to take your place - you've been so energetic."

"I was very surprised to hear what happened tonight, Mr. Corfe," said Akulov taking me aside. "What happened exactly? ... It's very unfortunate," he added at last. "Mr. Corfe, I know it's not for more than two months when I give my lecture on the Soviet Union, but I wondered if we could meet for lunch and discuss it."

"I'ld be happy to assist you anytime, Mr. Akulov," I said.

"Could we meet at noon tomorrow at the Sillankorva restaurant,?" he suggested. "It's near your home, so you wouldn't have far to go."

I readily accepted this invitation but was astonished that Mr. Akulov had already anticipated in his mind that the restaurant was only a stone's throw from where I lived. I was intensely curious for I strongly suspected that Mr. Akulov had other motives in asking me to lunch with him than wishing to discuss his forthcoming talk.

Perhaps I should here remark that some days previously I had met Mr. Akulov in Unioninkatu by the Botanical Gardens and that on stopping to exchange greetings, I had handed him one of my newly printed cards, whilst expressing the hope that he enjoyed our cultural evenings. This may possibly have persuaded him to advance on that friendly gesture at our next meeting.

At ten the next morning I arrived at Castrén and Snellman's office in Aleksanterinkatu. Rowland Hill, Anders Enblom and Ron Evans were also there, and for some time we were kept waiting in an outer office. Evans looked nervous, smoked constantly and said little. Enblom said he had arranged that my telephone would be collected on the following Tuesday. Rowland Hill was greeted by one of the senior partners who was an old friend, and then we were shown into the office of another lawyer, Mr. Bertel Åkermarck, who was going to act on the Society's behalf.

But when the time came for signing and dividing the proceeds of the Society, it was discovered that Enblom had forgotten to bring the cash box with him, and so as he returned to fetch this, the rest of us were kept waiting impatiently for another three quarters of an hour.

"I don't know where my boss is going to think I am," said Evans glancing anxiously at his watch.

At last everything was ready, and as we crowded a second time round Bertel Åkermarck, Enblom emptied the contents of the cash box onto his desk. Mr. Rowland Hill counted the money, checked the accounts, and then paid out my share of 400 marks plus four.

"That's for luck," concluded Rowland by way of dropping me a tip, and with that, the Society was stony broke, with a deficit of a hundred marks.

Then came the signing of the Agreement, which included the following words in addition to the main four paragraphs: "As the official founder of the International Society Finland, Mr. Robert Corfe shall always recognise and respect the duly elected Committee and at no time attempt to interfere, criticise or influence the management of the Society, unless he be elected onto the Committee or be elected as a Chairman or a President of the Society. He shall also be bound by all the rules of the Society, excepting only where provisions are made by the Society as regards his Honorary membership. Any misconduct or public scandal arising from his behaviour at any time and wheresoever it might take place, may incur the withdrawal of his Honorary membership and any special club privileges that the Society may be pleased to confer upon him. ... Helsinki, February 27th 1964." I felt that the above would serve as a sop to any excess that might have been seen in my demands.

Two clerks were called into the office as witnesses, and in an atmosphere of solemn formality, the six signatures were appended to the Agreement.

"All quarrels are now at an end," said Enblom.

"Let's hope so," added Rowland Hill.

CHAPTER 15
This is libel

"Cunning is the dark sanctuary of incapacity."

Lord Chesterfield, *Letters*, p. 656.

It was past noon and I rushed to the Sillankorva restaurant, for already I would be late for my appointment with the Second Secretary of the Soviet embassy.

In my pocket I carried the recently completed pamphlet, *Towards A Federal Europe*, for I entertained the possibility that I might be able to make some use of it that very afternoon. Mr. Akulov was the highest ranking diplomat who regularly attended our meetings. He was friendly and approachable; he had introduced guests and at least one other member; he seemed agreeable to the aims and environment of the club, and I liked the impression he had made. As a member he was equal with all, and I felt he was fully entitled to the privileges of the club, and to the protection of his good name against any untoward and unfounded suggestions that might be rumoured as to his motives for being in our midst.

Not only was the club non-political and indeed opposed to propagating any ideas, religious, humanitarian or other, but we were privileged to be living in a country which was neutral, and after three years residence I had come to pride myself on having achieved successfully a supreme Scandinavian objectivity, admittedly more Swedish than Finnish in outlook. I now enjoyed a curious perspective on world affairs and such a dispassionate outlook, as cannot be experienced or even imagined by an Englishman or other NATO European unless he has lived in and absorbed for some considerable time the mentality of neutral Scandinavia.

This perspective entailed a wholesome contempt for both the Soviet Union and the United States as being deviations from the true path of Europeanism (or civilisation), with its balance and maturity resulting from a synthesis of centuries of ideological conflict. During the following five years I was to expand on these ideas through the

Helsinki Appeals Court

(the Marble Palace) formerly the Villa Keirkner, where Ron Evans was tried behind locked doors. It is now Finland's Labour Court.

columns of the Finnish press.

In view of this I was confident that we who enjoyed the valued privilege of living in such a country as neutral Finland could mix easily with those from any part of the world with impunity. Certainly I felt a greater freedom here than in Britain in this regard, for living in a country caught up in the Cold War unhealthy inhibitions are held in thrall to undesirable partisan prejudices. But here in Finland - blessed by a happier state - there were no camps and no tension, and in addition, there was the opportunity to disentangle oneself from the distasteful ideological conflict with its half-truths and subjective falsehood. Some might contend that the achievement of this neutral Scandinavian outlook amounted to little more than an ivory tower mentality, but at the time, I saw it in the light of achieving a higher realism.

At the time I did not appreciate fully the necessity for *Realpolitik*, or the essential wisdom underlying the political philosophy of Niccolo Machiavelli. In retrospect, I now realise that my attitude was reminiscent of that of the ruling classes during the last centuries of the declining Eastern Roman Empire, i.e. the contempt of a refined but militarily weak state for a barbaric Latin civilisation in the West, and an equal contempt for an Oriental tyranny in the East - an overweening attitude immediately prior to the final conquest of Byzantium and Constantinople by the Turkish hordes.

At the time I felt contempt for the pettiness of those American diplomats, who apparently out of spite and baseless suspicion, were reputed to have put a bar on their personnel visiting our club. It was typical of their attitude! On the other hand I was sorry not to enjoy their presence in our company, and I hoped that with the passing of time we would gain their confidence before welcoming them into our midst. Already a number of Americans, not attached to the embassy, were regular patrons and I hoped that these would spread the good word.

As I arrived in the ground floor foyer of the Sillankorva, Mr. Akulov rose from a settee to greet me. He was immaculately dressed as always in a conservatively styled well-pressed suit, and after apologising for my lateness and leaving my coat with the doorman, we made our way to the restaurant. As we mounted the broad staircase I noticed the neatness of his haircut, and he conveyed an impression of such affluence and stockbroker respectability, that it was impossible to dislike the man. He was well on the way to adopting Western habits and I was pleased he refrained from using that dreadful scent most Russian men of the better class customarily wear in their own country. If the Soviet Union was to fall under the influence of such a class of men, I reflected, there was a good possibility that the spirit of Communism would wither away before the state, and if this was realised, a conservative and aristocratic elite might emerge cherishing values which varied little from those of the upper classes in Western Europe, and I found this a comforting reflection.

A table had been reserved for us and we were shown to a secluded part of the restaurant. Menus were placed before us, choices were made, and then we began on an excellent lunch including oyster cocktails, schaschlik, and plenty of vodka and beer. Mr. Akulov wanted the full facts behind the story of my unexpected expulsion from the Committee and Chairmanship of the Society.

"It doesn't sound right," he said. "You see, I'm very curious. I could bring some more friends to the club, but if there's something wrong - something of a scandal - I'ld have to be careful. We Soviet diplomats have to safeguard our reputation. We wouldn't like to find ourselves caught up in anything."

"Of course," I answered. "As with all diplomats you have to maintain an absolute discretion."

"Exactly! Your health," he said downing his vodka at a draught, and I followed suit then and frequently afterwards during the course of the lunch during which a bottle was consumed between us.

"As a member you're entitled to know everything about the Society," I said.

I outlined the full story of my conflict with Ron Evans, taking care to draw him in the worst possible light, as a purely malicious schemer. Mr. Akulov then questioned me on all that I knew about Evans, including the social status that such a man would hold in Britain, and from this we moved onto a general discussion of class differences and resentments in England. He then questioned me on why I had founded the club before turning to my personal background, examining me in the minutest detail as to spare time activities, place of birth, upbringing and education, career history and even ancestry, but his questioning was of so easy and friendly a manner that it was impossible to take offence.

He indicated no scruple in pursuing his curiosity, and I took this beguiling characteristic as an ineradicable tendency in the Russian character. I remembered having read in a novel of the Westernised Turgenev, a chiding reference to the Russian vice of asking personal questions as the only way his countrymen had of maintaining a conversation, and I attributed this traditional characteristic to my host, so that after several hours he had been afforded the opportunity of searching deeply into my soul, for of all nations, the Russian through his literature, had developed a reputation for delving most deeply into the soul of humanity. I had nothing to hide as to my past - no skeletons in the cupboard - so I had no fear of committing an indiscretion or the need for circumspection.

Reciprocally, he too was frank about his own background, explaining that he came from a town of half a million in Far East Asia, some 500 miles to the north of Vladivostock. He assured me that racially he was a pure Russian, and I concluded that his ancestors may have well contributed to extending the boundaries and building up the great Russia of the Tsars - originally perhaps, in the status of malefactors.

"Do you make much money teaching,?" he enquired.

"I can live comfortably," I replied.

"Your father must be disappointed your didn't follow his profession," said Akulov. "There must be more money in dental surgery." I was touched by this percipient understanding for my welfare. "Someone with your energy and initiative should be in business. That would be far more lucrative than what you're doing now." I felt the expression of such capitalistic sentiments from a Soviet diplomat unusual. I told him that after completing a correspondence course a year previously, I had taken steps to set up a business importing from Britain, but that the Commercial Section of the embassy had been so unhelpful and dilatory in answering queries, that I had eventually been forced to drop the project.

"That was a good idea," said Akulov. "There's a need for British goods here. Your country and mine are Finland's two greatest trading partners - you know that, don't you? - but the import of British goods here is negligible. There's too much imported from West Germany. The Germans are too strong here."

On only one occasion during the luncheon did he touch on party politics with, "I think Wilson'll be a good man in the Labour party, don't you?" I steered away from the topic but I clearly indicated that I had little sympathy for either Wilson or the Labour party. At that time I was more influenced by the liberal, "You've never had it so good" Conservatism of Harold Macmillan - a far cry from the viciously selfish Conservatism which was to develop at a later period. Towards the end of our meeting I told him about the expansion I had made for publication purposes of my speech on the 15th of January. As he expressed an intelligent interest in this I took the pamphlet from my pocket and handed it to him.

"I'll study this with great interest," he said, "and give it back to you at next Wednesday's meeting."

I was glad he had swallowed the bait, and realised that if I could arrange for an American diplomat to read the same, it could be the first step towards a dialogue I could enjoy with both before formulating a synthesis enabling each to see the ideology of the other in a different light. The purpose of several sections of the pamphlet were aimed at gently undermining the separate ideologies of America and the Soviet Union, whilst also emphasising the invaluable role that Europe as a neutral third world power bloc might play between East and West.

On arriving home shortly after 3 o'clock that afternoon, I felt so ill that I had to lie down for several hours. The consumption of alcohol had been so great that my stomach revolted and my head swam with a dizziness and buzzing. Mr. Akulov, despite his small size, seemed capable of consuming unlimited amounts of spirit, and I had felt that in failing to empty my glass whenever he did might be interpreted as a gesture of ingratitude or unfriendliness, as well as reflecting badly on the International Society as its founder, and on Britain as an Englishman. I had prayed that he would pour no more of the stuff into our glasses, but he had continued to do so, and so maintaining what fortitude I could, I cooperated with each hospitable gesture, and at the end of the luncheon, he had in no way triumphed over me in this respect and we parted as equals.

The following afternoon I met von Etter, and together we visited Count Werner von der Schulenburg, press attaché at the Legation of the Republic of Federal Germany. There was a problem over the programme entitled, *Life In The Federal Land of Bavaria*, that he was due to give next Wednesday. Count von der Schulenburg had all those characteristics generally associated with the traditional aristocrat: he was tall, fair and good looking, with a cool demeanour, civilised and charming manner, and a mild sense of humour reflecting a balanced temperament and an objective view of the world. I was glad that I had brought a Finnish aristocrat with me, and I hoped that I could interest the Count in an active involvement with our affairs.

As soon as we were seated he pointed out an inaccuracy in our programme describing him as attached to the Embassy of the Federal Republic of Germany, when in fact there was no such embassy. In the cause of neutrality and appeasing both West and East Germany - as well as other states - Finland had refused recognition to both countries, granting them merely legations. I said I hoped the mistake would be seen in the light of a friendly gesture and the Count accepted this with a laugh.

He then explained that he was not a Bavarian, had not been to Bavaria, and knew nothing at all about the place. He was a Prussian and proud of this, and asked if he might talk in general terms on Germany, in addition to presenting a film, and this was settled. He was to honour us with his presence on several occasions and to mix freely with diplomats in our midst from other powers.

During the interval of Count von der Schulenburg's programme, Mr. Akulov returned me my pamphlet as promised.

"It was most interesting," he said, "particularly the part you didn't include in your talk. I agreed with nearly everything, except - and this is because I'm a Soviet citizen - certain terminology. If certain words were changed there'ld be very few points of disagreement from official thought in the Soviet Union. It would be interesting to discuss the pamphlet over another lunch sometime."

I was pleased with Mr. Akulov's response.

On Wednesday the 11th of March we had the pleasure of

welcoming His Excellency the Ambassador for Israel, Mr. Yehuda Gaulan, who delivered a talk on Modern Israel: *A New Country In An Old Land*, but before the start of the meeting, a duplicated circular on the forthcoming election was handed out to members. I had only read the first few lines when I was struck by an outrageously misleading statement followed by a downright lie, viz., that the Finnish authorities had clearly indicated their preference that those foreigners in leading positions of the Society should be in possession of Long-Term residence permits, and that Mr. Corfe had resigned because of this.

The circular was signed by Evans and Lambertsen, and I pocketed the offending document, determined that this would be used as incriminating evidence in lodging a complaint with the Ministry of the Interior.

"What's the meaning of this - you know it's untrue,?" I said bounding up to Gösta and Ingrid at the reception table. I told them my complaint.

"Don't be so fault-finding and petty. What does it matter if it isn't true? It's merely academic."

"No it's not."

"As you don't intend standing for the Chairmanship again, I don't see the difference."

"Who told you I don't intend standing for the Chairmanship again? I've every intention of standing for election. I've never concealed the fact."

"You can't do that - not after all the money we paid you just a fortnight ago," said Gösta in mounting exasperation. "It's not right."

"I was entitled to the money."

"Not for the telephone."

"I only got the phone because of the club. And besides, there's nothing in the Agreement about my not being entitled to put up for the Chairmanship."

"The Agreement's nothing to do with it. It's a moral issue."

"It was a moral issue when I was kicked off the Committee."

"I thought we'd settled everything nice and peaceably at the lawyer's office," said Anders approaching us.

"We did, but this is another issue," I said.

"You can't do this to us, Bob," pleaded Gösta.

"Listen, you started introducing legalities into this Society, and that's what I'm standing by. I can play the lawyer just as well as you can."

"You're being a tyrant," said Gösta.

"Ask Ronald here. He said I could put up for election."

Mr. Evans moved awkwardly and then said, "Well, I don't know about the Chairmanship, but as far as the statutes are concerned, you can put up for the Committee - you'ld be welcome there."

"Anyway, that's not the issue now. What I'm concerned with is this circular," I said taking the paper from my pocket. "I regard this document as libellous on grounds that it contains falsely misleading statements contradicting established facts; and since that paper has already been mailed to members, it's not only irrevocably damaging to my cause but personally hurtful.

"Furthermore, I would contend that even if these falsehoods are recognised for what they are by our members, an implication might be read into these statements that the authorities are not entirely happy with my personal character. As I am - and I say this confident of the truth - a man of untarnished character in the eyes of the law, I regard this circular in any circumstances as libellous, and possibly, even as defamatory."

"You ought to be a damned lawyer," said Evans.

"What do you intend doing,?" asked Enblom.

"Tomorrow I'll lodge this paper with the police, filing an official complaint."

A cackle of excited voices broke forth, uttering abuse and veiled threats, shaking their heads and interrupting one another as to what I could and could not do. I walked away and fixed some election literature on the board I had for that purpose, but during the interval, I noticed Evans (who by now had been goaded into a spiteful mood) surreptitiously tear it down. In his present state of mind there would have been little to achieve through direct confrontation.

Through careful canvassing, however, I was able to drum up considerable support from members, and secure promises for votes and attendance on the 25th - only a fortnight hence. Several electioneering factors contributed neatly to my cause. Firstly, on that very evening membership of the Society was closed to Finnish nationals in an attempt to create an equal ratio between Finns and foreigners.

In a test case a girl friend I had brought to the club that night, had been refused membership of the Society, and the report of this incident was met with shocked surprise. Secondly, a stipulation on the current election circular of the Evans cabal stated that only 40% of Finnish members would be allowed voting rights at the General Meeting on the 25th. This decision seemed grossly arbitrary and unjustifiable in that it might exclude a majority of persons in the Society who already regarded themselves as established members. What this stipulation eventually did was to spread apathy instead of inspiring a will to secure what might be lost, with the result that many Finns absented themselves on the 25th.

As I was moving around the hall, collecting names and addresses, and asking for active volunteers, I was approached by an American girl who exclaimed: "You should emigrate to our country, Mr. Corfe. You'd do so well in the States. You've got the pioneering spirit - you'ld sure make something there. America needs people like you."

Due to the pressure of teaching work during the next few days, I refrained from immediately carrying out my threat to the Committee members of lodging a complaint with the police on that Thursday morning, but on the following Monday I drafted a letter to Mr. Kovero, Departmental Chief in the Ministry of the Interior responsible for foreigners. This letter detailed my complaints, requesting that the registration of the Society be postponed for the time being, urging that in view of the many irregularities, that I alone should be held by the Ministry of the Interior and the Ministry of Justice as the only true representative of the Society entitled to confer with the authorities on the question of registration. Together with relevant documents, I took this letter by hand to the Ministry, requesting a personal interview with Mr. Kovero.

After a wait of twenty minutes I was ushered into his spacious office, and together with an interpreter and two other officials, I outlined my complaints and we began discussing the matter. Mr. Kovero was most helpful in his attitude. He assured me that the Society could anyway not be registered until after Easter, and he requested my copy of the offending and libellous circular so that this could be taken to another department for examination.

"We know some people who could be very interested in this paper," said Mr. Kovero significantly, "and it might be useful to your case. All this is very mysterious indeed."

He suggested that I visit the Registration Office to examine the latest version of the Constitution, comparing it with that supposedly final version read out to members on the 5th of February by Ron Evans. On the following day I carried out this - what transpired to be - timely piece of advice, in the company of my scholarly friend, Seppo Lipponen, who had a critical eye for pointing out discrepancies in legal documents. We were three hours examining the two sets of documents and discussing their implications. At the end of our research we were enlightened by many factors and both of us were deeply shocked.

"I'm glad I'm out of this," said Seppo shaking his head. "It's dirty - really dirty."

He then spoke at some considerable length with the Departmental Chief, Notary Rissanen, explaining how members of our Society were being deceived and misled by the Evans cabal.

"The two constitutions are entirely different," said Seppo to the lawyer. "It seems to me as if the Society is falling under a dictatorial clique."

"The Constitution that I had drawn up was a members' Constitution," I added. "It was democratic, and guaranteed members their rights. This Constitution takes those rights away."

I knew that I had yet more ammunition in fighting my cause on the 25th of March.

CHAPTER 16
Scrape with death

"We never are but by ourselves betrayed."

William Congreve, *The Old Batchelor*, Act III, Sc. 1.

The meeting on the 18th of March was well attended, but it led to an incident which was to culminate in a criminal charge being preferred against a Committee member.

Mr. Esan El'din Hawas, press attaché to the embassy of the United Arab Republic gave a talk and presented us with a film and a nicely printed and illustrated programme that members could retain as a souvenir of the evening. He brought a number of friends with their wives along, and it was clear that his charm and generous manner had made him popular in the diplomatic community, for officials from a number of embassies warmly greeted him that night.

This was the last event before the General Meeting, and there was much electioneering, shuffling of papers and secret whispering, finalising details so that the election might go off without a hitch for the group which had seized power. By this time, however, it was realised by the Committee that there was nothing to prevent me standing for the Chairmanship, but nominations had to be completed on the appropriate forms, and I took several of these from the table where they lay strewn about.

As soon as I had done this, Gösta who had been following me with an eagle eye, exclaimed, "You're not going to do that, Bob" - in a tone like that of a nanny chiding her disobedient charge. I brushed aside his annoying interference, went up to a member and promptly secured the signature of a Proposer. For a moment Gösta stood aghast, and then bounded up to me, exclaiming rhetorically, "What are you doing?"

"You know what I'm doing," I replied.

At this point the account can be taken up by the statement I lodged with the Criminal police the following morning:-

"He said: 'You are causing trouble for the Society and I shall do everything in my power to prevent your nomination.' I said: 'Are you threatening me?' He said: 'Yes, and I shall follow you round the hall all the evening and tell members not to sign this paper.' I said: 'That's intimidating members of the Society.' He said: 'I've a right to do it.' I said: 'You've not a right to do it in that way. It's against the law because it's plainly intimidation.' He then insulted me, calling me amongst other things a 'dictator' and that I would made a 'good Nazi.' I said: 'I don't want to speak with you any further. Would you please go away.'"

During this dialogue Count von der Schulenburg and Mr. Akulov were standing close by. Some minutes earlier I had been pleased to see these diplomats in friendly conversation, and it reminded me of the *entente* which had once existed between their countries in the great Bismarckian era, but at that moment, the Count had his back to us, whilst Akulov was observing the squabble with an expression of bemused indifference, moving backwards and forwards on the balls of his feet.

"How dare you use that word in the hearing of Count Schulenburg,!" I whispered into Gösta's ear in attempting to make him behave better before our honoured guests. My hint was of no avail. The police statement can take up the thread again:-

"I walked away from him but he followed me at my heel. I walked the length of the hall twice in an attempt to throw him off my track, but he was still at my heel. I stopped at a table and solicited a lady for her signature to nominate me for the Chairmanship. Mr. Kelter said to the lady: 'Do you know why he's no longer Chairman? Ten Committee members signed a paper saying he must resign as Chairman.' The lady was plainly embarrassed and so was I."

It may be interesting to note that although I was denied the opportunity of seeing the document expelling me from the Committee, with such excuses that the paper was lost or no longer valid following the settlement at Castrén and Snellman's, signatures were still being appended in an attempt to give it greater credence.

The police statement continues:- "I left the table and approached Mr. Evans and pleaded that he tell Mr. Kelter not to follow me around the hall in this way. Mr. Kelter facetiously replied: 'I'm following you because I like you so much.'"

Following the libel and police threats of the previous Wednesday,

Evans was keeping well out of my way - he had always been terrified at any mention of the police - and indeed, he was never to molest me again.

To continue the account:- "At that moment, another lady approached me and said: 'Of course you should be nominated as Chairman - you started the club!' Mr. Kelter repeated the same words he had said to the first lady. The second lady signed the nomination paper. Mr. Kelter then said to me in a highly threatening tone: 'I promise you're going to regret this for the rest of your life.' He then ceased to molest me."

The most significant move of the Evans cabal that night was the extension of the Committee to twenty persons, and the work involved choosing and nominating these to satisfy both the requirements of democratic form and the needs of the registration authorities. Mr. Akulov, either through accident or design, happened to bring five smiling faces from the Soviet embassy along that night, four of whom, including Sokolov and Akulov himself, were to find their names on the circular listing members for election and re-election together with their proposers, which was handed out on the night of the 25th. Also on this paper was listed the aforementioned mysterious and cringing Pole, suitably supported by Soviet friends, amongst names of other persons who were hardly known to the club.

In attempting to create an opposing clique on the Committee, I too canvassed for prospective supporters, but with little success, firstly, because of the intimidation of the Evans cabal, and secondly, because a number of Finnish members were already leaving the Society out of a feeling of disgust at all the intrigue. I approached Count von der Schulenburg to stand on the Committee, but he laughed off the suggestion, exclaiming only, "Good gracious no - I wouldn't do anything so daring!"

Despite the tension and panic of the Committee to complete these arrangements in such a way as to obviate the possibility of strife or the election of the wrong persons, there was much dancing and gaiety in the upper hall that night after the cultural evening had been concluded. Late in the evening, however, after the lower hall had emptied, a sub-committee meeting presided over by the great Rowland G.P. Hill himself was held in the latter. The door was ajar, and as a friend and I put on our coats to leave, it was impossible not to overhear from the foyer, the babble that was happening within.

"We couldn't stop him," said Gösta.

"But what can we do,?" cried Enblom in despair.

"I must impress upon you gentlemen," said Rowland Hill maintaining his usual sang froid, "whatever we do, we must remain calm. We'll find a way somehow."

They knew where the popularity stakes were placed, but not even Rowland Hill with all his experience and ability was to emerge from this struggle unscathed.

About an hour later, on returning home, I encountered an experience of great unpleasantness as I turned into my street. On crossing Pitkänsillanranta towards the Sillankorva, a blue car answering to the description of Gösta Kelter's, sped down from Siltasaarenkatu, swerving out of its course in an apparent or feigned attempt to run me over. I stood my ground in the street, apprehensive as to the driver's next move. The car reversed violently at the street corner by the alcohol shop, and then sped towards me a second time, mounting the pavement - clearly attempting to knock me down - but I ran back, jumping onto the steps of the Sillankorva for protection. I saw two figures in the front seats - a man and a woman - but too indistinctly to distinguish their features.

The car sped back to Siltasaarenkatu and disappeared towards the city centre as it drove over the Long bridge. I was left stunned by the incident. There had been no time to register the car number, and then unluckily, there were no witnesses in the street to bear out my story. On arriving home I soon recovered my composure and was resolved on a course of action. The incident together with what had happened previously that evening, capped my decision, for tomorrow I would lay a criminal charge against Gösta Kelter for intimidation and threatening divers persons on the premises of the International Society.

The following morning I drew up a detailed statement suitable for use as police evidence in a court of law, and lodged this with the Criminal police at their central department. The statement was a personal request to bring a criminal charge against Mr. Gösta Kelter in that he "did threaten Mr. Corfe against obtaining signatures for nomination to the Chairmanship of the Society and did intimidate individual members of the Society against signing Mr.Corfe's nomination paper." The request was supported in view of the following factors and circumstances:- 1. "To uphold a basic purpose of the law in preventing further threats and perhaps physical violence in the Society;" 2. A belief that "Mr. Kelter has an instability of mind making him prone to resorting to physical violence," and, 3. In view of the strange occurrence which took place in Pitkänsillanranta at about 23.30 hours on the night of the 18th of March.

Towards the end of the statement was appended a request, "That police be posted within the premises of the International Society Finland, on the 25th of March, the day of the official founding meeting of the Society, to ensure the prevention of any outbreak of physical violence," followed by the remarks that, "the threats and intimidation of Mr. Kelter is merely the climax to a number of deceitful and entirely irregular actions pursued by certain members of the Society. Please see the attached paper further elucidating this" - the latter being a reference to a copy of the letter I had laid before Departmental Chief Kovero two days previously.

The police fully recognised the gravity of my statement - particularly the attempt to run me down in the street - and asked me to see Prosecutor Mäkelä the next day. This I did.

"What kind of Society is this,?" he exclaimed in incomprehension after pausing meditatively. "Is it a political society?"

"It's entirely non-political," I replied more intent on conveying my hopes than in reflecting the truth. "We're purely a social and cultural club."

"I don't like this reference to 'Nazi,' - it's political," said Mäkelä.

"I think it was intended merely as a general insult," I explained.

"It's an insult a Communist would use."

I said nothing. He seemed to be drawing the wrong assumptions.

"What's this - a letter to Kovero,?" he exclaimed. "Now I see! This is a matter for the foreign police. We'll confer with them before laying charges. Maybe they can tell us something more about this Society."

Having pressed my accusation as best I could with all available

SCRAPE WITH DEATH

evidence I agreed to sign a warrant of attorney, so handing over the responsibility for any prosecution to the police. Several days later Gösta Kelter was arrested at his office and held in custody for eight hours for questioning. The police had dropped the matter concerning threats and intimidation, saying that this was a civil matter, but they questioned him with regard to the misuse of his car. No proof was found to secure a conviction and so he was released by the early evening.

Since the night of the debate with Eric Jakowleff, a month earlier, and the visit of the HISC members to our club (some of whom had since joined the Society or at least begun to frequent our cultural evenings), reports of malicious and highly defamatory rumours reached my ear, but as so often with slanderous whisperings, I found it impossible to discover those who were spreading this talk, as well as difficult to penetrate exactly what these slanders were. I only learnt about these rumours and the fact that they were rife through oblique references, often expressed in a humorous vein, and because of their obscurity and because they were not aimed directly at myself, it was difficult to take them out of their context in the general conversation by way of taking the speakers to task.

The slanders bore no relation to fact, being purely the result of a twisted imagination, but nonetheless, I felt reason for concern. Such rumours, true or false, could be (and as I afterwards discovered were) invaluable to the Evans cabal. I felt that any sign of showing offence at the existence of these rumours would only tend to confirm the foundation of their claim in the minds of those who heard them.

One such ridiculous rumour was that I had been expelled from Sweden for drug-trafficking, another that I had been a political prisoner in East Germany, and yet another, that I had beaten-up my landlord in Berlin when I had stayed in that city for some three months, during the Summer, a year previously. The latter two were so absurd as to defy credibility except to persons of the very lowest mentality, but the first rumour was more disturbing - in every way more shocking, and I felt that some measure should be taken in counteracting this with proof to the contrary.

Accordingly, I visited the Swedish embassy on the 21st of March and discussed the matter with an official called Lundvik. On his advice I sent off a letter to the State Commission for Foreigners in Stockholm that very afternoon, from whom I was satisfied to receive an *ex officio* document a fortnight later testifying that I had "not been expelled from Sweden for any wrongful or suspected wrongful action."

As I was writing my letter to the State Commission there was a knock on the door. A messenger from Castrén and Snellman's handed me a letter to which they required a signature for safe receipt. Hullo, I thought, here comes the next offensive from the Evans-Rowland clique. I was not disappointed in my suspicions. The letter read as follows:-

> Having been requested by the board of the International Society Finland to check that all candidates for the forthcoming elections have a long-term residential permit required by paras. 4 and 7 of the statutes, I would be grateful if you kindly could take the trouble of coming up to my office on Monday morning, March 23rd with your passport in order to have this formality clarified before the meeting.

The letter was signed by Bertel Äkermarck whom I promptly phoned.

"What statutes are these you're referring to,?" I asked.

He was taken aback for a moment and I heard him shuffle some papers on his desk.

"Why, the Society's statutes of course," he answered.

"You had me confused," I said. "I thought you were referring to *legal* statutes. The board you refer to is merely a provisional body that doesn't exist yet as a legal entity, and as to the statutes, they're merely clauses from the Constitution that the registration authorities have not yet approved. Also, do you know that in Finnish law there's no such thing as a Long-Term residence permit?"

"I think it's in the same statutes," said Äkermarck.

"It's not."

"Then you'll have to ask Rowland Hill."

"It all sounds too arbitrary to be law," I remarked.

He was still confused as I put down the phone but I had revealed his letter for the bluff it was. Nonetheless, I agreed to go through the pettifogging mummery he had arranged for Monday as it meant upholding my cause. In view of the mounting tension of the struggle (and neither knew what action the other might take) I made a further appointment with Kovero for the purpose of filing a libel action against Evans and Lambertsen - for on this I was determined. I phoned Rowland Hill the next day.

"What's the Society's definition of a long term residence permit,?" I asked.

This time I had him on a spot, for he was obliged to give a clear definition, and his befuddled procrastination betrayed his acute discomfort.

"The board have stipulated three years," he replied at last as if the matter had been a foregone conclusion.

My confidence was revived. I held a three-year residence permit and now there was no legal disqualification to my re-election to the Chairmanship.

CHAPTER 17
No opposition, please

"Every man wishes to be wise, and they who cannot be wise are almost always cunning."

Dr. Samuel Johnson, *The Idler*, No. 92.

At 9 o'clock on Monday the 23rd of March I arrived at the Ministry of the Interior armed with all the Society's documents, letters and other slips of paper, determined not to leave the building until I had an assurance of support and witnesses in opening a libel action against Evans and Lambertsen. I was not a rich man but out of principle and the sheer joy of wreaking a well-earned vengeance, I was fully prepared to spend my last penny in the civil courts to ensure justice.

I felt convinced that my case was not only morally justifiable, but was clear cut according to the legal code, and would be assured of support in the eyes of the public. Hitherto the epithets of "tyrant" and "dictator" had been indiscriminately thrown at me by the Evans cabal, but who would be seen in the light of tyrants in my single-handed legal combat in such a libel case?

The above must be borne in mind in all my actions which were to follow in pursuing an exclusive resolve in making a weapon of the law, and if extraneous circumstances were to appear to put a different light on my actions, then these were an accident of fate having no connection with my affairs, and therefore, not indicating that I should budge an inch from my single-minded course of action. Certainly all that I was to do, despite the dropping of hints by officials from various Western embassies, was to leave me with no regrets, and if several individuals (of value to their own countries) happened to be sucked into the maelstrom, such accidental misfortune could only be blamed on themselves in that they stood in the way of my personal struggle in an unpleasant feud.

After half an hour's wait I was shown into Mr. Kovero's office and was surprised to be greeted by four other officials, and after handshaking all round the six of us settled at a coffee table at one side of the room.

NO OPPOSITION, PLEASE

The file on the Society, already bulky from the papers of its internal strife, lay on the middle of the table, and several gentlemen took papers from this and passed the folder around. I was not so much flattered as surprised that our Society warranted so much importance and attention, but I was curious and felt that something more serious must be afoot.

"We understand there's been some trouble in this Society of yours, Mr. Corfe," announced one of the officials solemnly.

"We must tell you we regard this as a serious matter," said another looking me in the eye.

"I'm glad of that," I replied, "because I too regard it as most serious."

"I believe you've come here with a complaint," said a third.

I handed him a copy of a letter I had sent to Mr. Kovero the previous Saturday, containing the following passages:- "Regarding the duplicated election circular of the International Society Finland, a copy of which is now in your possession, I should respectfully like to request that you send a letter to Mr. Lambertsen the Vice-Chairman and Mr. Evans, the Secretary of the Society, instructing them to inform members and associate members of the Society, that the statement: 'It became clear that the Finnish authorities would prefer foreigners with long term residence permits in leading positions of the Society' is untrue. ... I should like to request specifically that this instruction be given orally at the General Meeting of the Society on the 25th of March and by written circular to all those persons to whom the said circular was sent."

"I'm afraid we can't involve ourselves in the Society's affairs," said the official.

I felt a twinge of disappointment at this definitive statement.

"Can you tell us something more about your difficulties,?" said another.

I described my struggle of the last weeks with regard to re-election to the Chairmanship, and showed them the alleged libellous circular and the letter from Castrén and Snellman.

"What kind of lawyers are these who send out a letter like this,?" said one of the officials to a colleague. "What do they mean by long term residence permit?"

"They have no authority to see your passport," said another.

"That's your personal document between you, the police and your embassy."

"I don't like it," said the first.

Returning to the libellous circular, I said that in view of the untrue facts included therein and the damage it did my cause, I wished to open a civil libel action supported by witnesses from the Ministry of the Interior to contradict the falseness of the claims.

"I'm afraid government officials couldn't get involved in that," said one. "The regulations are clear and don't require the need for official witnesses."

I was not to take no for an answer and was to doggedly maintain my determination in securing official help in pursuing a libel action against Evans and Lambertsen. If civil servants could not be retained as witnesses then perhaps I could secure assistance of another kind from these government officials, and the interest that was then being shown clearly indicated the possibility of this.

"Who are these people who're against you,?" said the official who was asking most of the questions. I named the Evans cabal, answering questions as to their various personalities.

"They've no right to do this," he said indignantly. "You started the club, and it remains your club alone, and your responsibility until such time as registration has gone through."

The expression of such opinions could not have pleased me more. In the letter to Mr. Kovero of the 16th March I had implied that my wishes should be made to override those of the rebel Committee, but I had not expected to achieve such unanimity of feeling. There now seemed no bar to complete cooperation in destroying the Evans cabal.

"It's all very strange, very strange indeed," said one of the officials thoughtfully.

"We're interested in the ringleader - this man Evans," said another. "We'd like to ask a lot more questions about him. There's another department who're very interested in this man, and if you've time now, we'd like to take you along with us to consider the matter."

The group of us rose and left the room, went down several flights of stairs, departed from the building by a back exit, walked across the courtyard and into another block, and climbed several more flights of stairs. We then stood before a steel door with a black and white enamel plate on which was written the single word, *Suojepoliisi* - Security Police. A bell was rung and we waited. After several moments the door was opened from within, and as we were conducted along several corridors and through antechambers without the exchange of a single word, it became clear that our arrival had been expected.

At the junction of several corridors we came suddenly to a circular hole in the floor, where we were met by another official who led us down a cast iron spiral staircase, and as our feet clattered on the metalwork, I noticed we descended through a reinforced steel and concrete floor some three feet in thickness into what had clearly been constructed as a bombproof building.

In the passageway below there was a bustling of footsteps as numbers of people passed busily to and fro, and as we went towards the end of the corridor, I noticed through the opened doors of the rooms we passed, groups of people in many kinds of dress, from leather jackets to workers overalls to business suits, seated at classroom desks or lounging about, reading papers or just waiting. We had entered into the heart of the Secret City, where schemers, gatherers of illicit information and other mischief makers were to be tracked down and to find their aims annihilated, in the cause of de-escalating rivalry for power amongst quarrelling foreign nations. The secrets of the world that this building held were beyond what the imagination could conceive!

Our group was shown into the spacious office of the head of the department, and after more introductions and handshaking, we were seated on comfortable sofas and in armchairs around the desk of the chief.

"We're very interested in this man Mr. Ronald Evans and would like to know how you first came to meet him," said the chief.

As I began my account, coffee and cakes were brought in and we enjoyed these refreshments in the relaxed atmosphere of the office.

"Now we'll move onto something else," said the chief on my concluding the first account.

He took up a file and I was surprised to see my own name written on the front, and on opening the folder, he passed several papers inside to a colleague on his right. I was astonished to notice newspaper clippings of the letters which had launched the club, and a moment later even more surprised to see clippings from *Viikko Sanomat* and the student paper *Ylioppilaslehti* with regard to an attack I had made on the Helsinki Cooperative Society two years before. The police had a detailed systematic record of the activities I had engaged in since my arrival in the country. Their thoroughness was a marvel to their credit!

"You're the man who doesn't like cooperatives," said the police chief with a smile.

"I understood at the time that the directors of HOK made an official complaint to the police requesting my deportation," I said.

"Who told you that?"

"I was told at the Passport Office on renewing my permits," I answered. "The authorities there seemed to regard the complaint as a joke."

"HOK's big enough to look after itself without trying to get its critics deported," chuckled another of those present.

"I later visited the directors of HOK and gave them an apology which they accepted," I said.

"We know that too," said the police chief with a smile.

"You're not afraid of speaking your mind, are you. I suppose that's a British characteristic."

I did not know whether to take this as a compliment or as a veiled warning to watch my step in the future.

"I think I was justified in attacking HOK," I said.

The attack on HOK arose from an alleged food poisoning episode after dining on a pork chop in the Porthania University restaurant in Hallituskatu, resulting in acute pancreatitis, three weeks hospitalisation, two of them on a drip-feed, six months medication, and loss of earnings.

"Can you tell us why you started the International Society," said the chief.

This I told them.

"How was it you were thrown off the Committee?"

This too I explained factually in great detail. They then concentrated on questioning me on Evans, plainly stating that he was the man who aroused most suspicion.

By this time I began to wonder at the magnitude of the accusations

I had invoked against the Evans clique. Was all this solely the result of the charges I wished to press against the two erring members? Had I so impressed the police with my complaints that they were determined to make a mountain out of a molehill out of any scrap of evidence available? At that moment it seemed as if either I had oversold the gravity of my case, or else, through some fearful mental lapse, that the police were being led astray. My sense of curiosity deepened at the thought that perhaps there really was some mystery or dark plot to be resolved.

"Why do you think this man Evans is against you,?" said the police chief at last.

For a moment I was lost for an answer.

"Personality differences, I suppose," I said at last. "I think Evans is the type of man to whom intrigue is second nature. He's genetically irascible. If he wasn't stabbing *me* in the back, then it would have to be someone else. He's humourless. He can only see the worst in those around him. He's a fussy little man who'll use the slightest pretext in the contravention of any rules or regulations in an attempt to destroy an adversary. He's envious, he's incompetent himself, but he doesn't like ability in others if it casts a shadow on his own light. Those are my opinions. That's all I can say."

"Has Evans ever discussed politics?"

"Never - apart from passing references."

"Such as what?"

"He said a lot of German Nazis were moving into Helsinki and had begun exploding bombs here."

The group laughed.

"Who did he say this to?"

"To the Committee, at a party, following a meeting at Enblom's flat."

"What was the reaction to this?"

"Scoffing laughter."

"So you think Evans is against you for personal reasons," said one of the group.

"I have no evidence for otherwise," I said.

"We think the reasons are political," said another significantly.

"We think this is part of a conspiracy."

"You see, Mr. Corfe, this is exactly how the Communists operate," said another official. "They cunningly infiltrate an innocent organisation; drive out the old leaders; put in their front men for maintaining appearances - that's your Rowland Hill or whatever his name is - and then use the club as a cover association for their own purposes."

I said nothing. These suspicions seemed so wildly incredible and without foundation, that at that time and for some weeks afterwards I felt sure that the police were leading themselves astray in a misplaced enthusiasm, or were deceived in seeing Reds under the beds, possibly through lack of employment in their special duties. The reader of this book may see otherwise, but then he (or she) knows its subject matter in advance. It must be remembered that until that time Evans had aroused no suspicion amongst any of his colleagues on the Committee as to actual law-breaking - not even from that of his most ardent adversary.

Even when he was most disliked, he still conveyed the impression of the fussy careful basically law-abiding little man who would never risk involving himself in trouble with the law. He was so prone to giving out criticism that one might too easily suppose that he himself was beyond it, and as for suspecting that he could be involved in the crime for which he was eventually charged, this was quite beyond the realm of the imagination. After all, spies are only people one reads about in newspapers and books - one doesn't rub shoulders with them in real life - or at least, hardly ever.

"We'd like you to assist us in our investigations, Mr. Corfe," said the police chief.

"I'd be only too pleased to assist in any project in fighting the Evans cabal," I replied without fully understanding the wide-ranging implications behind my commitment.

"Would you object if we asked you to cooperate with one of our detectives,?" said another.

"Not at all," I replied.

"We must make one thing absolutely clear," said the police chief. "Your cooperation with us is purely voluntary. You don't have to answer any questions we put to you, and neither are you under any other obligation."

"I believe we can see eye to eye in wishing to pin down Evans, and since I can't expect any other kind of help from you in pursuing my libel action, I'll be happy to cooperate with you in any way if it assists my personal cause."

At that time I was still convinced that the police must be terribly wrong in their intuition, for investigations are often made without culminating in criminal proceedings, but I hoped beyond all else that I was wrong in my conclusions.

On leaving the Security police, I rushed to Castrén and Snellman's, for it was already passed noon, and I was immediately ushered into Bertel Åkermarck's office. He received me politely, but was apprehensive and hesitant, for he knew that I was not to be easily duped by his devious intentions - or those of his client.

"Do you still intend putting up for election to the Chairmanship,?" he asked.

I told him yes, and he requested to see my passport, from which he copied down details of the permits.

"Do you think you've been living in the country long enough to be Chairman,?" he asked diffidently.

"Yes," I replied.

"Is the Society going to be registered,?" he enquired, and this question seemed to indicate that either he was remarkably ill-informed on the Society's affairs, or that he held the opinion that I had an influential sway with the registration authorities.

"I don't know," I replied.

In view of the mounting tension in the Society, and of the determination and ruthlessness of the Evans clique, the occurrence of physical violence had now become a very real possibility at the meeting of the 25th. The most likely tactic would be an attempt to prevent my entering the main hall, possibly with the help of the HISC thugs who were now frequenting the Wednesday night meetings, and who were invariably unfriendly to the point of rudeness if not arrogant towards me.

To intercept the likelihood of violence I enquired as to the possibility of police protection, and accordingly visited the Chief of police for Traffic and Public Order at their headquarters in Sofiankatu.

If I could persuade the chief to post a detachment of uniformed constables in the premises of the Society in the same way as constables were placed in public dance halls to ensure public order, I felt the awe that this would inspire might considerably dampen any extraordinary measures that the Evans clique would entertain. I was shown through a number of palatial rooms through double doors into the office of the Chief of Police who was impressively dressed in the uniform of the highest-ranking officer in the force.

He was a towering figure, almost seven feet tall, and he motioned me to sit in the leather-upholstered chair in front of his desk. He listened to my story with sympathy and interest, and his impeccable manners and mode of conversation displayed him as a man of high intelligence and culture. He regretted, however, that it would not be possible to place a contingent of his men in the premises of our club that night, firstly because the premises were private; secondly, because our General Meeting would be of a private nature not open to non-members; thirdly, as our Society was a private association at no time open to the general public; and fourthly, because as tenants we could not have police posted in the building without the knowledge and permission of the landlords. Police could only be posted in a public building if there was thought to be the risk of riot or disorder, but he assured me that if an affray did occur that night at the club then the police could be called in by request to break it up.

At 8 o'clock I arrived at the Society accompanied by my valued helper, Mrs. Anja Hytönen, armed with duplicated election circulars I had prepared in her office, together with all papers pertaining to the Society's progress. Tonight would be one of historic decision! On taking a copy of the duplicated list of those for election and re-election, I was angered at noticing that my name had not been included, although there were the names of four Soviet diplomats amongst those of other East Europeans, one Indian, an Arab, a Frenchman, and two Americans in addition to Finns. Most surprising of all was the fact that four members had been co-opted onto the Committee for re-election, when they had never been nominated at any time previously, two of whom stood out significantly: Mr. Rowland G.P. Hill (the new and "legalistic" Chairman) and Mr. Eric Jakowleff, who had only once shown his face on the Society's premises and who had sought to destroy the club almost at the time of its inception.

"Why isn't my name on this circular,?" I asked Rowland Hill.

"There was a legal hitch - it'll be explained at the meeting," he answered nonchalantly.

"We'll see about this," I said. "Your lawyer, Bertel Åkermarck, seemed to confirm everything as correct."

A control was supposedly placed at the entrance to ensure that only members were allowed into the club that night, but as the hall filled, I noticed many faces that had never been there before, whilst a number of regular - and particularly Finnish - members were absent, it is to be assumed out of disgust at the corruption and unpleasantness of the previous weeks. The HISC group were there in number. I began to hand out my two page election circular.

With regard to the Constitution it contained the following amongst other remarks: "Mr. Corfe feels that the Constitution now awaiting the approval of the authorities is undemocratic and therefore unsatisfactory in serving the needs of the Society. ... A member who wishes to bring up a matter before the Society, must put it in writing and submit it to the Committee who must be given due time to consider the matter. No time limit is given as to how long the Committee might be entitled to shelve a matter. This clause leaves the way open for the Committee to exert arbitrary power in the running of the Society whilst greatly restricting the freedom of individual members. For example, there is no stipulation safeguarding the right of a member to put a matter on the agenda of a general meeting. It is rather unusual to find such a clause in the constitutions of societies in Finland."

Evidence that the HISC group had been prompted in advance as to the attitude they should adopt could be gauged by the heat of their feelings almost as soon as they came into the hall. Several crumpled my circular and threw it contemptuously onto the floor without even glancing at its general content. One of the group, a moody reticent American who went by the name of John, an employee of the Academic Bookshop, a Communist sympathiser and an alleged World War II deserter, tore up my circular with a threatening oath.

"Perhaps you'ld like to discuss your grievances outside," I said.

He followed me towards the foyer - I had no more idea than to give him a piece of my mind - but Rowland Hill, anticipating violence, grabbed him by the shoulder and firmly told him (but in a comforting tone as if to indicate that things would finally work out all right) to return to his seat, and this the American did.

The Evans clique were all smiles and friendliness, as usual when there was some evil afoot, except for Evans himself who gave me a wide berth. Only Gösta betrayed any feelings of resentment: "You're not my friend any more," he said. "I've got better things to do that sitting all day in a police station. I'm a respectable businessman. I don't run people down in the street. And anyway, I've got proof and witnesses that I was nowhere near Pitkänsillanranta at the time."

No meeting could have been better rigged. It began with the reading of a prepared report viciously attacking me on grounds that I had exerted a tyrannical control over the Society, and had sent out letters without due authorisation, and had prevented the infusion of new blood onto the Committee. None of the accusations were factually supported as indeed they could not be as they were baseless. My interruptions were shouted down by the Committee with the reminder that question time came later.

Several other prepared statements were then read out followed by the presentation of a long document entitled, "The Eligibility of Foreign Citizens for Membership To The Board of The Society," signed by Bertel Äkermarck, and as if to underline its emphasis, thrice read in Finnish, Swedish and English. Mrs. Evans read the Finnish version and Mr. Lambertsen the English, and as if to make sure that I fully understood its import, he looked me in the eye from the far end of the hall, and read it in the manner of a judge passing a death sentence on a sheep stealer.

The sixth and concluding paragraph of the document read as follows: "As regards Mr. Corfe's candidature to Chairman of the Board it must be noted that according to the said rules the Chairman signs the name of the Society. As Mr. Corfe's residential permit is valid until 18.3.1965 and thus is not at the date of the election valid for the required period of more than one year, my opinion is, that Mr. Corfe cannot be elected Chairman or other member of the Board with the right to sign the name of the Society. ... Helsinki, 24th March 1964."

This was such an outrageous piece of pettifogging nonsense that it had to be answered at once and I raised my objection.

"There'll be time for questions later," exclaimed Rowland Hill.

"Question time is now," I answered.

"We've overrun our time and we've put question time after the interval."

"But that's after the election," I cried, "and nobody is going to have an opportunity to discuss any points beforehand."

"That's how it's being arranged," said Rowland Hill.

"Stop trying to wreck our meeting," said Mr. Lambertsen.

"What kind of meeting is this,?" I cried. "It's irregular by any standards. The floor are being denied any effective opportunity to participate."

I protested forcefully that I should be allowed to put my case now before any further proceedings, and at last Rowland Hill said, "You can speak now, but only for five minutes. No member will be allowed longer."

"That's impossible," I answered, "in view of all the evidence I have to present."

An Indian member, a Brahman from Calcutta married to a niece of von Etter, intervened in the dispute.

"It's a pity to have all this quarrelling, and as a new member I don't know what it's all about," he began, "but I do know that Mr. Corfe started the Society, and it would seem fair if he was given a proper opportunity to speak."

This was met by murmurs of agreement throughout the hall, and Rowland Hill sensing the mood suggested that I be allowed to speak for seven minute periods after which a vote would be taken before authorising me to continue, and this was agreed. I spoke for thirty-five minutes: attacking the Constitution for its undemocratic content; describing what I had done for the Society; explaining how unfair was the accusation that I had ruled the Society tyrannically in view of the fact that I had been obliged to take over the duties of sick or otherwise ineffective members; and outlining the dishonest and cowardly scheming by which I had been victimised by the Evans cabal.

After every seven-minute period, except for the last, I was granted permission to continue by a unanimous vote, but then through my own foolishness, I fell into the trap of negating further sympathy. In mounting my attack on the irregularities of the rebel Committee, I made a passing reference to police disapproval of such tactics, and that their weight might be added in refusing registration, and some minutes later, there were shouts of "No!" in reply to a further vote on my right to speak.

As soon as I had sat down, Rowland Hill stood up and delivered the following little speech: "There've been many slighting references tonight to our Secretary, Mr. Ronald Evans, and these have hurt him a great deal. I've been asked to inform the meeting that he's not only an entirely respectable person but that on three occasions the Finnish authorities have offered him Finnish citizenship. These offers he modestly declined, but do you suppose for a moment that if he was in the bad odour of the police, as Mr. Corfe has clearly indicated tonight, that they would have been made in the first instance? I want you all, ladies and gentlemen, to give your full support tonight to our valued Secretary, Mr. Ronald Evans."

This was followed by some feeble clapping. The story of the declined citizenship sounded to me as absurd as Caesar's thrice-times boasted rejection of the crown. The election went off without a hitch, but the results of voting for the Chairmanship were interesting: for Mr. Rowland Hill: 14; against: 12; abstentions: 32. My fight proved a moral even if not a tactical victory, and the following day, whilst discussing the matter with Mrs. Hytönen in her office, I decided to continue the struggle.

"You must go on," she urged. "You must send a letter to the registration authorities requesting they withhold approval of the Society until a proper founding meeting has been held. The Committee were not even properly elected according to their own rules for the Society, and as for yourself, you were illegally prevented from standing for election."

We then drafted another letter to the authorities.

CHAPTER 18
Only an April fool

"Well skilled in cunning wiles, he could make white of black and black of white."
(Furtum ingeniosus ad omne, candidor de nigris et de candentibus atra Qui facere Adsueret.)

Ovid, *Metamorphoses*, Bk. XI, 1.313.

As yet I had little idea of the incredible slanders and unbelievable lies that the HISC group were circulating throughout the foreign community in Helsinki out of pure hatred and malice, but these slowly reached my ear one way or another. The significance of their danger to my cause in Western diplomatic circles can only be fully appreciated when it is understood that certain leaders amongst their group who were closely connected with the American embassy had allied themselves to the Evans cabal, and both this cabal and the HISC group of its own volition, were aiming a two-pronged stab in the back to bring my downfall.

Geoff Gee, the main slanderer (although not a frequent visitor to our Society) was the artist and interior designer who had recently completed decorating the marines' mess and then the bar of the embassy according to the specifications of His Excellency the Ambassador, Mr. Cullen. At least five members of the HISC group (all of them British), regularly drank in the US marines' mess on Saturday nights until the early hours of the following morning, and most recently, Geoff Gee had begun drinking on Saturdays with the affable, Mr. Cullen, referring to the ambassador as his "old mucker."

The exchange of *mis*information between these two, together with the file accumulating weird and disconnected facts which must have been hidden away on some shelf in the deepest recesses of the Pentagon, filled me with horror. Following the Society's rigged meeting, even Ray Reed began to appear regularly at the Wednesday meetings, and this despite all the despicable things he had once said about the club.

Two days after the election an unpleasant incident occurred on Friday night in the Insinööritalo restaurant. I was drinking with Martin

Summerhill, Rolf Erlewein and several other friends, when we were disturbed in our discussion by interruptions from a neighbouring table, occupied by a group of HISC members and an abusively drunken marine. The group occupied a cabinet divided only by a curtain from the main room, and after some time, they became increasingly rowdy, and the curtain was drawn back and the marine began hurling abuse at those at the nearby table. On at least one occasion, the uniformed doorman had threatened to eject the group if they failed to keep their voices down, and then the head waitress refused to serve them with more liquor.

The marine rolled on his chair, as with a blurred countenance he eyed me insultingly, but as so often occurs with those in an inebriated state, he soon began throwing out opinions and suspicions that might never have passed his lips had he remained sober. I had encountered the marine on previous occasions and disliked him. For one thing, he was surprised and jealous that as a self-employed language teacher I earned more than he did as a low-ranking soldier; and for another, as with so many of his countrymen, he was insensitive to the environment of the country in which he was privileged to be posted as a guest.

At last he moved over to our table, and after abusively insulting behaviour and veiled inferences as to my past, he then dropped references of a more specific kind. His drunken arrogance was an embarrassment to us all, and we dared not contradict or antagonise him, for fear of being involved in a fracas which might culminate in us all being ejected from the restaurant. The head waitress continued to observe us critically, and her discretion alone gave her police authority to ensure our expulsion if we raised our voices to an undesirable level, and so we could only humour the drunken marine.

"I hear you was chucked out of England," he exclaimed. Then he continued, "You'd never get into the United States - not in a lifetime. The United States government would never allow you further than the entry checkpoint. The United States has got you taped for every evil day of your evil life. We've got you down as a Red. You're a filthy lousy Commie!"

Several of my friends tentatively put in an allusively defensive remark such as, "Why are you picking on him,?" or, "What about yourself,?" but the marine then began to toy dangerously with an empty beer bottle which he swung about. The most painful and unpleasant aspect of the situation was our impossibility to retaliate, for if we were to brawl with a marine, not only would the US embassy have regarded me with an even more critical eye, but the Finnish authorities might have deported us all from the country.

Eventually the cowardly abuse of the marine became so acutely painful to us all, that one of our group, a Bohemian writer called Jean Louis, a French Canadian, teaching at the Quinta Language School, discreetly called me outside into the foyer, where he delivered an impassioned plea for my "good sense" in best safeguarding my interests.

"For God's sake, Bob, get out of this Society - cut yourself off from it. I'm warning you, it'll prove your ruin - there are rumours being spread around Helsinki you could never imagine. You've got enemies here - real big enemies - and you'll get nowhere fighting them. You're a small man, just like me, and you can't hope to take on the world. These people'll stab you in the back - they'll use the filthiest lies - they'll do anything to pull you down. You can't hope to win. Promise me, Bob, cut yourself off from this Society and get out of it."

There were tears in his eyes, but I made no promises, and after we had shaken hands, we returned to our table again. By now the marine had begun to sober up - or at least he realised that he had created such an unpleasant atmosphere and placed himself in such a bad light with his companions - that he began to make amends for his earlier behaviour.

He liked my tie and wanted to exchange it for his, and for a laugh at the table, I agreed to this, and finally he was slapping me on the shoulder and calling me a "great guy." However, my thoughts were elsewhere, and I was more determined than ever to press a libel action against Evans and Lambertsen. What Jean Louis had told me was shocking if true, but it was also an additional argument for the necessity of my cooperating as closely as possible with the Security police in clearing my name from malicious rumours and in vindicating my cause.

On the morning of April 1st the day of our next Wednesday meeting, Mrs. Hytönen came to my flat to say that a Det. Heinonen had phoned, requesting that we visit him that afternoon. We made an appointment for 2.30 pm, and on our way to the Security police, I called in on Äkermarck, picking up photocopies of his unimaginative document frustrating my election to the Chairmanship.

On arriving at the police, we were conducted into the bombproof section of the building, again by the same entry point as before, and we were then shown into a barely furnished room, with only a desk and chair at one end and two chairs placed with their backs to the opposite wall. We waited several minutes and were then introduced to a young police officer called Det. Heinonen, who was to direct an investigation into the affairs of the Society. I soon came to regard this man in the light of a lawyer prosecuting my case in a personal feud with an arch-enemy. Mrs. Hytönen and I placed before him all the evidence for our grievances, and again I related the story of our Society.

"There's something very strange about this Society," he said, "and I want it watched very carefully. You might witness some interesting happenings there within the next few weeks."

I assured him of my closest cooperation.

"I want the names of all members and guests," he continued.

"You have a list of members on the desk," I said.

"And I want a report of who associates with who and an account of anything strange or unusual. Almost anything could prove a vital clue in our investigations."

After one and a half hours we left, and I dined with Mrs. Hytönen in a luxury restaurant to celebrate the recruit of what we considered an intelligent and invaluable ally in our conflict with the Evans cabal.

Two revealing films were shown at the club that night, *Peking Today* and *The Countryside of China*, presented by the embassy of the People's Republic, and the two diplomats who brought along the reels were smartly dressed in the Western style, modest and civil, and each closely observing every action and word spoken by the other. They gave no introduction to the films but agreed to sit informally together and answer questions afterwards. The fun of the evening, however, began after their departure.

Two men arrived at the entrance hall and there was an apparent argument with Gösta Kelter who seemed to be hindering their entry. After some moments Gösta moved to the middle of the room and made the following announcement: "Ladies and gentlemen, I'm afraid we have something rather serious to say. The police have arrived and wish to see identity cards and passports. Would you kindly remain seated whilst they pass around the hall."

There was a stir as everyone glanced round at his neighbour with a quizzical look. The Soviet diplomats reacted with agitation and reached for their pockets until Akulov prompted them to remain calm. Ron Evans was almost petrified by shock, and with his mouth gaping, he moved from one foot to the other without leaving the spot where he stood.

"I say, is this in order,?" said Mr. Rowland Hill moving towards the two men.

"I'm afraid so," said one of the men.

"We've come with a warrant from the Security police," said the other.

"But what's supposed to be the problem,?" said Rowland Hill almost losing his cool.

"They say an undesirable person's infiltrated the Society," explained Gösta.

"It sounds a likely proposition to me," said Rowland Hill. "I've a mind to see my lawyer about this tomorrow."

"Anyone without an identity card will be arrested and taken into custody," said one of the men, and indeed, as they moved around, they picked out certain individuals and asked them to stand by the door, and this they shamefacedly did.

"You can't do this to these people," said Rowland Hill desperately. "I'll go to my lawyer tomorrow. I'll do more than that, I'll go to my embassy!"

"And what about your passport, Sir,?" said one of the men to Rowland.

"I don't carry my passport about with me."

"Then we'll have to take you into custody as well."

"But this is outrageous,!" exclaimed Rowland.

As soon as the two men had been around the hall, they moved into the centre of the room, took off the hats they wore, whilst one of them exclaimed: "Ladies and gentlemen, it's the first of April! We wish you an enjoyable time and all the fun in the world."

"It's bad luck to play an April fool after twelve o'clock," said someone.

There was a murmur of relief and some sickly laughter, and before the two men departed, I perceived Ron Evans wipe some beads of sweat from his forehead.

"Ladies and gentlemen," began Gösta Kelter once again, "that was only an April fool, and I hope that my partners from the office didn't frighten any of you too much. Now in all seriousness, let me assure you that we are a respectable Society and we its members are respectable people. During the past weeks there has been too much irresponsible talk about the police, and too much talk about informers and spies visiting our club. Let me assure you that the police have no interest in our Society, and let me for the last time assure you that this is not a place the police would have any interest in visiting. We are all nice people only out to enjoy ourselves with our innocent pleasures. Thank you for your attention - and have a good evening!"

This speech was punctuated with cries of, "Here, here,!" murmurs of complacent self-satisfaction, and its conclusion was met with loud applause.

"I'll endorse everything Mr. Kelter has told us," said Rowland Hill taking up the same topic. "We're an entirely respectable group of people who are only here to share each other's culture, and to enjoy our harmless games and amusements. It's only some of us are obsessed by the police," he continued dropping an innuendo in my direction, "but the rest of us can carry on in the satisfaction of our own clear consciences."

This was met with laughter and applause. Some minutes later I overheard Ron Evans remark to Anders Enblom: "I can take a joke, but that was too much. Someone should have stopped him - it might have caused an incident with our diplomatic friends and then we'd have really been in trouble."

The rest of the evening was occupied in childish games conducted by Mr. Kelter, and it seemed as if his companions and he were intent on creating a false jollity by way of suppressing any suggestion that they had gone too far, or to counteract a feeling of uneasiness which might have been created through their prank. I could not refrain a smile as I watched grown men and women pass oranges from under each other's chins, tittering in such a way as if this was their merriest hour.

As I circulated amongst members, a Dr. Olof Lille, a distinguished white-haired gentleman, approached me, and with a strange smile, remarked, "I understand from Mr. Evans you left Sweden in unusual circumstances some years ago."

"I can assure you that anything Evans told you was untrue," I replied.

"Why is it that all you Englishmen hate each other,?" he asked. "You're abroad and you should all get on well together. You should be friendly and help one another, but instead of that, you stab each other in the back and spread hatred. I can't understand it."

"That's a difficult question to answer," I said, "but I think you should ask the troublemakers themselves."

Dr. Lille's allusive remark to the circumstances in which I left Sweden was proof enough that Evans was guilty of slander, and I decided to penetrate deeper into what he meant at our next meeting, but he never came again. He was the same man, incidentally, who had asked that pithy question of Mr. Bauer of the Kulturzentrum as to why there stood a Wall in Berlin.

On the 8th of April Mr. A.A. Camara, Second Secretary of the Brazilian embassy presented a film and a most interesting programme about his country. The film was followed up by a talk and then a discussion and a lengthy question time. Since the previous week I now attended the Society as an ordinary member and could fully partake of the social and cultural facilities offered by the club, and on this particular evening, I asked numerous questions showing especial interest in the possibilities of opening a business in Brazil.

At the end of the programme, Mr. Akulov approached me and suggested that we might meet for lunch at Königs restaurant tomorrow, and I happily accepted the invitation. Königs was one of the older and better restaurants in the city centre, situated in Mikonkatu, and I met Mr. Akulov at noon the following day. Again we enjoyed an excellent lunch, but again I was reluctantly obliged to drink great quantities of vodka as well as several bottles of beer.

It was clear that Mr. Akulov enjoyed my company and he began to open a dialectical discussion around my pamphlet, *Towards A Federal Europe*. The only term he really found objection to was my use of "satellite" regarding the Soviet Union's friendly neighbours, and then we moved over to a discussion of the Marxist theory of class warfare, and I forcefully argued that Marx had based his theory on false historical premises, explaining that class conflict in society had only emerged at the time of the Reformation after the gradual breakup of the medieval order. Mr. Akulov gently stated that I was wrong in this, as I was failing to take into consideration the factor of "false consciousness," but he did not push the point too far, and he then steered the discussion to maintaining the balance of power in Europe.

"Now Count Schulenburg - he's such a nice boy - a very nice boy," said Akulov, "but he's so terribly wrong about Germany's place in the world. I've been arguing with him for months now, but he still doesn't see the question in its correct perspective."

Later Akulov returned to the question of my personal future.

"You're very energetic and ambitious. There are very few people like yourself, and you should go a long way. I was very interested in your questions at yesterday's meeting. You carried the evening after the speaker had given his talk. I think you should really go into business, and earn what your ability entitles you to. That's your right!"

Finally, he returned to enquiring as to the circumstances behind my expulsion from the Committee, and then asked searching questions about various Committee members as to my friends and enemies, and I saw no reason for suppressing frank answers.

"And Peter Martin, he's just a funny man - there's nothing serious behind him?"

"Yes, he's a funny man," I said, "but he's been useful to our club as a Social Host."

"I should just accept the situation of your expulsion as a *fait accompli*," he finally concluded in an undertone, and indeed, if he had made an issue of that point, he would have found himself embroiled in a heated argument.

At the end of the meal the waitress brought the folded bill on a saucer and laid it before the diplomat, but I took the saucer, and despite a short tussle of words, insisted on paying the bill that was in excess even of that at the Sillankorva.

"It was my turn," I said, for I regarded Akulov as an equal, and would have felt put out had he succeeded in adopting a patronising attitude, and certainly I should have failed in achieving my ultimate aims with regard to him.

"I'll pay next time," he said.

On leaving the restaurant shortly before three, my head was buzzing as loudly as on the previous occasion I had parted from Mr. Akulov.

"I've got to drive to Lahti now, for a talk I'm giving a working men's association," he said as we stood on the step of the restaurant. "If I didn't have CD plates I wouldn't do it, but that's the advantage of being a diplomat."

As he climbed into his Mercedes and I waved him off, it seemed remarkable that a man could consume so much spirit and yet remain so sober, and as for driving after the consumption of so much alcohol - and such a distance (some seventy miles) - the possibility was beyond my comprehension. Was vodka so much in his blood that to drink it was the Water of life? There was no other answer I could find.

CHAPTER 19
A man is missing

"The Town small-talk flows from lip to lip;
Intrigues half-gathered, conversation-scraps,
Kitchen cabals, and nursery mishaps."

George Crabbe, *The Borough* (1810) Letter 3,
"The Vicar," 1.70.

There was a lower attendance for our French programme on the 15th of April than there had ever been before, but Mr. Rowland Hill positively contributed to this factor by turning away those who failed to give proof of membership. As he stood in the foyer watching a group of Finns arguing with the Subscription Manageress that they had regularly attended meetings in the past, he pompously exclaimed, "This place isn't open to anyone, you know. It isn't the Mässa Halli" (the Earl's Court of Helsinki), and with that they departed.

The character of the club was to change with the emergence of the new Chairman, but although he stood at the entrance with the demeanour of a commissionaire before an exclusive London gaming house, eyeing every arrival, a number of new people still slipped through the net of this stringent control.

Mrs. Evans arrived in a state of apparent excitement that night, and as she began to move busily around conferring with various Committee members, my suspicions were immediately aroused. Where was her husband? Was she acting on his behalf? What was the excitement and the need for all the serious looks and the pensive nodding? Someone suggested he had left the country.

"He's had to return to England - his mother's been taken suddenly ill," explained Anders Enblom.

"I'm sorry to hear that," I said.

"His mother's been ill for a long time," said a friend of Evans who had not been to the club before.

The mysterious and newly elected Pole approached me.

"Where's Evans,?" he asked urgently.

"I don't know," I replied.

A MAN IS MISSING

On the following week the Pole fixed me with an angrily unfriendly countenance, as if I had done him an injury, and then he disappeared and was never seen at the club again.

"What's wrong with Ronald's mother,?" I asked Mrs. Evans, mustering all the sympathy I could.

"I really don't know exactly," she answered vaguely but in such a tone which clearly indicated her thoughts were far removed from my question.

"I hope it isn't too serious," I added.

"It might be necessary to have a temporary or even a new permanent Secretary for the Society," said Rowland Hill to a member. "This is a very critical time for us in view of our registration problems."

During the interval the hall began to buzz with rumours as to the whereabouts of Ronald Evans, for the assembly was filled with one of those intuitive feelings which inexplicably arise when it suspects that something out of the ordinary has occurred. For the first time my suspicions were aroused that perhaps Evans really was involved in an illegal activity. Perhaps he had fled the country to avoid police investigation, and in the light of this, his fear of the police made sense.

That Friday I had my first tip-off from a diplomatic quarter to stay clear of the club. Jim Hammond was an old friend amongst a group of cronies frequenting the Kolme Kreiviä. He was a security guard at the Canadian embassy, a rough diamond of a man, well into his sixties with a well-furrowed complexion, and well liked by all. Often Rolf Erlewein, Martin Summerhill, Peter Martin, and others in our group were invited to parties at his flat, and because of his generosity and the ample thirst of some amongst his companions, his friendship was too easily exploited for his duty free liquor - a bottle of Scotch costing him only four marks whilst in an alcohol shop the price was thirty-five.

He was dressed like a typical North American of his generation with wide-brimmed hats and suits with large lapels, and whenever he appeared in the café a place was made for him at our table, but another American characteristic was his big talk with descriptions of exploits of long ago. It was for this reason that I took everything he said with a pinch of salt, although others would listen with gaping credulity. Martin regarded him almost in a spirit of awe, reminding us that when he ate in our company he was "slumming" after parting from the confidence of His Excellency the Canadian ambassador.

"It's the ambassador who's slumming when he eats with Jim Hammond," I had corrected, "not the other way round."

Sometimes his talk carried him too far and his contentions proved baseless, and this is important to bear in mind in view of his warnings about the Society and my reactions to them. He loved the Finnish women, exclaiming, "Boy, they wouldn't believe me if I told them back home what I do over here. They'd string me up in Canada if I did half the things I do here," and on one occasion, he boasted of having just "screwed" a demure twenty year old girl back at his flat, when she had only left our table five minutes before after sitting with us for two hours. He intimated he knew the secrets of all the great powers, saying that "Castro wouldn't be alive today" if the public knew the real facts behind the Kennedy assassination (but he never actually told us what those facts were); and he was constantly complaining about those "goddam Russky agents" in the guise of cleaners who were always bugging his apartment.

These last contentions soon became a joke amongst us all, even though they may have been based on truth, and sometimes we would exclaim, "Oh, don't spoil their fun by throwing out all those hidden mikes, I'm sure they get some kicks out of what goes on in your apartment, Jim!"

His favourite stories though, were connected with his exploits during the Second World War. "You should have known me thirty years ago - I was really something then." He recounted how shortly after his arrival in England in 1940 some "stuck-up limey RSM with a pace stick began hollering" at him on breaking a "stupid" prohibition against walking across a drill square, and how he met the limey at the other side, and beat the daylights out of him.

"Boy, I got nine months inside the glass house for that," he concluded.

"It's incredible that Jim's got any employment at all with the government," said Peter once. "He's been inside so often for insubordination." But then Peter failed to understand that ruggedly rebellious individualism is placed highly in the North American scale of values. Such behaviour would have been regarded as so intolerable in any European society, that he would have been kept at the very bottom of the social ladder.

Three days after the French evening, Jim took me aside in the Kolme Kreiviä, and glancing around with his characteristically wary expression, like a cowboy waiting for the next draw, to ensure that no one could overhear, he exclaimed, "Stay clear of that Society, Bob. This is top secret - I'm warning you - it's being watched. The police have infiltrated. Things are going on in there you'ld never suspect in a life time. I can't tell you more - it's secret intelligence. Just get out of that Society and stay clear."

This was said with such melodramatic effect that at first I wanted to laugh, but not wishing to offend my friend, who treated such matters with deadly seriousness, I acquiesced and thanked him for the advice. Then I thought that perhaps he was pulling my leg, for the saga of my conflict with the Evans clique was now turning into a bit of a joke amongst the foreign community. During the following few weeks, however, Jim persisted in his warnings, always urging, "Stay clear of that club," and by then I realised he knew more than any of us in our circle, but I maintained that I was morally obliged as the founder of the Society to help "clear up the mess," for it was already rumoured that I was assisting the Finnish Security police.

Jim never questioned me on the activities of the Society, and although I knew he was aware of my contacts with Finnish security, he never referred to that fact or suggested that I should cease cooperation. Further, he never took me deeper into his confidence as to why I should stay clear of the Society, and because of his cryptic attitude, I saw no good reason to heed his advice either for my sake or for the sake of Western intelligence to which he never directly referred. Jim Hammond was a big talker, sometimes a leg-puller, and when he was serious he was far too serious.

Some months later on having learnt a great deal more and seeing the case in perspective, I suspected that perhaps the British embassy or intelligence had approached him with regard to contacting me, in an attempt to remove me from the scene of the club, so that MI6 could move in and have a free field. British intelligence might only have been motivated to do this in view of my contacts with the Finnish authorities, and they might have seen Jim Hammond as a convenient medium for this. If this was the circumlocutionary approach of MI6 then they had failed in their attempt, and some months later it was a failure the results of which they must have deeply regretted. On no occasion did British intelligence approach me directly in any attempt to put a bar between my new allies and I in our struggle to destroy the Evans cabal.

On the following Tuesday I received a message from Mrs. Hytönen to visit Det. Heinonen, and I phoned and made an appointment, and saw him that Wednesday morning at ten, sitting in the same barely furnished room.

"A lot more has happened with regard to that Society of yours since we last met," he said.

"Really,?" I said surprised.

"We're now treating the matter with very grave concern."

"What's happened?"

"Have you heard anything at the club? Did anything strange occur last Wednesday?"

"Not really. Evans wasn't there though."

"Isn't that strange?"

"It is."

"Where do you think he is?"

"I don't know. They say he's returned to England to visit his sick mother."

A disbelieving smile passed over Det. Heinonen's face as he shuffled some papers on his desk.

"I don't believe it," he said slowly. "It's too much of a coincidence. I think he's fled the country. I think he's mixed up in some spy business. - Was there any other talk at the club as to where he might be?"

"No."

"It's all very suspicious. Don't you think so?"

"Yes."

All the while Det. Heinonen was looking me closely in the eye, often with long pauses after an answer and before the formulation of his next question.

"Where do you think he's gone?"

A MAN IS MISSING

"To England, I suppose. There's nowhere else for him."

"I don't think so. I don't think he wants to go there. If he landed in England, the British would put him inside for thirty years. Anyway, not less than twenty."

These words were spoken with such impassioned emphasis in conveying an apparently repressed anger, that they left me stunned with surprise.

"He must have done something pretty big," I said.

"I think he's gone to Russia," said Heinonen. "He'd find his own level there."

"I've no idea where he is."

Heinonen gave me a long searching look.

"Have you been in East Germany,?" he asked.

"Only through it - to and from Berlin."

"Someone's told me you were arrested in East Berlin a year or two back."

"Who,?" I cried angrily at the circulation of yet another ridiculous rumour and wanting to get at the bottom of it.

"Just somebody," said Heinonen with a smile.

"Then it must be one of the HISC group," and I launched out attacking the HISC group, describing the kind of people of whom they were composed, and relating the various slanders and lies they had maliciously spread, and all the while Det. Heinonen was smiling gently at me, enjoying the display of my anger but also as if to suggest that I might be on the wrong track in accusing the HISC members.

I then clarified the origin of such a rumour, explaining that I had been held up at gunpoint in Treptow on the East side of the Wall in August 1963 on walking within the fifty metre limit, but that I had never been taken into custody. I had only been told to move off.

"That's nothing - we don't call that arrest," said Heinonen.

"It was unpleasant enough, having a gun pointing at you," I said.

"And you've never had any other involvement with the East German authorities?"

"Never," I said, "and here's my passport that'll account for all my movements and places of residence during the past six years."

"May I keep this until tomorrow,?" he asked.

"Certainly. I've nothing to hide from anyone."

"You see, some people lead exciting lives and stories are easily made up about them," he said thumbing through the pages of my passport, "and you seem to be one of them."

"I've never looked for excitement," I pleaded. "It's just come my way - by chance."

"Mr. Corfe, can I - and you don't have to answer me on this - can I ask what your politics are?"

"Certainly," I said. "That's no secret, but it would take a long time."

"That doesn't matter. We have time."

I began to outline my radical and individual political convictions: my belief in a society based on justice and equality of opportunity, and free from the destructive psychological barriers of class differences. I expressed the conviction that a society divided by a dual left and right wing party system could only strengthen class prejudices and feeling, and eventually would prove morally and economically destructive to that country. I praised proportional representation within a multi-party system, as in Finland, or better still government by referenda as in Switzerland as contributing towards the building of a more genuinely democratic community. I expressed my belief that democratic government was only of value as an instrument in serving the democratic aims of society, and that if it failed in this, it was sterile.

I emphasised my belief that what was of most significance in maintaining the morale and stability of a community was the criteria of its ultimate values, and I praised Education as the ultimate Scandinavian value, and Work as the German value, in contributing towards the success and happiness of their peoples, contrasting them with the British value of "Image," which was degenerate and could prove destructive. I was soon to learn, however, that the open expression of these political ideals was not what Det. Heinonen required, and that my lecture was only confusing the issue.

"That's very interesting," he said at last, "but where does your sympathy lie - take your own country - with the Conservative or the Labour party?"

"I'm equally against both parties."

"Then you're a Liberal."

"I'm just as much against them."

He was perplexed, and I was soon to learn that a person whose politics could not be neatly packaged and labelled, is likely to arouse misunderstanding.

"And now what about foreign politics? Are your sympathies pro-American or pro-Russian?"

"I'm neutral," I replied, trusting that the expression of such a sentiment could hardly give rise to objection in a neutral country. Det. Heinonen was not to be satisfied.

"How do you mean?"

"I believe in Europe - in the creation of a third world power bloc serving her own interests."

"That's what you argued in your talk on the 15th of January, and it interested me in you"

"Did you know about that?"

"It told me you were a political animal. Go on."

I expatiated on Europe at some length, describing how I felt above all else a European, with loyalties to Europe in everything she meant in terms of culture and civilisation. I argued that the ethos of American and Russian civilisation were two deviations in opposite directions away from the true norm of Europeanism. Again Det. Heinonen tried to penetrate deeper in forcing a commitment one way or the other - East or West - but I stubbornly maintained I was neutral with regard to the world's greatest ideological conflict.

"But you must have some feelings," he insisted. "You're British. Now in your country you have a phrase, 'blood is thicker than water' - surely that means something in terms of the American NATO alliance and Britain's place in the world."

"Power politics isn't always coextensive with the social and cultural needs of peoples," I said.

At last Det. Heinonen became impatient, and then he rose from the desk exclaiming, "I think you're a Communist,!" and he stormed out of the room slamming the door behind him. I was left alone for some minutes in the silent and empty room, filled with horror at the response that all my talk had achieved. A Communist! No one - apart from a drunken marine - had ever thrown such an epithet in my face before. I loathed Communism and I loathed Marxism in their every manifestation; in their undermining the natural bonds in society and the value of the individual. The only Socialism for which I felt any sympathy were the ennobling ideals of St. Simon, Robert Owen, Carlyle, Ruskin, William Morris, and their brethren. Then I realised Heinonen must be joking - using a tactical device - for no one but a madman could throw such an accusation at me, and I understood the purpose of his examination and the way I had frustrated his task.

After five minutes he returned to the room. I assumed he had been changing the tape recording our discussion.

"I'm sorry about that," he said. "Now tell me, are you pro-American or pro-Russian?"

"If you put a gun to my head, I'm pro-American," I answered.

"Good, that's just what I wanted to hear," he said relieved, "and now we can work together. So you're pro-Western?"

"Most certainly."

"That's the only basis we talk together in the future. That'll be our investigation into the International Society. I think there's a Communist plot in the Society, and that's what we'll set out to prove."

On leaving the Security police that afternoon, I went for a long walk around Kaivopuisto and the South harbour to reflect on all that had happened that morning, and for the first time, I realised that something was seriously wrong in regard to the International Society I had been responsible for establishing. One thing was clear: it was for me to assist the police to the best of my ability in extirpating the evil which had somehow penetrated the club. This was a moral issue!

That night attendance at the club was lower even than on the previous Wednesday, and there was a curious atmosphere that something was amiss. There was none of the relaxed amiability as usually at the club, and there was an awareness that everyone was watching his neighbour. Mr. Rowland Hill and I exchanged a few polite words, but as we stood in the foyer greeting members, guests and newcomers, there was a suspicion that kept us worlds apart. There was no more conflict in the club and no resentment, and together with the cordiality and smiles which marked my outward relationship with the rebel Committee members, there was an icy coldness which destroyed the possibility for any natural riposte between us.

As we stood there, Rowland and I, a tall lean man with a sallow complexion and jetblack hair, well greased and brushed back, came into the club and approached the subscription table.

"Are you a member, Sir,?" enquired Rowland Hill striding forward.

"I'm a close personal friend of Mr. Evans," said the new arrival drawing out a card. "This is my first time here and I'ld like to join the club."

Give him an application form," said Rowland peremptorily to the Subscription Manageress.

I introduced myself to the newcomer as the founder of the Society and wished him every enjoyment in our midst. He was to be a regular member, not missing a single forthcoming event, and he threw himself into the spirit of our festivities as if he had always been amongst us. He handed me his card: Mr. Eric Cross.

"So you're a friend of Ronald. Do you know where he is,?" I asked him. "I hope nothing's happened to him."

"I understand he's returned to England for a fortnight," said Mr. Cross, "to look after his mother."

"I hope he won't have to stay too long," I said. "The Society needs its Secretary."

"That'll depend on how ill his mother is. She's very old now."

"It's a long way to go to nurse one's mother. I hope she isn't too sick."

"Ronald was always very attached to his mother. He's a good son."

"I'm sure he is."

"I'm particularly interested in meeting Ronald's friends. He's told me so much about the club."

"We're all his friends. Come into the hall and join the others."

Mr. Cross began to circulate. He was an enigmatic personality: friendly yet also withdrawn in a way that was odd. I disliked him from the first, despite his amiability that I returned in kind, but perhaps my feelings stemmed from the prejudice aroused through his friendship with

Mr. Evans.

Before the start of the programme, I noticed Mr. Cross sitting beside Sokolov, both steeped in an interested discussion, and after several weeks, it soon became clear they had formed a close and inseparable friendship, for the one was never seen without the other. So that's why he's here, I said to myself, he's come to take Evans' place - although I had never remembered seeing Evans in conversation with Sokolov.

That evening there was an American programme presented by Mr. Lauri Noriela, Chairman of the ASLA Alumni Association, but he rushed so quickly through the colour slides he had come to show, that he clearly wanted to be out of the building as quickly as possible. At the end of his illustrated talk on a, *Journey Through The USA*, he hurriedly packed up his belongings, dropped a curt apology into the ear of the Chairman, and then dashed out of the building without a word to another person. The American embassy did a good job in frightening him off, I thought.

The next morning I was back with Det. Heinonen for I had agreed to visit him on the morning following every meeting of the Society with a full report.

"Anything interesting last night? Anyone new,?" he asked.

"This suspicious weirdo turned up," I said throwing Cross's card onto Heinonen's desk. "He spent the evening in close consultation with one of the Soviet diplomats."

"What did you make of him?"

"It struck me he was at the club for a purpose. He said he was a close friend of Evans. Perhaps he's continuing his work."

"Perhaps he's from the other side," said Heinonen.

"What do you mean?"

"A British agent."

"I would hardly think so."

"Thanks for the card. We'll see."

Heinonen then moved on to enquiring about the various Soviet and other diplomats who had visited the Society, and in the course of our discussion, I casually remarked I had dined with Akulov.

"Have you been with Akulov,?" exclaimed Heinonen jumping up

Haiko, formerly the palatial country home of Waldemar von Etter overlooking the Gulf of Finland, where at a weekend party information was passed between Soviet and Western intelligence agents. Today the villa is the luxury Haikon Kartano Hotel.

from his desk.

"Yes, why?"

"He's the most dangerous man in Helsinki. He's the bane of every Western embassy."

"Why?"

"He's the top Soviet intelligence agent in the country. He's the king of the KGB."

"If that's true, then why don't you kick him out?"

"Because it's one of those things that everybody knows and nobody can prove. He's a highly dangerous man. What did you discuss with him?"

"We didn't discuss party politics."

"That's what everyone says."

"I don't see how he could be dangerous to me. I stood my ground with him all right."

"He's a clever man. Akulov can have people working for him before they know it. - Why do you think he took you out to lunch?"

"I don't know. He said to discuss the Society."

"Akulov doesn't take people out for lunch with him just for a cosy chat."

"Then why do you think he asked me out?"

"He probably had a job in mind for you. He's got lots of jobs going."

"What kind of jobs."

"Cover jobs. He can set-up people in any kind of business - possibly anywhere in the world - and then put them to his own use. - How often have you met him?"

"Twice."

"Don't meet him again. You're always doing very suspicious things, Mr. Corfe."

"I've come along this morning to help contradict that impression," I said opening my briefcase. "I'm a one hundred per cent respectable and law-abiding citizen and here's the proof. I told you I had nothing to hide. Look, here are my tax papers; my account books with all my earnings; and here are my diaries for the past two years."

"I don't really need all this," said Det. Heinonen smiling.

"Yes, go through it - satisfy yourself."

"Well, only to satisfy you. You mustn't be worried by everything I say though. I'm paid for being suspicious."

"In the diaries you'll see the dates and times I met and parted from Akulov and everyone else for that matter."

"It's useful to keep a diary. I'll bring it back to you tomorrow. It could be useful in investigating the Society. - Getting back to something else, when you were in Berlin last summer, did you beat up your landlord?"

"I certainly did not," I replied angrily. "Who's been telling you these nonsensical stories? Is this the HISC group again?"

"No, they're not involved," said Heinonen with a teasing smile. "It's just something I heard from a little bird."

"Who?"

"Wouldn't you like to know," replied Heinonen enjoying my discomfort.

"It's true I had a dispute with my landlord and I had to call in the police to settle it. The facts are I gave statutorily sufficient notice of vacating my room when my landlord seized my skis and camera in lieu of the following month's rent. The police recovered my possessions and I went to stay with friends. That's all there is to it. - I'll tell you another rumour too. They're saying I was kicked out of Sweden for drug-trafficking."

"I know," said Heinonen smiling.

"You know.!" I cried. "Then why don't you do something to stop the slander?"

"Don't worry about that, Mr. Corfe. We have friendly relations with the Swedish police, and if there was any truth in the suspicion you'd been handling drugs, you'd never have been allowed into the country."

"I'm not worried about what *you* think - it's everyone else in Helsinki."

Det. Heinonen smiled, pausing.

"Mr. Corfe, if you and I cooperate to destroy this enemy of yours, Ronald Evans, then perhaps these stories'll just whither away."

"If we find him, that is."

"I think we will. He hasn't the money to go far."

"I'll tell you another rumour going the rounds of Helsinki. They say I'm intending to flee the country. I heard that one the first time in the Kolme Kreiviä, two nights ago."

"I've heard that one too, Mr. Corfe," said Det. Heinonen with a smile.

CHAPTER 20
Festivity macabre

> "Ay, now the plot thickens very much upon us."
>
> George Villiers, 2nd Duke of Buckingham, *The Rehearsal*, Act III, Sc. 2.

To help counteract the damaging effect of the wild rumours circulating through the foreign community of Helsinki with regard to my mysterious past, I decided it would be a good move to approach the embassies of the leading Western powers and tell them all by way of clearing my name. At the same time I hoped that they might also throw some light as to the whereabouts of Ron Evans, for his disappearance was now forming an uncanny impression in my mind.

But how to do this with discretion without attracting the attention of clerks, doormen and all the other minor personnel of the embassies before finally reaching the confidential closets of the consuls? This was an important question. The embassies were staffed with at least some Finnish nationals, who could well be informers for their own country, and I dared not at this stage risk any action which might undermine the trust of my new friends and allies at the Ministry of the Interior.

The reception counter at the Consular Section of the British embassy, for example, had for years been manned by a gorgon of a woman who had won a fearsome reputation amongst Britons and foreigners alike for frightening enquirers and keeping nuisances away from the Consul, and she was a Finn, although her manner and speech and even appearance were so English - so officiously civil-service like - that no one would have suspected it unless they had been told.

She doubtless projected the image expected of her by the embassy and she was doubtless valued as a most efficient employee, but for my liking she knew too much about everybody's business, and then again, she was a Finn and to my mind a too risky barrier to pass through before reaching the confidence of the Consul. Demure little Finnish girls would approach the large glass window behind which was the domain she ruled, to be discouraged by a sharp, "You can't work in England without a permit from the Home Office," or, "We can't help you, you must do that yourself," whilst Britons would be met by, "What do you want to see the Consul about - he's a very busy man?" Every Briton had a right to see the Consul on a confidential matter without the obligation of having to explain his or her business to a third party, but that was a right I was unprepared to declare in the delicate situation I found myself.

It was then that I remembered the Rev. Masters, Chaplain to the embassy, and it seemed he might be a suitable medium to approach in conveying all that I had to say to the upper echelons of the embassy staff. Peter Martin, who loved to insinuate himself into the better circles, frequently attended the Sunday morning services of the English Church which were followed by coffee, and most lately he had been approached there with the question, "What do you know about this International Society,?" to which he had replied, "I know nothing at all about it," for after my expulsion from the Chairmanship, and possibly also, after a tip-off from his good friend, Jim Hammond, he had decided to cut off his last links with the club. The Sunday services clearly offered an opportunity for the exchange of gossip or an approach to the embassy staff, and I finally decided to take advantage of this for it meant that I had no need to go anywhere near the embassy building.

The Rev. Masters was a large rotund man, amiable and gregarious with a resonant voice, good-humoured, well-liked - the personification of the priestly prototype. Sometimes he ate in the Kolme Kreiviä where we enjoyed his company at our table, and Martin Summerhill remarked that he was the only Englishman in Helsinki who spoke a "fine Johnsonian English," and indeed his figure and the ideals he expressed conjured up an impression of the great lexicographer.

He was especially liked by Peter Martin, but the Chaplain gave the clown of the International Society short shrift when it came to an exchange of opinions. Peter would change like a chameleon to reach the confidence of the man whose trust he sought - there was no hypocrisy of which he was incapable - and after the baptism of his son that February (Jim Hammond had been godfather), he began to expatiate with indignation on the alleged "generosity" of the younger generation of Finnish women, to which the Rev. Masters had aptly replied, "I would describe you as a very typical co-respondent type." This sharp rebuke, however, was not to upset Peter's liking for the man, and he continued to attend the Sunday services, "to gather his thoughts," as he expressed it, and as soon as he had been sounded out there on the question of the International Society, he told me immediately.

"The embassy's curious - they want to know what goes on there, but I disclaimed all knowledge of the place," he said.

"That was foolish," I replied. "They must know you were mixed up in the business."

"They did keep on at me, but I don't want any further involvement in it," he said. "I'm sick of the name of Evans and the whole damned Society. It might be a good idea for you to go along there though. You might be able to tell them something useful."

Shortly after I realised it might be to my benefit to make contact with the embassies, I decided to attend the next service of the English Church that was situated in an old apartment block in Fredrikinkatu. As I made my way to the church that Sunday morning, I realised that the Rev. Masters might well be a more suitable man to approach for more reasons that I had previously anticipated. He was at that time the man with the largest Anglican bishopric in the world, being responsible for the souls of every Church of England member in Finland and Soviet Russia from her Western frontier to the Pacific Ocean five thousand miles to the East, and for this reason, it was sometimes necessary for him to visit that other flock in Moscow, but most recently, the Soviet authorities had inexplicably frustrated his returning to his other congregation, and a diplomatic tussle had followed because of this, but still to no avail.

If the Soviet authorities had grounds for a genuine grouch (and who could bring proof to the contrary?), then possibly the Chaplain was in some remote way involved with British intelligence, and if this was so, there could be no better man to approach with my story than the Rev. Masters.

The Church service was a suitably English event, some thirty or forty conventionally-dressed people including married couples and children, crowded into pews in a small room; and as the congregation mumbled through the prayers with a self-effacing sincerity, I could not help being struck by two over-dressed and particularly odious American children standing in front of me, who with closed prayer books were ostentatiously reciting at the tops of their voices, so that their Yankee twang could be heard above the soft English threnody.

During the coffee break which followed, I recognised several elderly ladies who had been regular members of the International Society - one was an Englishwoman (married to a Finn) who had been resident for two generations in the country - and I met Mr. Rogers, who had presented the film for the Canadian evening, and I circulated freely, sipping my coffee and exchanging polite compliments and urbane points of view.

The Rev. Masters was not easy to reach, for as the centre of attention in his own place of worship, he was surrounded by diplomats wishing to shake hands or say a word or two, and on this particular Sunday, the ambassadors of three powers were present - of Britain, Canada and the USA. At last, and then only with reluctance, I was forced to push my way into his presence, and after an introduction, I came straight to the point in expressing a wish to discuss confidentially with him on the question of the International Society and the unpleasant nature of my conflict with Ron Evans. He listened with sympathy but the other diplomats stood around with interest, intent on not missing out on a word I said.

"He knows it all," chuckled an American diplomat to the Chaplain, and then he added, "I shouldn't worry about this man Evans if I was you. He's merely an idealist, not a professional."

"So you know something about it,?" I said turning to the American.

"Only through rumour," he replied taken aback.

"My interest is to track down this man and prosecute him for a criminal libel - possibly for slander also."

"Look here, Mr. Corfe," began the Rev. Masters, "why don't you come round to my place on Tuesday morning when we can discuss the whole matter over a cup of coffee."

My curiosity as to the outcome of this meeting was great, for possibly the Chaplain might be as inquisitive as to the affairs of the Society as I was to know the whereabouts of Evans and to seek the clergyman's advice. As it happened, the meeting differed from my expectations. The Rev. Masters had a ground floor flat in an apartment block in Freesenkatu, not far from the Parliament House, and he welcomed me warmly on my arrival at 11.0 a.m.

"I'm glad the ice has melted at last," he said from the kitchen where he was preparing coffee and laying out cakes on a doily. "The streets are so slippery in winter, and with my weight, when I fall I fall heavily."

I told him the full story of the International Society and of my conflict with Evans, and he replied with reassuring advice and some curiously terse comments, but showed no curiosity to delve more deeply into my past.

"I shouldn't worry about your position in the Society," he said, "but I suggest it might be better for yourself to completely throw up the project as it has a 'smell' about it. I can't see any danger for you, but I would advise that you be discreet in everything you say. Don't speak too loudly, and moreover, don't be persuaded to say things people might tempt you to say. Be on the watch for those who may be out to compromise you."

I expressed the fear that I might have aroused the deep displeasure of the American authorities.

"Goodness me, don't worry yourself about those people," he said contemptuously, "the slightest thing puts them in a flutter. I remember when I was in Cairo at the start of the McCarthy nonsense, and you should have seen the poor things at their wits end, searching through library shelves and destroying books by the hundredweight. You don't want to measure your actions by their standards."

We then returned to the topic of Evans and I said that I wished to find his whereabouts.

"I expect he'll turn up one of these days," mused the Rev. Masters. "I don't think he can go far."

"What makes you think that,?" I asked.

"Just a hunch I have. You've no idea where he could be then,?" added the Chaplain after a pause and looking me straight in the eye.

"None at all - that's why I'm asking you," I said. My suspicion was at once aroused by this curious exchange that the Chaplain might possibly know far more than I did as to the whereabouts of Evans, but I could pursue this line of questioning no further.

"Have you met Evans,?" I asked.

"Oh yes, several times," said the Rev. Masters. "He has a charming wife - charming, and three most delightful children. I went to dinner on one occasion - there was everything there for a complete household - nothing was missing. I didn't think much of the man himself though. His wife was obviously the boss in the home - she decided what was what."

"That coincides with my impression of the man."

"I'm not implying I thought him stupid. He spoke quite intelligently about the religious upbringing of his children. He was most worried over the dilemma as to whether they should be brought up in the Church of England or in the Lutheran Evangelical faith. I advised they should be brought up as Lutherans."

"I'm surprised you should say that in view of the strong opinions I know you hold with regard to episcopacy," I said.

"I advised it for purely practical reasons, for his children speak almost no English, and it is the Church of the country. I don't know what decision he made in the end. Mind you, I didn't like the man. I don't like him now either. He was living well when I saw him - probably far above his means. I should think that such a man would probably be lucky to get a basement flat in England."

This last was spoken with such an undertone of malice, that it surprised me as being quite out of character in the man, but I realised at the same time that this expression of contempt would not have been made unless there had existed circumstances of which I was unaware.

Despite the Rev. Masters' exhortation that I should not worry my mind about what the Americans thought, I still considered it wiser to take measures in clearing my name in their books, firstly because as the leading Western power they might have a primary interest in the Evans case if he had in fact compromised their interests; and secondly, because I did not wish to find in later life a bar arbitrarily raised against my entering the United States. Accordingly, I visited the American embassy on the afternoon of the following day and related my full story to their Mr. Nelson.

"I shouldn't worry, Mr. Corfe," he said, "it'll all be cleared up."

"I only came here for the purpose of clearing myself with the

American authorities," I said. "If you have any further questions or require additional information at any time I'm at your call."

"You've got an incredible memory for all the facts."

"I only hope you've got everything down on tape," I added.

"Don't worry about that, Mr. Corfe," he said with a smile as I departed.

That evening at the club was the Grand Party to celebrate the joys of Spring, for it was the 29th of April, and tomorrow would be Walpurgis night followed by the celebrations of the 1st of May, the most festive event in the Finnish calendar, when the population of the country would turn out in the streets dressed in funny hats, and papier mâché noses and all the other paraphernalia of a carnival; and students, past and present, proudly wearing the student cap of their particular "Nation House;" and carrying balloons, young and old alike, would parade up and down the major streets of the towns, displaying all the merriment of which the Scandinavians are accustomed.

The club's party that night held to give our members an opportunity to express their sense of joy at the approach of Spring, turned out to be the weirdest mixture of forced gaiety, nervous reticence and obligatory culture, as could be imagined. Few could have had their thoughts on what was supposedly the centre of attention, and all were dressed in such a way as to contradict the underlying mood of the party. The hollowness of the atmosphere - far exceeding what is called pretence - could never have succeeded in bringing together a more meaningless assembly, where every word spoken and every action undertaken amounted to bizarre absurdity. Such a party could only have been aptly described as a macabre festivity.

The hall was fuller than on previous weeks, some 60 or 70 members attending, but there were so many new faces that I almost felt a stranger in their midst, and as soon as the festivities began, candles were lighted on all the tables in the room, the electric lights turned out, funny paper hats, false noses, masks, papier mâché walking sticks, squeakers, rattles, cardboard trumpets and all kinds of cracker oddments were handed around to assist us into the festive mood. I noticed Sokolov playfully blow a squeaker into the neck of a companion, whilst another Soviet diplomat solemnly adjusted his false nose, and at the next table a fat East German struggled desperately to put on a tissue ruff.

"Come on everyone, the party's begun," said Gösta Kelter encouragingly. "We've lots of fun and games to suit you all tonight."

Sven's gesture was met by a few empty laughs intended to rally the faint-hearted, but there could hardly have been a heavier atmosphere in the hall. All were now suitably dressed in their festive attire, stiffly sitting around tables, obligingly grinning to brighten their neighbour's view, or occasionally giving out a guffaw as a measure of their high spirits.

"Before we start our games we're going to have some culture from several countries," announced Gösta. "Several of our members have kindly agreed to read to us some literature from several languages. First, ladies and gentlemen, our new Chairman, Mr. Rowland G.P. Hill."

There was some feeble clapping and nods of approval. Mr. Rowland Hill strode pompously up to the long table at one end of the hall with a fat book in his hand, and began, "I'm going to read to you tonight a passage from one of my favourite authors, P.G. Wodehouse." He expounded on this writer in the manner of a headmaster giving an end of term lecture to the school, and then he delivered a reading that lasted for three quarters of an hour.

During this time I observed a certain amount of restive activity in the room: several East German diplomats were passing notes and making signs to one another across the hall; Sokolov was in deep consultation with Eric Cross; several men were snoozing, whilst our dear Committee member, Inge Kainulainen, had fallen into a deep slumber and was snoring gently.

At the end of the reading I anticipated an interval, for we had heard a great deal of clattering from the direction of the kitchen, and the smell of cakes and the whistling of kettles, but we soon learned that we were not yet due for a respite. Gösta announced that his countryman, Anders Enblom, was going to read a poem. Enblom was at last in his element - he had been waiting for this moment since the foundation of the Society.

"I wanted to read you a Spanish poem tonight," he began, his resonant voice filling the hall, "as I am particularly attached to Spanish poetry. But unfortunately the anthology in which the poem is published was out of the library when I went to fetch it two days ago. That ladies and gentlemen is the way life is." (Polite murmurs of disappointment.) "However, I'm going to read you a poem from my own country - an old Swedish ballad about the fall of a poor innocent country lass who came to be corrupted in our great city of Stockholm. Written in the 1840s it tells the true story of many a poor girl leaving the poverty of the countryside to seek her fortune in our magnificent capital."

Anders read the amusing poem that carried the comic refrain, "Det war den första gång" (It was the first time), and those of us who understood the beautiful Swedish language laughed at the sardonic lines of the ballad. This was followed by an Australian singing a couple of folk songs on the guitar, and then Gösta gave out an announcement before the refreshment interval that next week's meeting (when Akulov was due to have his talk) had been cancelled by the Committee. This was a surprising piece of news, and I asked no questions as to the why or wherefore, only sidling over to Gösta with the ironical remark, "I hope you're not going to offend our good Soviet friends - whatever next?"

"We don't want people like that coming to the club," he only replied, and I assumed that from then onward the Society wished to project a purely pro-Western image - something not reflected by those who formed a great part of the assembly that night. Akulov's talk, however, was deferred until the 20th of May, but that fact was not published then.

Sima, a yellow cordial with raisins, drunk usually only in the month of May, and seasonal cakes, including *tippaleipä*, a curiously entwined honey biscuit (also a Spring delicacy) were brought in, and we began to enjoy these refreshments. I circulated through the hall, introducing myself to new and welcoming old members, and sometimes I was approached by strangers with a greeting or a curious remark, and I was overwhelmed by the number of East Europeans in our midst. "Soviet embassy," exclaimed a man with a dunce's hat in an undertone; "Legation of the German Democratic Republic," said a masked figure; "Bulgarian embassy," exclaimed a man with cardboard spectacles attached to a false nose in a discreet tone; "Hungarian Trade Commission," said another secretively.

A little man ran up to me, and glancing around furtively, he whispered into my ear, "Where's Schlitz?" "Who's Schlitz,?" I answered?" "There's only one Schlitz," he said. "I'm afraid I can't help you," I replied. What had brought all these East European diplomats here,? I asked myself. What were they doing? What did they expect to find? - for some were sitting around with an expectant look as if awaiting contacts. The festive clothes covering so much incongruity and pretence created a surreal environment.

"What happened at the International Spy Society last night,?" were the first words with which Det. Heinonen met me the following morning, and he was to refer to our club in these terms forever after. I described the evening in detail.

"I think Akulov cancelled the programme himself," said Heinonen when I told him about Gösta's announcement. "I don't think that he'll like going to your club any more."

"That wasn't my impression," I said. "Although I must say Akulov wasn't there himself last night."

"Have you heard anything about where Evans might be?"

"Nothing," I replied.

"It's strange, very strange," he said. "I wonder where he could be?"

"He's probably in Russia by now," I suggested.

Heinonen then covered old ground, questioning me extensively on my motives for founding the International Society and as to what I hoped to gain from it, and he showed particular interest in my opinions on the Committee members, sounding me out as to how they stood financially.

"I don't like people who live too well or spend a lot of money," he said. "They're suspicious. I like to know where they get their money from."

He then began on the old tack that I too was suspicious, concluding with the words, "Who are you working for?"

"I'm not working for anyone," I replied. "I just work for myself. And as for living too well, I don't think you suspect me of that. You've seen my accounts and you've been to my flat."

"You don't have to live too well to work for someone else," he said cryptically.

"I know that too," I laughed.

He did not appreciate my humour.

"Are you a Russian agent or a British agent?"

"I'm nobody's agent. I work for myself and that's an end to it."

He looked me searchingly in the eyes.

"You'd be useful to the Russians," he said at last. "I suppose in England you'ld be what's known as an upper class type. The Russians need your type. They make good front men - they can live well, travel where they want, spend lots of money - and they're not suspicious. It's part of the great Russian plan for world conquest: infiltration of front men into commerce, business, the professions - even politics. Slow but sure - it's better than the old way of marching armies. No one gets hurt so much."

"You should know about Russian conquest."

"We've fought the bastards three times this century alone - and beaten them. We intend to keep it that way."

"But that doesn't have anything to do with the suspicions you're trying to pin on me. I thought I'd already made a clean breast of everything. I've told you I've nothing to hide, consciously or unconsciously. Listen, if you've really got suspicions, then you've my full assent to put me under a truth drug."

"I don't believe in truth drugs," said Heinonen with a chuckle. "They don't produce facts. They only induce the suggestions you want."

He went on in this accusing manner for some time until I put up a show of defensive anger.

"Listen, Mr. Corfe," he said at last, "if you've got nothing on your conscience you've nothing to fear at all."

"I've nothing on my conscience," I said. "The only thing I'm afraid of, because of all this trouble, is not getting my permits renewed."

"How long do you intend staying in Finland?"

"Probably some years yet."

"You enjoy yourself here, don't you? I've been reading your diaries," he said with a suggestive smile.

"I've never done anything against the law," I answered.

"Let me assure you, Mr. Corfe, you don't have to worry about your permits. If you're in the clear, you can spend the rest of your life here. I think we like the look of your face by now."

"I've heard stories of foreigners who've had permits withdrawn for no reason at all - and they've been given a month or less to leave the country."

"We never do that. There's always a reason. Providing you live in our country in good faith and don't get mixed up with intelligence - of any power that is - you'll be safe."

"All my life I've tried to be respectable, bourgeois, conventional and dull. Those have always been my ideals," I confessed. "But things just haven't worked out like that. Events around my life have always been unintentional - a series of accidents. That's not my fault. I don't like being talked about behind my back any more than the next person. But I've become a subject for gossip and wild rumours - none of them with an ounce of truth - amongst the entire foreign community here in Helsinki."

"Just keep your nose clean and your head down and you'll be all right," said Heinonen.

In the years ahead in Finland, I was to keep my nose clean but I was not to follow the other half of Heinonen's advice. The work of a freelance journalist is not conducive to keeping your head down, and some of my articles were quite sensational.

On the following Wednesday, May 13th, Mr. Thadani, chargé d'affaires of the Indian embassy gave a talk on his country, but its bias annoyed me intensely. Our Society was strictly non-political, and up until that date we had welcomed speakers from all kinds of countries in all parts of the world, and none had yet abused their trust in maintaining a polite discretion, but on this particular night, we were obliged to hear a talk that was distinctly anti-British. Britain was made the scapegoat for all of India's present ills! So much for the spirit of the Commonwealth, I thought, but this washing of dirty linen on soil that was foreign to both our countries made it an especially distasteful performance. I was glad to be a private member that night, for during question time, I took Mr. Thadani to task and made him retract much of what he had clearly implied.

Mr. Akulov bounded up to me during the coffee interval with his usual good cheer and enquired as to whether I knew the whereabouts of Mr. Evans.

"I'm afraid I don't," I replied abruptly. "I now have nothing to do with the running of the club, and I don't know what the Committee's up to."

I exchanged no other words with Akulov that night, but I was surprised to see Mrs. Evans hurriedly moving around the room as she conferred with other members. She had not shown her face at the club since the mysterious disappearance of her husband a month earlier, and I refrained from speaking with her, for I felt that even if she knew the whereabouts of her husband she would not divulge the secret to me.

Det. Heinonen said he was busy when I met him the following morning, but suggested that we meet at the Insinööritalo restaurant tomorrow at noon.

"I've something very important to tell you," he said. "I think it'll be of interest to you."

CHAPTER 21
It's on the headlines

"Having watched the form of our traitors for a number of years, I cannot think that espionage can be recommended as a technique for building an impressive civilisation. It's a lout's game."

Rebecca West, *The Meaning of Treason*, 1982 ed., Introduction.

"Well, Mr. Corfe," said Det. Heinonen after some introductory chit-chat and as soon as we were settled with a beer awaiting the hors-d'oeuvre in the Insinööritalo restaurant, "have you heard the news today?"

"What news,?" I asked.

"Haven't you read the papers?"

"I've been working all morning. What's in the papers?"

"I'm surprised you haven't heard."

"What's in the papers?"

"We've charged Evans."

"Charged him,?" I exclaimed bewildered.

"Yes, I've an apology to make. You see, we've had Evans under arrest for a month now. I wasn't allowed to tell you before. We had to do it that way for security."

"So no one knew?"

"Only your Consul. We had to inform him as Evans was a British subject."

"So Evans has been in custody for a month!"

"We wanted time for carrying out additional investigations."

"And what'll happen now?"

"He'll be sentenced shortly. He was tried behind closed doors."

"I'm overjoyed," I replied, "but I'm so stunned with surprise I find it difficult to express my feelings. In a way it was expected, and in another way, it's just too good to be true. - But what were the charges exactly?"

"Espionage."

"So he was a Soviet spy?"

"He was, but we don't publish that fact. It might upset our 'friends' across the frontier. The charges were that he spied for one power to endanger the security of another. We only made it clear that Finland's security wasn't compromised in the case. I think that's a sufficient clue for the Western press to draw the right conclusions."

"So poor little Finland has to intervene in the Cold War in adjudicating in an East West espionage case!"

"We don't like getting involved in this kind of business, but someone's got to watch all these foreigners in the country. If we didn't take action in stamping out East West espionage on Finnish soil we'ld incur the wrath of both great power blocs, and eventually we'ld be sucked into the sphere of one or the other."

"And so in maintaining your neutrality you not only have to safeguard Finnish security but also that of the Western powers and the Eastern bloc."

"That's about it. It costs us a lot of money."

"Was it a clear cut case?"

"It was. Evans fully confessed to his part in the espionage set-up. It was a ten day trial or thereabouts - merely the presentation of written evidence. His defence lawyer wasn't able to do much - just say what a nice guy he was."

"I bet he had to use his imagination for that," I laughed.

"What I want to prove now is political conspiracy. We know that Evans passed over confidential documents on the premises of the International Spy Society, and what we now want is proof that he took over the Society for use as a Communist front organisation."

"You have my cooperation," I assured him.

"What kind of information did he pass over?"

"That's something I can't tell you. It's top secret."

As we continued our lunch, we entered into a long discussion on the East West political conflict, and the vigilance necessary by all powers in preventing a direct military breakthrough in any part of the world where armed force was allowed to fall below a certain level. Det. Heinonen especially criticised the multifarious "Peace" movements throughout the world as offering the greatest danger to undermining world security.

"They're the biggest headache we have to handle," he said. "If they went unchecked, in only two decades they'ld lead to a situation either igniting the Third World War, or making Communist domination inevitable. They all serve as Communist front organisations - even when they're not backed by the Soviet Union or some other power. The people who get mixed up in 'Peace' movements know nothing about the eternal realities of politics or history. They'ld only have to pick up a book on ancient Egyptians or Greeks to know that Peace movements serve only as front organisations to foreign powers - or for traitors - the principle's always the same. That's how Evans got mixed up in espionage. He was an idealist. He was a 'Peace' man. He thought he was doing good. But he's ignorant - he knows nothing about the realities behind international conflict. That's what happens when technicians or scientists start dabbling in politics - in things they know nothing about."

After lunch we sat for two more hours drinking coffee and glass after glass of cognac, and I congratulated him on the fine French brandy he had chosen.

"The government pays for it," he said with a smile. "I think you're worth more than our local *jälloviini*."

"I thought perhaps you'd got all the information you wanted from me by now."

"You could be useful. There are still a few more things to clear up you've brought to our attention."

"Really,?" I said. "I'm interested."

"I can't tell you any more than that I'm afraid," he said with a smile.

He then moved over onto Finnish politics but I saw a trap and stayed clear.

"I don't like President Kekkonen," he said. "Do you know that back in 1939 Kekkonen was working in my department. He was a lawyer and a security man. He was doing a good job then. He's not like Paasikivi. Now Paasikivi was the one man who could stand up against Stalin, and no one, not even Churchill could do that."

"Kekkonen gets on well with the Russians."

"Oh yes, he can dance in front of them balancing a glass of vodka on his head, and they like that, but that's not enough."

President Kekkonen was widely criticised in Finland as heads of state mostly are everywhere in the free world, but I felt that Det. Heinonen was leading me along a path of argument to induce a free expression of opinion that might put me in the light of a British agent.

Later that afternoon, I rushed home in a state of elation, went out for a sauna and then visited my friends in the Kolme Kreiviä. The news had already reached them, and I frantically turned over the pages of the daily papers to read the news reports, but the Finnish press merely published the official statement put out by the Ministry of the Interior. Clearly they wished to hush-up the case in view of Finland's delicate situation as a neutral state on the edge of a great power. The statement said that Ronald Evans had been spying for a period of three years and during that time had received 3,500 Finnmarks (about £400) for his services. I was congratulated by Peter, Rolf, Martin and others for having achieved a moral victory in my conflict with the Soviet spy.

"I wouldn't mind betting the police are pretty suspicious of you by now," said Rolf Erlewein.

"Why,?" I asked.

"After all, you gave the Ministry of the Interior a pretty hard time in urging them to prosecute Evans for libel."

"So what?"

"You forced them to get out their files and look into Evans. Now they must have suspected Evans of his espionage activities for some time. You must have tipped the scales in getting them to prosecute."

"Where does the suspicion of me come in?"

"The British have known about Evans for a long time," said Jim Hammond. "That's why they refused him membership of the Embassy Club a long way back."

"So the Finns might well suspect me of being a British agent? I still don't get it. If the British knew about Evans all along, why didn't they turn him in to the Finnish authorities themselves?"

"They may have done," said Rolf, "but that doesn't mean the Security police got their finger out as soon as they had the tip-off."

"Things take time in this country," said Peter. "You know how bloody slow the Finns are."

"The Security police could have suspected you of working on instructions from British intelligence in putting a bomb up their backsides," said Martin Summerhill. "You must have scared the daylight out of them with all the publicity you made over the Evans conflict. If you weren't worrying them you were worrying the Criminal police, and if it wasn't them, you were worrying the police for Traffic and Public Order. You've been on at them for weeks now."

"You should be entitled to a reward from the British government for all you've done," said Olav.

"They're too bloody broke," said Martin.

"The least they could give him is a medal," said Rolf turning to Martin. "Surely they can afford that."

"You know what I think, I think the Russians turned Evans in themselves," said Peter. "He had given them all they wanted and he was getting round their necks. Besides, I don't think the Russians like their spies having the limelight of being secretaries of international societies."

Later I visited my valued helper, Mrs. Hytönen, who was overjoyed at the news, and that night I went to the UPI office of my journalist friend, Pentti Kiiskinen (to whose memory this book is dedicated and with whom I enjoyed many drinking sessions throughout the decade of the sixties) and there saw the telex tapes of the Evans story being transmitted to a central bureau, and from there to news offices throughout the world. We then went to the Press Club and drank and discussed the Evans case until the early hours of the morning.

The following day millions of people throughout Britain awoke to be greeted by the smiling countenance of Ron Evans and his family on the front pages of their morning papers, but I was sickened by some of the human-interest appeal that the British popular press had read into the case. Evans was described as a 44 year old radio engineer with a Finnish wife and three children: 12 year old Gwyneth (Evans' daughter from a previous marriage); Peter, aged 6, and 5 year old Henry. He was born at Sheerness, moved with his family to Glasgow during the War, was educated at Alan Glen's High School, and had met his wife, Marja Tuulikki, in London whilst she was working in a London hospital. He moved from Wood Green, London, to Helsinki in 1955, where he shortly afterwards married his second wife. He was employed by the Philips television concern until three years before, when he moved over to his new firm Aga, a Swedish-Dutch Philips subsidiary.

When his mother, 70 year old Mrs. Ethel Evans of Galway road, Sheerness, heard the news of her son's arrest and trial, she broke down and cried, exclaiming, "It's too ridiculous for words. I am sure there has been a terrible mistake. I knew something was wrong. I hadn't heard from him for three weeks, and he usually writes every week. It must be a terrible blow for Marja and the children. She is a wonderful wife and is a governor of the grammar school in Helsinki which Gwyneth attends."

The case against Evans had been heard at a closed session in the Helsinki Court of Appeals, which deals with all espionage cases, and only the charge had been made public. The authorities and also the British embassy had refused to reveal any details of his alleged activities except that he had been working in Finland "on behalf of another country against a third country." The Finnish authorities had only commented that there was much spying in the country but that "most of the known agents were spying against each other rather than on Finland."

It was stated that Evans was known as a Communist sympathiser in Espo (the district in which the town of Tapiola is situated), and that he was a pacifist and a member of the Defenders of Peace Society, an organisation subsidised by the Communists. However, Evans' defending lawyer, Mr. Risto Brax, had claimed that his client was an "idealist," adding nonsensically, that he would not have defended him had he been a Communist. He added that Evans had acted out of "thoughtlessness." Evans had pleaded guilty to spying from 1961 until April 1964 - the time of his disappearance. He had been found guilty; the state had ordered the confiscation of his ill-gotten gains; and he had been further remanded in custody for a period of up to 30 days within which period under Finnish law, he would receive his sentence.

There were only twenty-six people at the next Wednesday cultural evening of the International Society, for the Evans scandal had ruined the club's better reputation, and in addition, Akulov was presenting his programme on *Life In The Soviet Union*. Mr. Rowland Hill and other Committee members met me sheepishly. I was not so insensitive as to make even an oblique reference to the Evans case, but neither did they then nor on any subsequent occasion attempt to offer an apology or other gesture admitting their improper behaviour towards me. They had fallen for every cunning manoeuvre that Ron Evans had initiated, and in doing so, they had ruined the Society and everything I had achieved since launching the club almost exactly six months earlier.

There were six Soviet diplomats as well as Akulov at the club that evening, and I mixed easily in their company during the interval, after their countryman had delivered an uninspired talk with numerous statistics describing the domestic economic achievements of Russia.

Akulov introduced me to his friend the Soviet Naval attaché, a well-proportioned fair-haired man.

"I like England very much," said the Naval attaché in his American accent. "I should like to improve my British-English diction. You have a wonderful Royal Navy. Some years ago I was in Portsmouth and I saw the Duke of Edinburgh then. A fine man! England's a great country."

"What do you intend doing in the International Society now? Is there to be a Summer programme,?" asked Akulov.

"I don't think so," I replied. "This Evans business seems to have knocked the stuffing out of the club."

"Was that the same Evans,?" exclaimed Akulov in surprise. "I remember reading about it in the paper."

"It was the same Evans alright."

"I thought it was another Evans. It's a common name in England - I know that."

"There's only one Evans in Finland."

"Such a nasty business," said Akulov sympathetically. "I hope there are no repercussions."

"Ladies and gentlemen, may I have your attention for just a moment," said Gösta Kelter from the far end of the hall. "We're arranging a weekend in the country. Mr. Waldemar von Etter is kindly throwing open his Country Club at Haiko to members of the International Society on the weekend of the 6th of June. Haiko is just outside Porvoo - less than an hour's run from Helsinki. Those without cars may take the Helsinki-Porvoo bus. There'll be opportunities for swimming, fishing, boating, hide and seek in the woods, and all kinds of other forest and water games. Those interested please put their names on the list on the notice board - but note there'll only be thirty-five places. It'll be the last event of the season."

"That sounds a lovely opportunity for us, Basil, all those open air activities," said Eric Cross to Sokolov. "What about putting our names down?"

"What a pity the club is closing down for the summer, Mr. Corfe," said another Soviet diplomat. "We've all enjoyed ourselves so much here."

CHAPTER 22
What happened at Haiko

"Once to every man and nation comes the moment
to decide;
In the strife of Truth with Falsehood, for
good or evil side."

J.R. Lowell, "The Present Crisis," *Poems: Second Series* (1848)

Det. Heinonen called at my flat the following Monday at 1.0 pm, and after I had described to him the previous Wednesday's meeting over a glass of wine, we went to the Sillankorva restaurant where we ate and drank till late in the afternoon.

"I'd like you to go to this von Etter's. It might be interesting," he said. "I'd like to know what Soviet diplomats are there and what they're up to. - What do you think of von Etter?"

"He's certainly not a Communist. He's the one Committee member who was not involved in the Evans' clique."

"Do you think he's an American agent?"

"I shouldn't see why he should be."

"There are two reasons," said Heinonen, "firstly, he's worked for the Americans - as a press man, and secondly, he's short of money."

"First you say you don't like people if they've got too much money, and now you say you don't like them if they've got too little."

"That's because they're both suspicious," answered Heinonen.

"I don't know if there's such a thing as a happy medium when it comes to wealth," I remarked.

"I think von Etter's working for the CIA for a little pocket money," said Heinonen with quiet confidence.

"Really?"

"He's spent most of his own on drink and women. Anyhow, put your name down and keep your eyes open."

The 27th of May was the last meeting that the Society held in its premises in Fabianinkatu - for me a sad evening because of this - and I placed my name on the list of those wishing to visit the Haiko Country Club.

On the 5th of June the papers announced that Evans had been sentenced to ten months imprisonment - Heinonen later explaining that the short term was given so as not to unduly offend the Soviet authorities.

It was now the most beautiful time of the year in Finland, long warm sunlit days, high blue domed skies, and white nights when a red rim of light lit up the horizon. The sea was a deep blue, contrasting with the red granite shore, and the forests of pines and conifers completed a picture that was peaceful and idyllic. In Helsinki the birch and other deciduous trees were bursting forth their buds, and in a few weeks flowers would be planted in the esplanades and public gardens of the city. The people looked forward to an outdoor life of sunbathing, and the women and children would leave the city for their summer villas and lakeside saunas for a three month break. The winter doldrums could be left behind until the shortening of the days and the approach of another November.

At 4 o'clock in the afternoon on Saturday the 6th of June I arrived at the Porvoo bus platform in the square behind Mannerheimintie, and shortly I was joined in the queue by others from our Society. Not far behind me stood Sokolov, his face bright and happy as suited the occasion, carrying bag and fishing tackle, accompanied by his new friend, Eric Cross; and as we mounted the bus, I had to hush down Anders Enblom, for he was telling me at the top of his voice how the police had recently called at his flat, enquiring as to his "country of residence."

We arrived at Haiko at 5.30 pm and Digmar, dressed as always in his brown tweed suit, welcomed us at the gate to his estate, and drove several of the older members of our group, in an old 1930s vintage car, to the entrance of his stately family home. Eric Cross, Sokolov (walking with brisk strides), several others and I strode along the wooded and winding drive, until we came to the palatial house dominating high ground with a magnificent view leading down through forest to the sea and islands in the Gulf of Finland.

"Isn't this glorious,!" exclaimed Salme overwhelmed by the surroundings.

"There's no better air anywhere in the world than in a pine forest," said Dr. Schenk, another of our members.

We were met at the door of the house by several servant girls, and the housekeeper read out the numbers of the rooms to which we had been allocated, and we were taken up the grand staircase and led to our various sleeping quarters. I was put into a large room with old-fashioned furniture and a marble washstand and water jug for washing, and from the window there was a fine view looking South across the sea towards Estonia only some sixty miles away.

Downstairs in the hall again, above which rose a glass paned cupola, I was met by von Etter's petite dark-haired niece who was married to the Indian. I had first met the couple three years before, and she proudly showed me around the house that had been in the family inheritance for generations, and in the loft we saw piles of unused bricks.

"They were going to build another storey and add a wing onto the house," she explained, "but then the civil war came, and the family lost their estates in Russia, and they couldn't afford to continue building."

In the drawing room downstairs at the back of the house was a large bay French window leading onto an impressive verandah. There were many pieces of baroque and rococo furniture (some in considerable disrepair) and many ancestral portraits dating back to the 17th century decorating the walls.

"That's Digmar's father," said his niece pointing to a portrait. "He was a Major-General and responsible for the Helsinki Command and thereabouts at the time of the civil war."

A son of von Etter, by a previous marriage, and some other relatives were also there.

"This house must have some history," I remarked to a distinguished looking lady.

"On several occasions the *Standart* was moored within sight of the house and Tsar Nicholas came here at least once - but his informal visits were always kept strictly secret. He didn't like fuss or bother on holiday. His father though, Alexander III, spent very much more time in Finland, fishing and hunting, especially at his lodge at Langinkoski outside Kotka."

At this point in the narrative it might be apt to relate something more about the life of this fascinating personality, Waldemar von Etter, in contradicting any impression which may be given in this book, that he merely led an idle existence of empty pleasure. At his death he was described as an estate owner and Engineer - the latter appellation alone giving him status in the eyes of the Finnish majority, in a country that set its democratic values on education and personal achievement. He was born in St. Petersburg in 1899, and educated at the Imperial Lycée, and so as with most upper class people in pre-Revolutionary Russia, intended for life in an international milieu, French was the main language of education. After matriculation in 1917 he was sent to the Ecole des Sciences Politique in Paris.

He attended the Army Officers School in Vaasa until 1920, and in the same year, during the War of Independence (the civil war), he fought in battles at the occupation of Viipuri, formerly Finland's second largest city, close to the Russian frontier. He was later employed by General Motors, and then in the advertising branch of the Dorland agencies in Paris and London until 1933, when he became managing director of Representation Propagande International (RFI). Meanwhile, he was elected a delegate and public relations representative by the Finnish Olympic Committee for the Olympic games in Paris in 1924.

In 1936 he returned to Finland to manage the Haiko estate, and was later appointed the Scandinavian correspondent for the *New York Herald Tribune*, and in later years became the Nordic advertising representative for the paper. He was also a member of the Civil Guard, an organisation suppressed by the peace treaty following the Second World War. During the Winter War of 1939-1940, he served at the front with the 23rd Regiment, fighting in battles in Northern Karelia and the Karelian Isthmus, and during the Continuation War, coinciding with Operation Barbarossa and Hitler's invasion of Russia (1941-1944), he served as a staff officer at the State's Information Centre. The above information is taken from obituaries in Finland's three largest dailies. He was married with several children but lived apart from his wife.

At 6 o'clock we dined on an excellent meal, some forty of us seated at six or seven tables, and I sat in the company of Cross, Sokolov and a group of friendly middle-aged Indians, and Cross was in especially fine fettle as he expostulated on his curious philosophy of life. Also at dinner I was surprised to see Sonja, the Swedish ambassador's Secretary, together with a girl friend. They were not staying in the house, however, but in a cottage in the grounds, and later in the evening, Digmar and an American friend joined them there, but were abruptly turned away by the offended or frightened girls. After the meal, began the fun and games, and I organised a hide and seek adventure. The first to hide were Digmar and a lady called Ellen, and as they ran off, we counted a hundred, but search as we did, we could find them nowhere, and they only re-appeared an hour later.

"I wonder where they've gone,?" I exclaimed.

"Don't be silly, of course you know where they've gone," exclaimed one of Digmar's fans spitefully, clearly upset that she had not been chosen as his partner in the game. "They've shut themselves away."

Later Digmar was showing Salme, Eric Cross, Sokolov and I the cellars of the house, one room of which was only furnished with couches whilst the walls were decorated with pornographic frescoes of nude couples in different sexual positions - obviously designed for orgiastic functions. Von Etter was particularly proud of this room - he had probably painted the nudes himself.

"Do you think Digmar would be offended if I suggested his pictures are in rather poor taste,?" confided Salme somewhat ridiculously to Cross and I as soon as our host was out of hearing. "I think it lowers the dignity of the house."

Before the sun set for a twilit night, Dr. Schenk, Anders Enblom and I made a leisurely stroll through the pine trees down to the sheltered inlet of the sea, and we walked to the jetty and boathouse and back, and the old man who had been so ill the previous Winter was now a decade younger. The main function of the evening began when Digmar organised a bingo session. A group of us sat in comfortable armchairs before an enormous log fire in the entrance hall of the house, but the chimney was faulty, for smoke came up from beneath the mantelpiece and rose towards the high glass dome where it escaped through a broken pane.

As Digmar read out the winning numbers in his reverberating voice, Sokolov became increasingly animated by the jovial atmosphere of the company, and began emptying the host's Whiskey into everyone's tea, irrespective of whether this was asked for or not. As I watched the smoke of the log fire rise to the cupola, I noticed several attractive young servant girls leaning over the upstairs banisters, laughing mischievously at the guests below, and I realised that this was a house where any adventure was possible at a late hour. Finally, at thirty minutes past midnight, the company began to make their way to bed, but before returning to our rooms, Cross, Sokolov and I strolled through the grounds of the estate, Cross reciting long snatches of verse he had learnt during the War whilst in the RAF, and Sokolov occasionally singing snatches from a Russian song.

I arose at 8.15 a.m. the next day, another bright morning with a promise of scorching weather, and during breakfast, Cross, Sokolov, Salme and I settled down to an interesting discussion on life attitudes and marriage. Cross began to ponder on the origins of the Celtic race describing those particular characteristics of their culture - he was himself a Celt (or rather boasted that he was) - and Sokolov soon pushed the discussion over to a consideration of the treatment of malefactors in the Soviet Union, where convicted persons were allowed to find their redemption after punishment through work and the trust of the state. Sokolov was a true idealist and it was impossible not to feel some sympathy for the man and some truth behind what he said. Cross was cynical and degenerate by comparison, inclined only to express views based on personal experience. We then began to discuss cultural differences between the women of different lands.

"I'll tell you who are the finest women in the world," began Cross. "There are no finer women than Arab women. The Arab and Egyptian peoples are the happiest in the world because they have the right philosophy of life. I lived amongst them during the War. I speak Arabic fluently. In fact I'm a Moslem convert. Look, here's my ring that every Moslem wears."

"But why are Arab women the best,?" asked Salme who was clearly hurt by the idea.

"Because they make the best wives as they do everything possible to please their husbands, and because of this, their husbands are always nice to them. Divorce is easier in the Moslem world than anywhere else, but it's very rarely resorted to."

"I was always nice to my husband but it didn't work out," said Salme. "I brought him his food on a tray in bed, and I laid out his slippers, but he still broke his promise and didn't let me continue living in Helsinki to study."

Here Sokolov broke into the discussion with the force of a sledgehammer.

"You're both wrong," he said. "Husbands and wives shouldn't dominate one another. They should be equal. Both of them should contribute equally in economic terms in helping to build up the home. That's justice! If the man has difficulties in his work or life, then the woman should give him psychological help. That's how it is in the Soviet Union. Anyway, that's my ideology."

As I browsed through the bookshelves in the drawing room, my eye caught a finely bound guest book, and I took this down and turned over its leaves, to find its pages entered with the names of Russian Counts and Countesses, Princes and Princesses, all written in French in a fine copperplate, and even the name of the great Marshall Mannerheim was there, formerly Supreme Commander of the White forces and Regent of Finland, and at a much later date, President of the country following the Continuation War. In his youth he had been an officer in the Empress Maria Feodorovna's Chevalier Guards, and subsequently, he had seen active service in the Russo-Japanese war in 1905, and then on the Eastern front during the First World War. The house had clearly seen better days when the Gulf of Finland had been the Summer playground of the Russian nobility.

Different outdoor activities had been arranged for that morning, and shortly after breakfast, on walking out onto the verandah, I met Sokolov dressed in thigh length boots and carrying his fishing tackle. He was waiting for the Russian serving woman (who had been employed since Tsarist times by the von Etter family) to prepare the rowing boat he was to use that morning. As he stood there, he looked the happiest man in the world. He stretched his arms in the sunshine, breathing in the fresh air.

"It's so refreshing to be a Communist," he exclaimed. "That's the life for a man - a challenge for body and soul!"

As Sokolov was conducted to his boat, Cross and I walked to the seashore by another route and for the first time we were alone.

"What do you think'll happen to Ronald when he comes out,?" I asked.

"It's hard to say," said Cross. "They may allow him to go to the Soviet Union, or they may deport him back to Britain. It's a great pity what's happened to him. He's a brilliant man and he was a wonderful friend. He got some incredible information out of lots of people."

"You know something about the case then?"

"I'm working in the same line of business, though my firm's the Cable Factory by Lauttasaari. It's terrible what the police get up to here. They never leave anyone alone. You have to watch yourself always. I don't like these people. Don't you get tied up with a Finnish woman. You'll always regret it if you do. They're so stubborn, it's unbelievable. I know, I've been married to two of them. I've still got my second. ... I'll tell you something you must never do in this country."

"What's that?"

"Hit someone."

"Why?"

"Because they lock you away in an asylum. It happened to me once. I was at a firm's Christmas party and I hit a bloke really hard. The next morning a couple of men in white coats came to the door, and they said, 'Did you hit Mr. Saarinen last night,?' and I said, 'Yes, why,?' and do you know, they took me away. I was kept inside for two weeks for observation and medical tests. You can't do anything unusual in this country without people thinking you're mad. It's a terrible place! They think all Englishmen are mad, but they wouldn't be so impolite as to admit it."

On reaching the seashore, we strolled along a peninsula to a small jetty, joining a crowd from the estate who were drinking beer and Whiskey, talking and dozing in the sun. There was a man with a monkey, and several others, including Digmar's American friend, who was starting a speed boat, and after bottles of beer had been pushed into our hands, Cross and I were invited for a trip around the bay, and during this excursion, we were soaked to the skin by the spray. On returning to the villa shortly before noon, it was so hot, that I changed into trunks and

WHAT HAPPENED AT HAIKO

began scything the long grass in front of the verandah. Lunch was at one, and after this I again changed into trunks and sunbathed for an hour, before a group of us walked to the house of the famous 19th century Finnish painter Albert Edelfelt, some fifteen minutes beyond the boundary of the estate.

Cross, Sokolov and I walked in a row along the forested path, and suddenly the Russian joyfully broke out, "Let's all walk in step," and he changed step in perfect military fashion. On returning from the Edelfelt exhibition, I spent the rest of the afternoon scything the grass, whilst a number of others sat on deckchairs on the verandah sunbathing, and occasionally chiding me good-humouredly for my "labour" - especially Digmar who thought it most amusing - and Sokolov took several snaps. In the middle of the afternoon we heard the echoing sound of a ship's horn, and looking down towards the sea, we caught a glimpse of the 60 year-old paddle steamer, the J.L. Runeberg, making her way from Helsinki to Porvoo, before she disappeared again behind a wooded island.

Later in the afternoon, however, on going several times into the house for drinking water, I was surprised to observe Cross and Sokolov engaged in a most interesting activity. Both were seated across a small table by the bay window in the drawing room, both tense with concentration, and Cross was dictating a list of numbers to the Russian and drawing some geometrical-like plans. From that moment I was convinced that Cross was the Soviet spy who had supplanted Evans, and I was to urge the police to carry out an investigation into Cross with the idea of securing yet another conviction.

The consequences of this decision were to have widespread if not disastrous repercussions. Cross and Sokolov, who had shared a bedroom in the house, left together at 4.30 p.m. to catch a certain bus back to Helsinki. I stayed on for dinner at 6.0 p.m. that night and was later driven back in Ellen's car.

CHAPTER 23
Death takes its toll

"Among the calamities of War may be justly numbered the diminution of the love of truth, by the falsehoods which interest dictates and credulity encourages."

Dr. Samuel Johnson, *The Idler*, No. 31.

I was still in bed when Det. Heinonen called early on Wednesday morning, and apologising for my lateness, I sat him in the armchair whilst I washed and dressed.

"How did you enjoy your weekend at Haiko,?" he asked.

"Fantastic,!" I said.

"I thought you'ld have a good time."

"I've got some incredible things to tell you. Cross and Sokolov were there, and if they weren't up to some spy business together, I'll eat my hat."

I briefly described the weekend.

"I want you to identify this Russian from some pictures I've got here," said Heinonen, and he took a large envelope from his briefcase and emptied some two hundred passport size photographs onto the table. "They're all Soviet embassy employees and I want to pinpoint the man."

I went through the mass of pictures, many of them officers in uniform with rows of medals, and it was not until I had been through two thirds of the pile that I eventually identified the man we were after."

"That's him," I said.

"Are you quite sure?"

"Without a doubt."

Heinonen took the picture and turned it over.

"His name's not Sokolov," he said.

"I don't expect it is," I agreed.

"He's an embassy chauffeur - or that's what we have him down as."

"He's a jolly intelligent chauffeur then."

I pressed my argument that Eric Cross was an obvious bolshy.

"What makes you think that,?" said Heinonen.

"He impressed me as a man who was a Communist but was clever in concealing the fact."

"Did he talk politics?"

"Of course not. If he was taking Evans' place, he wasn't going to compromise himself."

"Perhaps he's working for the other side."

"What, a British agent? You must be joking. The man's a way out weirdo - he's even been shut away in an asylum. He's even a Moslem convert - showed us his ring. Do you think the British could put their trust in a man like that? He might be spying for the Arabs though. He loves them."

"The British are very clever. It could be a front."

"They wouldn't go that far. The man's been twice married in Finland alone, and God knows how many wives he's had before that."

"I know."

"He's unstable. You can't employ a man who's unstable as a spy. You need to have a tough character for that. How could British intelligence put their trust in a man who leads a life like that? He's got to have a balanced personality since how else is he going to behave under stress? It stands to reason."

"You make me suspicious again," said Det. Heinonen with a smile. "You seem to know a lot about British intelligence."

"I'm just using my head," I replied.

"There are a lot of weird characters involved in intelligence - even amongst the professionals. The world is more complex than you think," said Heinonen.

"I still find it insulting to both my intelligence and to the British secret service you could imagine that my country could employ a man like that."

Det. Heinonen laughed.

"It may be that only weird characters are attracted to spy work or counter-intelligence," he said.

"I'd suggest you put him under surveillance," I urged. "He's a Commy for cert."

"We'll see, Mr. Corfe. - How about meeting for lunch later at the Insinööritalo?"

"I'd love to but I'm going to a big party this afternoon. The biggest social event of the season."

"What's that?"

"The Queen's birthday reception at the British embassy residence."

At 5.30 p.m. that afternoon I arrived at the British embassy residence situated in the best area of the diplomatic quarter adjoining Kaivopuisto park. The winding uphill street approaching the embassy was already crowded with big cars carrying the flags of many countries, in addition to the many Finnish military vehicles and those carrying number plates indicating that they were in the service of the state. As I slowly walked along the drive leading to the house entrance, following the line of senior civil servants, diplomats and high ranking Finnish officers in their steel grey uniforms, highly polished jackboots, tasselled swords, epaulettes and rows of clinking medals, it was impossible not to be impressed by the august assemblage which was arriving that afternoon to honour the birthday of the Queen of England. We ordinary mortals who were resident in Finland were allowed to these annual parties as a special privilege without the need for a formal invitation.

There was a great crush and the noise of busy chatter as I entered the building, and as soon as I had shaken hands with our host and hostess, their Excellencies Sir Anthony and Lady Lambert, and taken a glass from a proffered tray, Mr. Akulov eagerly leapt up to me from out of the throng.

"Why, Mr. Corfe, I'm so glad to see you here," he said. "I've been trying to phone you for weeks but there's never any reply."

"The Committee took my phone away months ago," I explained.

"There's so much I'ld like to discuss with you. I always enjoy your company and it's a long time since we last met. How about meeting at Königs at noon tomorrow?"

"I think that would be alright," I said hesitantly. "I'll phone you tomorrow morning to confirm it."

"See you then, Mr. Corfe," he said and dashed off.

I had no intention of meeting Mr. Akulov or of phoning him, but had used the ruse of complying with his wishes to further avoid his company. Det. Heinonen was subsequently to regret that I had done this as he wished me to find out Akulov's attitude to the Evans' case and its repercussions for the Society.

Several of the HISC group were also there, including Ray Reed and his wife - he chewing on his pipe as ever - he was never one to miss an opportunity for free booze - and so was Rowland G.P. Hill together with his fiancée, Miss Ingrid Andersson, the Society's Subscription Manageress (in a delightful pink dress), and Rowland and I exchanged a few polite words as to the future of the club. Ingrid and he were to be married the following month.

"There may be a chance of getting the Society registered in the Autumn if there's a change of government," said Rowland nonchalantly. (It struck me that that was a bit of a long shot.) "It's really a matter that can only be settled with the right people over a good dinner. The authorities have put a spoke in the works. The real trouble in this country is that the judicial system here is still a part of the old Tsarist set-up. They're dictated to by the police instead of the other way round. There's no democracy in that. The police are the only stumbling block to getting the Society registered."

Jim Hammond was also there, slapping the behinds of the female embassy staff and plying them with drinks, and in his jovial good nature, calling them "honey."

I circulated freely, exchanging compliments with diplomats and friends from many countries, but as I stood sipping a sherry with Martin and Rolf, Peter bounded up to us laughing and holding his hand over his mouth in apparent embarrassment. We sensed at once that he must have been implicated in some frightful boob.

"Do you know, Bob, I've just committed the most awful *faux pas*," he exclaimed laughing. "Do you see that man by the window with all those medals? Well, I thought he was one of ours. I met him at the club and he always spoke American English. I've just been telling him all about my top secret technical work in the RAF. Well, really, do you know, he's from the other side. He's the Soviet Naval attaché. I felt such a fool, and you should have seen the look the British Consul gave me!"

"You twit,!" said Martin. "You've been ten years in the RAF and you can't even tell the difference between a Russian and an American uniform."

"These naval uniforms all look the same to me."

"Americans don't wear their uniforms at functions like this - you should know that," said Rolf.

"The trouble with the Americans is that they're too visible when they shouldn't be and too self-effacing on those occasions when they should be making a bit of a show," I said.

"In less than a month they've got their own July the 4th celebrations just across the road," said Peter. "And you know what they dish up there: hot dogs and coca cola. It makes you puke to think of it. It's not as if they didn't have the money. It's just they haven't got the style."

"British is always best,!" put in Martin ironically.

The most impressive looking officer in the entire assembly was undoubtedly the British military attaché, Col Robinson, and as he limped around the room sipping his drink, he seemed positively weighed down by the iron of spurs, medals, stars, chain mail epaulettes and sword, and together with his finely cut toothbrush moustache, he epitomised the image of everything that the British officer should be. As I glanced at this gentleman, over-awed by his finery, reflecting what a pleasure it must be to wear such a uniform, Peter whispered into my ear, "I dare you, Bob, to ask him for a twopenny return!"

Towards the end of the reception I was buttonholed by a young lady employee of the British embassy called Mrs. Anja Stubinsky, who claimed that she knew me and was a member of the International Society, although I never recalled having seen her before. She began questioning me at some length on the future of the Society, saying by the way that she was of Finnish nationality, recently separated from her Yugoslavian husband, and had been living in England for ten years.

After we had spoken for some twenty minutes or so, I suspected she might possibly be working for British intelligence and I therefore invited her back to my flat where we could discuss the Society in greater depth over a bottle of wine. She declined this invitation but instead invited me to accompany her and several others, belonging to the British Embassy Club that was holding a party at the Casino that night (one of Helsinki's most expensive restaurants), and I reluctantly agreed to be her guest for the evening.

Mrs. Stubinsky, however, was obliged to ask permission of the club's chairman before confirming the invitation, for there were place settings at the Casino, and she searched through the crowd for a Mr. Cook, at last finding and bringing him over to introduce him to the prospective guest. Cook was an embassy guard or doorman, a short man with an insolent manner and an East End accent, and after looking me up and down in a disapproving manner, and then disappearing and returning again several times, and repeatedly asking my name and making offensive grimaces, he exclaimed at last, "I've never 'eard of you." His odd behaviour and eccentric mannerisms could only be interpreted as contrived rudeness, and I took an instant dislike to him, and I was soon to learn that our feelings were mutual. He had the coarse effrontery of a Sam Weller, and he was to instigate an unpleasant situation that was to embarrass my relationship with the embassy.

At 7 o'clock we left the embassy (one and a half hours before the end of the function) and drove to the Casino restaurant, a large palatial structure situated on the seashore, on the island of Kulosaari to the east of Helsinki.

"It's so nice to get away from those horribly stiff functions - they're such a bore," said Mrs. Stubinsky. I said nothing for I disagreed with her.

At the Casino about a hundred of us sat in small groups in the bar drinking beer until we were called into the restaurant and were seated at long tables and immediately served with champagne (which together with Martini was poured out to us by the bucket for the rest of the evening) and we had to suffer an interminable wait for the arrival of food, during which time I became increasingly impatient, bored and hungry.

To my distress, Cook sat himself opposite me, and then demanded that we all pay him five marks to cover the cost of champagne so that we might drink as much as we liked, and we dutifully took out our wallets and placed five mark notes on the centre of the table. The club's chairman leered at me all the while with an insolently inquisitive expression, occasionally making hideous grimaces, but he made no attempt at conversation, and in view of his oddity and rudeness, I was not prepared to be the first to break the silence between us. Perhaps he was jealous or curious as to why I was accompanying Mrs. Stubinski, or perhaps he knew me by reputation as the founder of the International Society.

At last food arrived, a few mushrooms and pieces of salad, and although I had several helpings, I was still hungry, and meanwhile, an old flame of Mrs. Stubinsky arrived and attached himself to her (to my understandable irritation) and so unsurprisingly, I felt increasingly moody. Since the start of the evening I had had a considerable amount to drink, I was surrounded by dull people whose company I had not sought out, and my head was swimming, and I thought it would be time for me to make a discreet departure.

Shortly before I left an incident occurred which was to have repercussions some months later. Cook who was a little less - or possibly a little more - inebriated than myself, began arguing forcefully with an acquaintance across the table, that he should take back his five marks, which the friend refused. Finally, Cook cried, "I don't want your damned money - take it back," and he threw the note down onto the table. Turning to others round about him, he then repeated the exclamation, saying, "Take back your money - I don't want your damned money," and he pushed Mrs. Stubinsky's note, and that of several other persons, towards them, and after ten minutes or so, the notes were returned to the wallets from whence they had come. Cook refrained from touching the note that I had contributed, and so it remained in the middle of the table, but after some time, I too, like the others, took back the note and replaced it into my wallet - and indeed, it was the last and only note on the table to be retrieved.

By now it was very late, and as I was feeling drunk and aggressive, and not wishing to reveal these feelings in public, I rose from the table, left the company without a parting word, and walked home through the night the three miles to my flat in Kallio.

The following two months were uneventful as often in Scandinavia in summer, but on returning from a three week holiday with Mrs. Hytönen in Greece, where we had surveyed the antiquities of the country, I was met by a tragic piece of news. On the evening of the day I returned, the 3rd of August, I was drinking in the Poly when I was approached by my old friend, Rolf.

"Have you heard the sad news of what happened whilst you were away,?" he said. "An old enemy of yours had died."

"An enemy? Who?"

"A member of the HISC group, Mike Spencer. He drowned in the sea."

I recollected that it was Mike who had almost wrecked the founding meeting of the International Society in November last and would almost certainly have succeeded had I not taken a strong hand in opposing him and the group with whom he was associated, and I remembered how saddened I was by his opposition in view of the fact that I had once befriended him.

"It seems as if all your old enemies are dropping lies flies," said Rolf. "If it's not loss of face, it's imprisonment, and if it's not imprisonment, it's death."

"I can only interpret it as some kind of moral retribution - if there's any interpretation to be made at all," I replied.

"The funeral's at nine o'clock tomorrow at the chapel of the Hietaniemi Cemetery. He'll be cremated there as well. Most of the English community will be there to give him a good send-off."

"I'll make every effort to be there."

Rolf explained that Mike Spencer had been drowned at a country house decorating party the previous Saturday, and that at midnight, after the decorating had been completed and after much drinking, the group of forty or so persons decided to take a moonlight dip, and that Mike (who was a non-swimmer) dived into water which was waste deep and was never seen again. His absence was unnoticed until the group had returned and dressed, when they became alarmed, and called the ambulance service, and on arrival, they walked into the sea and almost immediately pulled out his body, but by then, any question of resuscitation was far too late.

"Those are ridiculous circumstances to die in," I cried. "I suspect the whole lot of them were drunk."

"Probably a combination of paint fumes and alcohol," suggested Rolf. "Also, it may have been connected with a relapse following the unpleasant bladder scraping operation he had a few weeks back."

"He was always a heavy drinker. He told me himself he liked to drink a bottle of cognac every week, and that he'ld always earn enough money for that, even if for nothing else."

This last remark began to spread round the foreign community in Helsinki, and when it came to the ear of his best friends, Ray and Shirley Reed, they took me seriously to task, saying that I was slandering the dead.

"He never drank," said Ray.

"When I knew him, which was before you came to this country, he always drank a bottle of cognac a week," I insisted, "and if he changed his habits since then, then I didn't come to know about it."

I overslept the following morning and so missed the function at the cemetery, but I later met Peter and Martin who had just come from the funeral, and we went to the Elanto bar in Kallio for a coffee.

"It was a very tasteful funeral, over forty people were there, and the Rev. Masters gave quite a touching sermon and had all the girls in tears," said Peter. "He said he didn't know Mike Spencer personally, but that judging by the number of people in the church, he must have been a 'very nice person.' That went down very well. Even the British Consul was there."

"If I'd known there'ld be so many people I'ld have turned up," I said.

"And why weren't you there,?" burst out Peter in mock anger.

I was embarrassed by this question for I felt a twinge of shame at my having made so feeble an effort to attend the funeral, and my first reaction was to gloss over my laziness with the easy excuse that I had overslept, but suppressing this, I came out with the truth, awkwardly exclaiming, "I just couldn't be bothered."

My discomfort drew a burst of laughter from Peter and Martin, and they rightly reproached me for treating the death of a fellow Englishman so lightly.

"You know, none of those girls who were crying in the church really liked Mike Spencer," mused Peter. "He never had a relationship with any girl. They were only crying because that's what girls do in a situation like that."

"The Finns love a good cry, anyway," added Martin. "It makes them happy. They like anything depressing or to do with death. Look at the way they gather in cemeteries during Christmas, lighting candles over all the graves."

"Mike Spencer only came to this country as a conscientious objector to escape National Service," explained Peter. "He certainly didn't come for the girls."

The International Society did not go out with a great bang like a rocket as might have been suspected on the weekend of the 6th of June, but rather continued to fizzle and splutter for a little longer, like the dying motions of a damp squib. On Wednesday the 7th of October, Det. Heinonen phoned Mrs. Hytönen to tell me that the Society's papers were still lodged in the Registration Office, and on the following day, he phoned again to enquire as to the general activities of the Society, and as to what I was doing, and as to whether I was still living at my old address. This aroused my suspicion in that perhaps Heinonen had heard some rumours about the Society and wished to probe me as to what was happening. Not wanting to contact him again without good purpose, I phoned Anders Enblom and asked how the situation lay.

Enblom reacted in a stuttering panic, sensing that I must have phoned him after I had again been in contact with the police. I had met him earlier in the summer after my return to Greece but shortly before I was due to depart for Spitsbergen on a small packet boat from Tromsö. "The police must have paid you a tidy sum if you can afford to take one foreign holiday right after another," he had insolently remarked. "The police paid me nothing," I had answered.

He said he was leaving for Menorca in a quarter of an hour, and without further prompting, he made a clean breast of the fact, that a Committee meeting of five or six persons had been held in the Primula café the previous night, to discuss the possibility of re-founding the Society. He added that Rowland Hill had not been amongst their number. An hour later I phoned Gösta Kelter who spoke in a slow measured manner, explaining that a meeting was held at his flat on the 11th of September attended by only five people at which Rowland Hill was also absent, but that the latter was returning from Spain that very day. He added that he had just met Enblom in the street who had told him about my call earlier, but I disbelieved this as being too much of a coincidence, and assumed that Enblom had phoned his countryman immediately after my contacting him. With this information, I phoned Det. Heinonen and made an appointment to meet him the following day.

We met at 11.30 a.m. at the Insinööritalo and Heinonen expressed his continuing strong interest in the Society.

"I still want to prove that Evans tried to involve it in a Communist conspiracy," he said. "I'm convinced he did. On the day of his arrest we asked Evans for all papers he signed on behalf of the Society, and he had to go home to fetch these. It was when he returned that we officially charged him, and his first words were, 'I wish I'd never got mixed up with the bloody Society. It all began with that.' That was suspicion enough to go on. ... Evans was lucky to be charged in this country and not elsewhere. He admitted himself that if he'd been in England he'ld have got twenty years."

"What'll happen to Evans when he comes out?"

"That's still undecided. He won't be allowed to stay in Finland - that's for sure. He regards that as the biggest part of his punishment. He'ld rather have his sentence trebled and be allowed to remain, but we don't like people of that sort in our country."

Det. Heinonen tried to persuade me to contact Akulov with the idea of finding out what he wanted with me and then feigning to cooperate.

"You're asking me to play a very dangerous game indeed," I said. "I'm not a professional informer and I certainly don't want to court all the implications that could arise."

"Alright, Mr. Corfe, it's your skin," he said with a smile.

On parting I promised to contact him in a month if I heard anything useful, but only three weeks later, on the 5th of November, whilst sitting with my cronies in the Kolme Kreiviä, I heard a rumour that Evans intended publishing his memoirs of the International Society and of his life as a spy. Two days later I saw Det. Heinonen in his office and expressed my fears over the libellous nature of such projected memoirs in view of Evans' malice, and asked him to enquire into the truth of the rumour.

"I can understand your worries," he said. "I'll contact the prison on Monday and find out if it's true."

"If he's writing his memoirs, I want them suppressed."

"We can't do that. ... His wife visits him every week."

"Does she? It would be easy to smuggle a manuscript out of the prison then."

"I don't think so. There's always a guard."

"Does he understand English?"

"I think so. Anyway, Evans nearly always speaks to his wife in Finnish. ... If he does write his memoirs you can only go to the civil court and take out an injunction against them - but that could be difficult."

"If he writes his memoirs, then I'll write mine," I said.

On the following day Rolf, Martin, Jim Hammond and I were discussing the Evans case in the Kolme Kreiviä.

"Bob, you're courting danger to be around when Evans comes out," said the North American melodramatically. "If you take my advice you'ld go back to England and steer clear of the limelight."

"If the Russkies wanted to use Evans again he could get very nasty indeed," said Martin. "You know how spiteful he is, and he might start laying down his own conditions. Now you know it's the easiest thing in the world to grab someone off the streets of Helsinki and put them on the Moscow train. And remember, that train leaves here every afternoon, seven days a week, and no Finnish official ever goes through it."

In view of these opinions and the fact that Martin's predictions on the dangers of founding a society had been proved correct, I began to wonder if it would really be better to clear out of the country, but on weighing the pros and cons, I decided to remain despite the risks. On the 10th of November I met Det. Heinonen again and we dined at the Don Roberto restaurant. He was able to completely allay my fears with regard to the strange warnings of Martin and Jim.

"If you've told me everything, you've nothing to fear from the Russians," he said. "They don't bump people off for the fun of it, and they certainly wouldn't allow themselves to be used by any grouch that Evans had. But if they do bump you off, Mr. Corfe, don't worry, I'll bring some flowers to your funeral. You're a good chap! ... Evans did have a plan for writing a book but he's given it up now. He's full of his own self-importance. He thinks the British, the Russians, the Chinese and the Americans are all going to have a go at kidnapping him as soon as he comes out."

Heinonen then returned to the topic of the Society.

"I'm still convinced the Society was started for the purposes of espionage," he said.

"How can you think that when I started it single-handed,?" I replied.

"You're a highly suspicious character. I think you're a British agent."

"Don't come back to that nonsense again," I told him.

"If I had my way I'ld kick all the foreigners out of this country. They're a bloody nuisance."

"That's going too far," I said. "What you really want to do is tighten your frontier controls and keep out undesirables. After all, most of us are a pretty decent bunch."

"You're a good foreigner, anyway," said Heinonen with a smile.

"I think we've served each other's interests, but I don't see how I can help you further," I remarked.

"Maybe you can, Mr. Corfe, maybe you can," concluded Heinonen in a cryptical tone.

CHAPTER 24
MI6 becomes a cropper

"He replied that I must needs be mistaken, or that I *said the thing which was not*. (For they have no word in their language to express lying or falsehood.)

Jonathan Swift, *Gulliver's Travels* "A Voyage To The Houyhnhnms," Chap. 6.

On Thursday 17th of December I was awoken by an unexpected visit from Peter Martin. I had not seen him for several months, and indeed, he had only returned to Helsinki the previous night after working as a partially successful salesman in Britain.

"How's England,?" I asked him.

"Lousy,!" he answered. "The wife couldn't stick it there. We had to come back. She couldn't stand all those slums and miles of urban development. It was so depressing. She wouldn't mind settling in Germany - she spent three years there - but England, never! The houses are so cold and it never stops raining."

"What brings you here at this hour in the morning?"

"This hour? It's gone nine o'clock, you lazy bugger - you should be up by now."

"I went to bed late."

"You always do! It's all those women. - Bob, can you keep a secret?"

"You know I can."

"Don't tell anyone, this is top secret. British intelligence have been onto me."

"No!"

"God knows how they traced me. Sent me a letter when I was in Birmingham. They wanted to see me in London, so I went there. They asked all about Evans and the International Society. They showed me pictures of a couple of Russians but I couldn't identify them. They did it very nicely though. There was a little old gentleman with gold-framed spectacles and a pin-stripe suit and they brought in coffee and we sat round in armchairs. I couldn't help them. I was only there for an hour."

"So they're still interested."

"They'll pull you in when you go back to England - just to make sure you're clean."

This prediction was not to be borne out. British intelligence were not to contact me then or at any time afterwards, and as will be seen, probably to their deep regret. It puzzled me that they had bothered to contact Peter Martin, a minor official of the International Society, whilst they made no attempt to question me on Evans and the affairs of the Society, and I was apprehensive as to the kind of picture Peter had conveyed to British intelligence about our club.

"I told them all about you - that you were very left wing - just to assure them," continued Peter.

"You what,?" I exclaimed threateningly.

"That was right, wasn't it.?" said Peter startled by my anger. "Left wing - that does mean you support the church, you're pro-monarchy, vote Conservative, and all that sort of thing?"

"It means the opposite," I retorted.

"Anyhow, I told them you were politically clean and had a good Army record. They can check that out for themselves."

"I hope you haven't told anyone else I'm 'very left wing,'" I said in concern.

"Not that I can recollect," answered Peter dismissively, but he didn't sound too sure.

Before the end of the day the "confidential information" which Peter had confided to me was already the gossip of the foreign community. Peter confidentially informed all his friends at the Kolme Kreiviä and elsewhere about the red carpet treatment he had received in Whitehall, and this aroused a new interest in the Evans case. Jim, meanwhile, continued to impress upon me the danger to life and limb of my remaining in Finland after Evans' release, but by now I took no serious notice of his warnings - perhaps he suspected I had at some time in the past somehow been politically involved in Evans' evil plans and that we had fallen apart.

When I told Martin and Rolf later that day that Peter had informed British intelligence that I was "very left wing," Martin Summerhill responded by saying, "You don't know what he told them about you in

Whitehall. He could have said anything. Have you ever heard Peter Martin say anything good about *anyone* behind their backs?"

"I suppose you just have to understand that about Peter and forgive his faults," I only remarked. "How else can you explain it?"

"Peter's world fell apart when his parents divorced in 1948," explained Rolf. "Everything before that date was good, and everything after it is bad. He's caught in a time warp. That's the reason for his cynicism about everything in life, and that's why he's unstable."

Some weeks later, on Monday the 4th of January 1965, on visiting the Consular Section of the British embassy for the annual renewal of the registration stamp in my passport, I was told the Consul, Mr. Marshall, wished to have a word with me.

"Mr. Peter Martin's been here and told us about his interview in Whitehall," said the Consul. "He says you told him you think you could be of value to British intelligence."

"Most certainly," I replied. "You've doubtless heard about my invaluable assistance to the Finnish authorities. I cannot understand why British intelligence should approach Peter Martin before coming to me. After all, I was the founder and Chairman of the Society."

"In what way do you think you could assist British intelligence,?" asked the Consul.

"I'm afraid that's highly confidential, and I'm only prepared to divulge any information to the right quarter. But I could tell them about a very interesting meeting that a certain person - a British subject - had with a Soviet diplomat at a country club not fifty miles from here."

"It sounds interesting."

"It is, and I could produce some very interesting documents and show them my diary. I'm only prepared to discuss this matter further in Whitehall. If British intelligence are interested they'll have to pay costs in advance to cover loss of earnings, hotel expenses, and naturally, my return fare by jet."

"Naturally," exclaimed Mr. Marshall in an ironical tone which I thought was quite uncalled for.

"By the way, how's Evans coming along?"

"He should be released about the 22nd of this month. I see him once a month - he's in the Riihimäki prison - but I must tell you that prison's done nothing whatsoever to reform his character. He feels as bitter and resentful as on the day he went in."

I felt like answering that he wasn't supposed to enjoy prison anyhow, but I said: "Where will he go on release?"

"It's still undecided," replied Mr. Marshall.

The interview with the Consul gave me food for thought. British intelligence was clearly still interested in the Evans case, and in view of the invaluable information I held with regard to Eric Cross (the embodiment of the Communist agent) it seemed as if it was clearly my duty to contact the British authorities in alerting them without further delay. Perhaps every hour counted, and the damage that Cross was rendering Western defence was increasing day by day. Mr. Marshall was too slow a medium to depend upon in liaising between British intelligence and myself, for the information I had to impart was of the utmost urgency. But to whom to write? The address of MI6 was not listed in the usual directories and so I felt finally obliged to address my letter to the Under-Secretary for Defence, hoping that it would be passed speedily through to the appropriate section.

The letter was necessarily long, but I clearly headed it, "The Evans Spy Case," quoting my passport and Army numbers, so that the identity and military character of the writer could be quickly verified through official records. The letter began with a preamble describing my visit to the Consul that day; outlined the several warnings of danger of my remaining in Finland that I had received from a Canadian diplomat; gave an account of the American embassy's alleged displeasure with the Society, and related the story of my struggle with Evans and how I became involved with the Security police through attempting to prosecute a libel action.

I said that I had been particularly upset by the suggestions of the Finnish police that I was a British agent when there was no truth in the suspicion, and I then dropped the clue as to my prospective value to British intelligence in the following words: "I was also obliged by the police to spend a weekend in the country mansion of a distinguished Finnish aristocrat (who honoured our Committee with his membership), where I observed some strange occurrences which I think would be of interest to your department." Finally, I said that I should be pleased to

Eric Cross

head of MI6 in neutral Scandinavia. On deportation to Britain he asked for police protection before being whisked away into secret hiding.

visit Whitehall, bringing all relevant papers with me, to tell the full story and answer any questions that might be put.

Although the letter was dated the 4th of January, it was not completed until the following day when for security reasons it was transferred via a relative in London. I received no reply to the letter. I sent a reminder on the 23rd of January. Finally, I received a small buff MOD Form 2 card from the Ministry of Defence dated the 26th, stating that the, "The Permanent Under-Secretary of State, Ministry of Defence, acknowledges receipt of your letters dates, &c., which have been forwarded to the appropriate branch for attention." The card was not even placed into a plain envelope.

When I subsequently told Mr. Marshall about this indiscretion of security, he exclaimed, "They must be mad in London." Still no letter came and when I did eventually receive a reply to my communication it was through personal contact, but by then, it was too late and irreparable damage had been done. It was to be a sad day for British intelligence. However, the writing of this letter was an act I never regretted, for it contained the proof of my good faith in safeguarding British interests in addition to a warning that could have prevented a disastrous situation.

Late on the evening of Wednesday the 20th of January, whilst wandering around the streets of Helsinki and looking into various cafés to spot friends and opportunities, I caught sight of Eric Cross in the new Columbia bar opposite the main railway station, and I joined him as an old friend and member of the Society. He was sitting with a particularly dour looking worker whose face bore the hardened and resentful expression of the traditional militaristic Finnish Communist - a type typical amongst the industrial proletariat - but he left soon after my arrival. After a short while we were discussing our supposedly mutual "friend."

"You can't help admiring Ronald for his guts," said Eric Cross. "He can push himself anywhere and get away with it. He's been a Communist since his youth. He joined the party in 1937, whilst working in a medical instrument factory. He became a strike secretary, and brought the factory to its knees. Now if a youngster could do a thing like that, what do you think he could do today if he did his best?"

"Then why hasn't he organised strikes here?"

"He's a foreigner, he's had to watch his step. He'ld be locked up if he did a thing like that. He was already unpopular amongst his work mates for his scheming. It's Marja who's the real Communist though. She's been a fanatic all her life - since she was so high," he said putting his hand some three feet above the ground. "Her father and other relatives were rounded up and shot by the Whites. She's never forgotten it."

This was yet another reminder that Finland stood as an example of the inadvisability of political executions during periods of civil discord, for the curse was passed on from one generation to another through the bitterness of undying hate. The contemporary Finnish Communist (or at least until the 1960s) was not to be identified, as in most countries, through his or her immediate class origins or economic environment, but through the historical circumstances of heredity. The Communist was sometimes a wealthy business person, or often a top professional, with the outward appearance and manners of an affluent bourgeois. It was in the dark secret alone of parents, siblings, or other relatives, who had been rounded up and arbitrarily shot as Reds, that their conviction as Communists was to be uncovered.

"How did Ron meet his wife,?" I asked.

"They met on a park bench in Trafalgar square. There was a peace demonstration. They married, travelled around England and then came over here. For the first year he had no employment and the family were living in the most appalling squalor."

"What information exactly did Ron pass over to the Russians?"

"It was a radio attachment fixed to the underside of small boats and submarines. I don't believe he only got three and a half thousand marks for what he did. The Finnish authorities made him look ridiculous when they pinned such a petty charge on him - it was insulting - but that's all they could prove at the time. I know he received a thousand marks alone for giving technical tuition in electronics to a couple of Chinese - and that was over a ten month period."

This information sounded most significant, but it struck me that Cross knew an extraordinary amount about Evans' espionage activities in view of the fact that he claimed not having even met him within the three year period leading up to his arrest. After the Columbia closed at

11 o'clock we then moved over to the station café, and after we had exhausted the topic of our "friend," Cross became deeply absorbed in describing to me his strange scientific theories.

He was a believer in flying saucers, had met people who had seen them, and he believed in the theory of vibration as an energy source. He was convinced that in the distant past a civilisation had existed in South America, scientifically in advance of our own, so anticipating the ideas of Eric Däniken and that this civilisation was the lost Atlantis which had once conquered the world before finally sealing its own self-destruction through nuclear power. He argued that the cause of cancer lay purely in the radio frequency of individuals and that it could be insulated against. He described the case of a Finnish nurse in Loviisa who had been given only three years to live, and how she was completely cured after copper plating had been placed on her bed and tiles beneath it, and how he had afterwards examined the house with a Geiger counter.

By the beginning of February Evans had still not been released - the Consul's prediction had not been fulfilled - and Mrs. Hytönen phoned the chief of the Security police on the 2nd of February to arrange an appointment for me to meet Det. Heinonen. On the same day Jim Hammond put through a request from his embassy to borrow the membership list of the International Society for a few days, and I agreed to this and the Canadian authorities had this in their possession for a week. On the 5th Mrs. Hytönen passed on the message that a luncheon appointment had been arranged for me at 2 o'clock the following day with Det. Heinonen at the Insinööritalo, and the subsequent meeting was perhaps the strangest I ever had with this police officer.

I enquired as to the date of Evans release, which was to be about the 22nd of that month, but as yet no decision had been made as to his eventual place of deportation - or at least, this was being kept secret by the authorities. I then described my meeting with Eric Cross a fortnight earlier, and tried to impress upon Det. Heinonen that this man was undoubtedly a Communist agent and that the sooner he was arrested the better for us all.

"I don't appreciate your sense of humour," was all he answered.

"I've never been further from joking," I said.

"Then you're teasing me."

"Not at all. I think you should arrest the man."

"Are you working for the Soviet bloc?"

"I don't understand you."

"I think you do."

"You're speaking in riddles," I said.

"No, it's you who're speaking in riddles," he replied.

"I've made myself quite plain."

"Perhaps you're a British agent. A last ditch attempt by MI6 to confuse the issue."

"I'm nobody's agent."

"You're either a Soviet spy or a British agent."

"Listen, I object to these slanderous insinuations."

Dat. Heinonen glanced at me with a surprised expression.

"Haven't you read the papers today,?" he asked.

"No."

"It seems you never do."

"What's in them?"

"We arrested Cross yesterday. Now you see why I'm suspicious."

"You surely don't think I'ld talk to you like that if I'd heard the news!"

"I don't know."

"Anyway, I'm glad to hear he's been arrested," I said. "Congratulations!"

"I don't think you'll be glad to hear it when I tell you he was working for the other side. He's a British intelligence man. You helped us a lot, Mr. Corfe, in catching our second man. We're indebted to you."

I was struck with astonishment, but at once, many things began to fall into place.

"What'll you do with him?"

"We can't tell you that, Mr. Corfe," said Heinonen smiling. "That would be a breach of Finnish security."

"Have you charged him?"

"No, he's just under arrest. You see, we're a neutral country and we have to watch both sides. I'm sorry it should come to me to tell you that we've arrested your man. I don't think we'll imprison him though. I think he'll be deported next week. There, that's a favour for you!"

Despite the clarification of the misunderstanding to which this short altercation gave rise, Det. Heinonen remained deeply suspicious for some time, and three times left the table to make telephone calls, and was away for many minutes on each occasion. As I was left alone, turning my glass of cognac between my fingers, I assumed he was speaking with the big boss as to what should be done with me. Finally, trust was renewed between us, and we began to talk about politics in general and the death of Sir Winston Churchill a few days earlier - "the last of the greats" Heinonen called him - and when we left the restaurant three and a half hours later, and after many coffees and cognacs, we parted as friends.

The arrest and revelation as to Eric Cross's true function was a great shock to me in view of the part I had played in ruthlessly tracking him down. On leaving Det. Heinonen I went immediately to the Kolme Kreiviä where I joined my friends Martin and Rolf and others, and I eagerly looked through the papers. The Finnish press was full of the story - splashing it across the front pages in a way it had not featured the Evans' case - and one paper displayed a large picture of the building in which his flat was situated, together with the forest of aerials he had set up on the roof for communicating back to his MI6 office in London. Not even his wife had been let into the secret that he was engaged in intelligence. There was no attempt to cover up the story as there had been following the secret trial of Ron Evans, for there was now no fear of embarrassing a powerful neighbour as there had been then.

Eric Cross was described as a 37 year old technician, twelve years resident in Finland, twice married, with two children, a 12 year old girl by his first marriage and a four 4 old son by his second. Most interesting of all was the account published by *Huvudstadsbladet* describing how several years previously he had been highly decorated and promoted to the rank of Major in the Intelligence Service by the British ambassador at a secret ceremony within the embassy before a highly-selective invited guest list. Since then he had been appointed chief of MI6 for neutral Scandinavia, being directly responsible for the activities of dozens of agents, and the names and addresses of these had been discovered by the police during the raid on his flat, with the result that Britain's entire counter-espionage network in these countries was destroyed overnight. As I read this, the enormity of what I had done became manifest.

"I warned you not to start that damned club, and now look at what you've done," cried Martin Summerhill pointing an accusing finger at me as he glanced up from the newspaper. "It was a damned stupid idea and we all told you so at the time. You can't start up clubs in a country like this."

"You'll be a marked man for life," said Rolf. "They'll never let you into the States now."

"You'll never get a civil service job either," said Martin. "You'll be on all the black lists."

"Who wants to work for the civil service anyway,?" said someone else at the table. "It's a bloody useless life."

"Do you realise, Bob," began Martin jutting his finger at me, "that you've actually been a Finnish agent - and the fact you haven't earned a penny from it doesn't make the slightest difference - working against your own country? How does it feel like? And the fact that you thought Cross was a Communist only goes to prove you were wrong."

"What do you think they must be saying about you in Whitehall now,?" said Rolf "They must be tearing their hair out in anger. MI6'll be out to get even with you, even if the Russians don't."

"Do you realise it takes years of painstaking work to build up an intricate counter-espionage network like that - not to mention a fortune to the British taxpayer - and now with your stupid blundering and your bloody International Society, you've gone and put the whole thing up the spout,?" cried Martin.

"Cross should have kept out of my way then."

"If I were the Finnish police, I'ld round up every member of that Society and chuck the lot of them out of the country," said Martin. "You're all under suspicion!"

On the following Tuesday I went to the British embassy. I was deeply disturbed by the accusations of my friends, and felt that some official apology was called for to the British authorities. I was embarrassed as to how I could best express this, but in clearing my name, I realised I was obliged to make a frank confession of all that had passed.

MI6 BECOMES A CROPPER

Whilst waiting to see the Consul, I was approached by the doorman, Cook, with a bundle of bills, requesting that I pay him for the food and drink I had had on the 11th of June last at the Casino restaurant. I was dumbfounded by the enormity of his insolence.

"It's rather late to present these bills," I said.

"You ran away before we could collect the money."

"Excuse me," I said, "but I was a guest at your club."

"But poor Mrs. Stubinsky can't pay for it."

"Why didn't you write to me at the time? You make me feel like a thief coming to me at this late hour."

"I didn't know who you were."

"You repeated my name enough."

"But I didn't have your address."

"Nonsense! It's always been in the files here."

At that moment I was beckoned to go into the Consul's office.

"I'll speak to you afterwards about this," I concluded, and I was red with fury at the thought that such a sordid dispute could be carried on in such a place and so long after the event.

"I'm so glad you've come along," said Mr. Marshall, "I was going to contact you anyway this week."

"I'm terribly sorry about Cross," I said. "I don't know how I can offer an apology to the right quarter. I feel awfully ashamed."

"It's a shocking business."

"The ambassador must be feeling very upset, having his name splashed over the papers in connection with MI6 - especially after decorating the man."

"The papers are full of rubbish. How could they know about a secret ceremony in the embassy?"

"In this city, nothing's secret for long. There must be some truth in the story - after all, *Huvudstadsbladet's* a reputable paper. It's not your twopenny tabloid."

"The papers distort everything," said Mr. Marshall in irritation.

"I've really come along just to apologise. I would never have pressed my accusations against Cross had I not suspected he was a Communist. He was such a weirdo - not my idea of our James Bond."

"I don't think British intelligence have any James Bonds, Mr.

Corfe. But don't worry about Cross. The man's a complete idiot," added Mr. Marshall with malice.

"It's a pity MI6 didn't find that out before employing him."

"Now, Mr. Corfe, I'll be contacting you very shortly to come along here. I'll drop you a card. There's someone here who'ld like to speak with you."

"I'm at your service at any time."

Out in the reception hall again I was met by Cook and we continued our sordid wrangle.

"I've got outstanding bills here for over a hundred pounds," he said, "and I've had to pay most of it to the Casino out of my own pocket."

"Then you're not a good organiser. You should run your club like I've run mine."

"It's most unfair. Everyone should pay their bit."

"That's nothing to do with it. Chairmen who run clubs in this country - especially if they're Englishmen - should be careful what they do. Besides, you were so drunk that night, you didn't know what you were doing."

"All I want is twenty-five marks from you."

"If I was to pay you that, it would make it look as if I'd been a thief."

"And if you don't pay it now, you always will be!"

"How dare you talk to me in those terms, Cook! Settle it with Mrs. Stubinsky - I was her guest," and with that I stormed out of the embassy.

I was so distraught by the man's effrontery, and even more so by the slanderous imputation behind his unreasonable demands, that I wrote a long explanatory letter to the ambassador asking him to adjudicate in the matter, but this was an even more foolish action, for it publicised an incident that need and should never have gone beyond Cook and myself. The outcome was that I eventually received a reply from the Consul stating that the ambassador declined to intervene in what he rightly regarded as merely a private quarrel between two individuals.

On the 9th of February Cross was deported to Britain, and two days later, I read in the British papers that he had refused to answer reporters' questions and asked for police protection on arrival at Heathrow to safeguard him from a Soviet assassination attempt. Also on that day, I met Mr. Flax, a member of the International Society and a prospective parliamentary candidate for the Swedish party, who told me he had met Stig Lambertsen who informed him he had been approached by Polish intelligence agents immediately after the disappearance of Evans.

On the 17th I received a letter from the Consul requesting me to visit the embassy, and on arriving there, he explained that the Military attaché had received my letter of the 4th of January addressed to the Under-Secretary for Defence. The attaché would like to speak with me but first would like sight of the documents referred to therein. This I was certainly not prepared to do, and so replied, "I should first like to know the basis on which the Military attaché wishes to inspect the documents." Mr. Marshall disappeared for a few minutes, after saying he knew nothing about the details of the matter, and on returning asked if I could meet Col Robinson next Tuesday morning and this was agreed.

Col. Robinson was an elderly officer of the "old school" with a classic military moustache and a tired manner, and leaning nonchalantly back in his chair, he began by describing how some days ago he "found himself in a certain department in Whitehall engaged in the normal course" of his business, when a "certain official" brought to his notice a "certain matter" not really his concern, and that this was my letter to the Under-Secretary, and that he had agreed to look into the matter. I told him the story of the Society and of my conflict with Evans, and that I was particularly worried about any lies that Evans might say about me to British intelligence on his release and deportation back to England.

"How interesting," exclaimed Col. Robinson when I described how Evans had pushed himself onto the Committee, and "How amazing," he exclaimed when I told him about Evans' lie that Peter was dissatisfied with my chairmanship, but somehow I felt that the colonel was unconvinced by everything I said. I showed him the Society's programme.

"So you had speakers from Western countries as well," said Col. Robinson surprised. This statement betrayed such a gross ignorance of the International Society - clearly indicating that the Military attaché had formed his prejudices about the club whilst ignoring established facts - that it did not warrant any reply. He was clearly a man with the most obtuse intellect with whom an open discussion was not an option. He plainly saw our Society only in the light of a Red conspiracy. On describing the weekend at Haiko he asked about those who had attended the party.

"So everyone had a good time there,?" he remarked.

"We all enjoyed ourselves," I replied.

"It sounds like something out of James Bond to me," said the colonel incredulously. "Do you recognise any of these people,?" he added pointing to a framed picture on his desk of a group of uniformed Russians. I recognised only the Soviet Naval attaché.

"Infernal nuisance, these people," exclaimed Col. Robinson under his breath, and clearly the entire matter was most distasteful to him.

"It's a pity the Ministry of Defence never contacted you earlier about this matter. I could have saved the situation had MI6 been on the ball. It's tragic you should have to call me in at this late hour."

"Don't worry about it," he replied. "I want you to rest assured that our interview here has been strictly confidential. No one knows about it except for Mr. Marshall, Whitehall, you and myself."

I disliked the colonel's suggestive tone that the interview had been "confidential" merely to assure me of my own safety. If I was to appreciate the secrecy of the matter it would not be for the sake of my own skin, but for the sake of the importance of the case in itself. Before leaving, he requested that I lend him the Society's documents, and I agreed to bring these in the following day.

"How much longer do you intend living in Finland,?" he asked.

"Until I find a wife, and then I'll return to England," I said.

"You won't you know," he answered with a chuckle. "If you marry one of these Finns you'll spend the rest of your life here. They like to keep their menfolk in the country. I was saying exactly the same thing to another English chap only last week when I was on manoeuvres with the Finnish army."

The next morning, Wednesday the 24th of February, I handed in the membership list, legal documents, Kelter police statements and other papers to Mr. Marshall to pass on to Col. Robinson.

As I was about to leave, and the Consul was locking his safe, he said: "Before you go, Mr. Corfe, I must tell you something - I hope it won't frighten you - but Mr. Evans left Finland this morning on flight" - and he repeated a flight number.

"Where does that go,?" I asked, expecting him to reply to Moscow or Peking.

"London."

"Why should that frighten me? I've nothing to hide."

"I just thought I'ld tell you," said the Consul awkwardly.

Everywhere I trod I had left a trail of suspicion and distrust.

*

www.ingramcontent.com/pod-product-compliance
Lightning Source LLC
Chambersburg PA
CBHW020746160426
43192CB00006B/261